EMPIRES
OF
SPYMASTERS

EMPIRES
OF
SPYMASTERS

THE SECRET WAR BETWEEN THE
BRITISH EMPIRE AND IMPERIAL JAPAN
1900–1941

PANAGIOTIS DIMITRAKIS

AMBERLEY

First published 2025

Amberley Publishing
The Hill, Stroud
Gloucestershire, GL5 4EP

www.amberley-books.com

ISBN 978 1 3981 2437 0 (hardback)
ISBN 978 1 3981 2438 7 (ebook)

British Library Cataloguing in Publication Data.
A catalogue record for this book is available
from the British Library.

1 2 3 4 5 6 7 8 9 10

Typesetting by SJmagic DESIGN SERVICES, India.
Printed in the UK.

Appointed GPSR EU Representative: Easy
Access System Europe Oü, 16879218
Address: Mustamäe tee 50, 10621, Tallinn, Estonia
Contact Details: gpsr.requests@easproject.com,
+358 40 500 3575

Look back over the past, with its changing empires that rose and fell, and you can foresee the future too.

Marcus Aurelius, *Meditations*

CONTENTS

PREFACE

On 7 July 2022, Boris Johnson resigned as prime minister. After his speech in front of 10 Downing Street, he compared himself to the infamous Lieutenant Hiroo Onoda, an Imperial Japanese Army intelligence officer.[1] He was a graduate of the Nakano school of espionage and sabotage who refused to surrender in 1945 and stayed in hiding in the jungles of the Philippines for twenty-nine years. The author cannot see the connection of the case of Johnson and Hiroo. Nevertheless, this clearly shows the well-entrenched bias of the British political elite towards Japanese warriors/officers. As we will explore in this book, a noted pro-Japanese politician was Winston Churchill – the politician Johnson admired the most. Almost nostalgic of a medieval past, British officials and officers assumed that the *samurai* and their descendants (the officers of the Imperial Japanese Army and Navy) were similar to English knights. This was wrong. In reality, by long tradition and practice, Japanese warriors and officers – and spymasters – were disobedient to authority to an extent inconceivable by British standards.

Indeed, the case of Hiroo, who did not obey when ordered to surrender, proves this. More significantly the attempted coup on the night of 14 August 1945 could have changed the course of history. As Emperor Hirohito accepted the provisions of the Potsdam Declaration for unconditional surrender after atomic bombs had devastated Hiroshima and Nagasaki, junior staff officers plotted a coup in which troops would storm the palace and 'protect' him. It was the last mutiny of the Imperial Japanese Army. The leading coup officers murdered Lieutenant General Takeshi Mori of the 1st Imperial Guards Regiment and searched for Imperial Household Minister Sōtarō Ishiwata and Lord of the Privy Seal Koichi Kido. Both officials were keeping Hirohito's recordings of the surrender speech to be broadcast. The plotters were unable to find them. Eventually, when no senior officers or other units joined the rebellion, the coup plotters committed suicide. Hirohito's speech was eventually broadcast.[2]

George Kenneth Young was a deputy chief of the Secret Intelligence Service (SIS) early in the Cold War. He once issued a circular to his staff:

> Men's minds are shaped of course by their environments and we spies, although we have our professional mystique, do perhaps live closer the realities and hard facts of international relations than other practitioners of government. We are relatively free of the problems of status, of precedence, departmental attitudes and evasions of personal responsibility, which create the official cast of mind ... And so it is not surprising these days that the spy finds himself the main guardian of *intellectual integrity*.[3]

Young's thoughts reflected the warnings of his predecessors on the rise of Japan as a threat to the British Empire in the Far East from the early 1900s up to 1941. From the turn of the century to the attack on Pearl Harbor, two opposing forces in Whitehall clashed in memorandums, reports and discussions; secret intelligence indicating the growing threat of 'militaristic' Imperial Japan confronted the argument that Japanese policies in the Far East should be condoned due to weak British presence in the region and because economic and commercial interests (squeezed by Japanese competition in cheap labour and low prices) would be put in jeopardy if there was conflict. Consecutive spymasters in possession of secret intelligence remained the guardians of intellectual integrity, though they were not allowed to influence policy; the pro-Japanese bias of key politicians and officials, as well as of figures who were paid by the Japanese, ensured that credible and militarily efficient means were not employed to deter Japan from attacking the British Empire in the Far East. The Japanese political and military leaders serving the emperor were 'men who spied opportunities and actively sought to manipulate events abroad just as they ordered their world at home', as Frederick Dickinson remarked in his seminal study *War and National Reinvention: Japan in the Great War, 1914-1919*.[4] In their eyes, Britain weakened year by year – and weakness invites assault.

Since 1905, British imperial strategists had reached the conclusion that Imperial Japan was on the rise, that it was an emerging militaristic power and that, unless it was granted continuing concessions, it would inevitably displace British power and interests in the Far East.

Ancient Athenian historian and general Thucydides authored the history of the war between Athens and Sparta (the Peloponnesian War), in which he argued that the war was inevitable because of Spartan fears concerning the growth of Athenian power. Historians and international relations theorists debate endlessly on the proper interpretation of Thucydides' thesis in contemporary world politics.[5] In any case, had he reviewed the interests of empires in the Far East in 1900–1941, he would have concluded that there were 'too many empires for diplomacy to hold the peace'.

The militaristic Imperial Japan can be likened more to Sparta, and Imperial Britain to Athens. Tokyo demonstrated a will for economic and military expansion at the expense of other imperial powers in the Japanese victory over Russia in the 1904–5 war. Both empires claimed influence over China, and Japan invaded in 1931, taking Manchuria before moving on Shanghai in 1932. In 1937, full-scale war erupted against the Republic of China. The Japanese army expanded its area of operations to an unprecedented degree that could not be checked by the Royal Navy, the key strategic weapon to defend the scattered constellation of British colonies in the Far East.

British imperial strategists had felt the change in the Far East before the First World War; Japanese aspirations could not be accommodated by the existing treaties, which merely delayed the fulfilment of evident Japanese ambitions. Nevertheless, London was as myopic towards the threat of Japan to British positions in the Far East as the modern British government was in its policy on Russian oligarchs' financial status in the UK before the 2022 invasion of Ukraine. Despite the constant complaints of British business communities in the Far East about the growing threat of Japan in the region from the 1900s until the 1930s, the British government accelerated the threat of Japan by providing – with nothing in return but money for defence companies like Vickers – advanced naval and aviation technology. Winston Churchill, as Chancellor of the Exchequer, dismissed any possibility of war with the Japanese. In this rather fertile environment of complacency, British officers spied for Japan.

British spymasters of the SIS and MI5, established in 1909, pointed to a Japan hostile to the British Empire. Already, at the turn of the century, British officers commended the performance and tradecraft of Japanese spymasters deemed resourceful and merciless taken into consideration the contemporary military ethics.

Imperialism was a driving force for Japanese strategy. From the end of the Napoleonic Wars to the First World War, the system of imperialism worked as an unwritten code of conduct between European powers in Africa and Asia. It was a 'Europeans only' club, whose members valued key factors like alliance-making, fair play and relative military strength in colonial regions. In the age of imperialism, the balance of power and diplomacy ended antagonisms that could lead to war between Europeans for their African and Asian conquests. However, imperial strategy and diplomacy began to decay from the start of the twentieth century, with the Boer War in particular turning into a trauma for the British.[6] Nevertheless, until 1945 the Japanese leaders remained fascinated with the concept of imperialism, unaffected by the aims of the League of Nations, which were disarmament, prevention of war through collective security, peaceful settlement of disputes between countries through negotiation and diplomacy, and the improvement of global welfare. Since the 1870s, generation after generation of Japanese leaders had aimed for their restless empire to be accepted by the others as the 'master' in the Far East. Their attitude is more reminiscent of Sparta turning against Athens than of a nineteenth-century European-style imperial power. This also is reflected in the way they viewed espionage: armies of spies in the thousands, devoted to the emperor, reporting on everything significant or insignificant, without the professionalism and rules observed by European powers.

Winston Churchill and Yamagata Aritomo, two overconfident imperial strategists, forceful characters believing in wars of races, are the leaders who influenced, repeatedly over the decades, cabinet members in Britain and Japan, determining official policy, mentoring officers and diplomats as well as spymasters. Both consumers of secret intelligence and keen strategic analysts appear and reappear in the maze of this history. For decades, Churchill discounted the Japanese threat to the British Empire. For decades, Yamagata advocated a cautious yet unrelenting strategy to claim British and Western interests in the Far East and in particular in China. As a young anti-Western paramilitary leader, he had witnessed the devastation of accurate Royal Navy guns while holed up in primitive coastal defences; he experienced defeat and humiliation. He was not to forget.

Indeed, as early as October 1893, Yamagata warned the imperial cabinet as well as a large number of officers and officials that he and his loyalists believed that 'our nation's adversary is not China nor Korea but England, France and Russia'.[7] Racial wars would soon break out in the Far East, he claimed. In 1914 he shared his conclusion with the cabinet:

> Recent international trends indicate that racial rivalry has yearly become more intense … the exclusion of Japanese in the state of California in the United States, and the discrimination against Indians in British Africa are also manifestations of the racial problem. As a consequence, the possible further intensification of the rivalry between the white and colored peoples leading to an eventual clash cannot be completely ruled out. When the present great war in Europe is over and order restored, politically and economically, nations will again turn to advantages and rights they might gain in the Far East. Then, the rivalry between the white and colored peoples will intensify, and perhaps it will be a time when the white races will all unite to oppose the colored peoples.[8]

During the early phase in the war of the Pacific, on 15 February 1942 Churchill said in a broadcast, 'No one must underrate any more the gravity and efficiency of the Japanese war machine. Whether in the air or upon the sea, or man to man on land, they have already proved themselves to be formidable, deadly, and, I am sorry to say, barbarous antagonists.'

British spymasters had pointed to the hostile intent and schemes of Imperial Japan against the British Empire since the late 1900s. Throughout the 1910s, 1920s and 1930s, the *consistent* Japanese strategy in Asia was more than evident. Japanese expansion meant squeezing out the British imperial and commercial presence. The strategists of Japan, generation after generation, in a parliamentary system with a strong military influence, aimed to expand their country's presence by any and all means. Neither the public, the business community, the intellectuals nor the parliamentarians disputed the anachronistic imperialism Japan claimed. After all, expansion meant more resources and more markets for goods.

This chronological study, focusing on espionage as a historical narrative, attempts to identify British perceptions of Japanese espionage from 1900 to 1941, and to identify the sources, the officials who boosted pro-Japanese bias inside the British government, the Royal Navy and the War Office. These officials were indirectly agents of influence by distorting assessments of Japanese intentions while it was known that Japan claimed hegemony in the Far East. It will also narrate the role of officers who spied on behalf of Japan or leaked secret intelligence and military technology while knowing that Japan was antagonistic towards Britain, and on the other hand will elaborate on the role and reports of spymasters who warned of Japan's hostile intent.

I

AN ALLIANCE WITH AN ANTAGONIST

In 1902, Britain and Japan signed an alliance treaty aimed at safeguarding their interests in China and Korea against Russia. Yamagata Aritomo promoted this treaty; he assumed that imperialist policy in the short term could be served in alliance with other imperial powers.

A spy's early background shaping his character, skills and thinking can be most valuable for a future politician and strategist. From the late nineteenth century to his death in 1922, Yamagata Aritomo (b. 1838) was the influential leading member of the élite group called *genrō*, composed of senior statesmen who promulgated imperialism and chose prime ministers in imperial Japan. He was born to a low-ranking samurai family; so low was his status that he was only allowed to attend classes in school by sitting in the corridor. At the age of thirteen, he became an errand boy in the village treasury office. At sixteen, he was a servant in a school building. The next year he was listed as an informer for the police. Aged twenty he witnessed a civil war in which the Tokugawa clan of the hereditary shogunate, armed by the French, British and Americans, concluded commerce treaties with the United States and other countries, disregarding the emperor. The emperor had appointed the shoguns who collectively were called *bakufu* and exercised local administration. Nevertheless, gradually the real power of the imperial court diminished and the shogun flourished.

Young Yamagata sided with the ideals of the burgeoning 'honour the emperor, expel the barbarians' movement. In 1858, he and five other young samurai reached Kyoto, ordered by their warlord to be his 'eyes and ears' on pro-Western officials.

It was Yamagata's first secret mission, and it would not be his last. In the summer of 1862, Yamagata went to Kyushu on an espionage mission in disguise, using the name 'Hagiwara'. He met local samurai with the same beliefs. In 1863, the imperial court sanctioned the ideal of 'expelling the barbarians'. Yamagata, still a humble samurai, joined the fight and encouraged the formation of the *Kiheitai*. A unique paramilitary organisation, this group contravened prevailing samurai code by admitting not only samurai of all social ranks but also farmers and merchants, and employing both Western and Japanese arms.

On the afternoon of 4 September 1864, French, Dutch, British and American warships commenced the bombardment of the forts of the feudal Choshu domain.[1] Yamagata remembered:

> During the fighting the four ships which made up the enemy's left flank fired continuously on the Dannoura fort so I was unable to give any assistance to Fort Maeda. In return we fired on the enemy ships from Dannoura and the sky was filled with shells which made it sound like a typhoon. However, the enemy's fire was far more severe, shells landing on the side embankment throwing earth and rocks skyward and causing much suffering. Shells landed in the hill behind the fort crushing and splintering the trees. Others exploded after sinking into the soft rice.[2]

Defeat and humiliation just made Yamagata more persistent. He was given a six-shooter revolver and was appointed leader of the *Kiheitai* until the final victorious restoration of the emperor in 1868. Yamagata effectively joined the new regime and took over the task of organising a modern Japanese army and shaping the apolitical General Staff in the service of the emperor. Throughout his long career, he continuously confronted influential noble samurai families and their political aspirations in the form of political parties after the establishment of the Diet. He urged commoners to take up arms and pushed for universal army recruitment to be introduced. In his eyes, the independent samurai tradition challenged the authority of the emperor – according to the Shinto religion, the emperor was the direct descendant of the solar goddess Amaterasu. Besides, Yamagata's lowly background meant he knew what it meant to be sidelined in society. At a time when British officers admired the samurai and their code of conduct, Yamagata was deciding that the wearing of swords should be prohibited. In December 1872, the Council of State proclaimed that members of the samurai class 'who wear two swords ... are indolent and arrogant and in extreme cases irresponsibly murder innocent people with impunity ... the samurai is no longer the samurai of former times and commoners no longer the commoners of the past; all are now equal in the empire and without distinction in their duty to serve the nation'.[3]

In 1869, Yamagata, after a request to the newly formed government, was allowed to visit Prussia and France in a private capacity. On his travels, he was impressed by the German military system and influenced by the political concepts of authoritarianism in domestic politics and imperialism in foreign relations.[4] He would use these influences when appointed chief of the army General Staff in 1878 (he would hold the role for four years, and then again subsequently). He had a reputation for listening to officials and officers of lower or middle ranks, diplomats, businessmen and scholars coming from abroad, debriefing them personally and 'bombarding them with requests for the latest data statistics, government reports and studies'. So much did he value personal observation that even when ill, in the last year of his life in 1921, he visited barracks to examine the latest weaponry. He did not enjoy universal acclaim, with sources mentioning 'his views that sometimes were not taken seriously by his cohorts'.[5] Yamagata called for the appointment of officials from Choshu, his birthplace. He chose subordinates with administrative skills and excellence in military affairs. His key protégés were future prime ministers Katsura Tarō, Kodama Gentarō, Terauchi Masatake and Tanaka Giichi. He established the soldier-statesman tradition, with Tanaka admitting that Yamagata 'achieved most of his success through the willing toil of his loyal followers who would stick with him through thick and thin'. The way Yamagata had with people was 'to become friendly in gradual stages, opening only one area of his interests at a time'.[6]

In the Japanese government, the seven members of the unofficial *genrō* were trusted advisers to the emperor who took most foreign policy and military decisions as well as working for the appointment of prime ministers and their cabinets. It could be argued that Yamagata did not represent the army, which was committed to territorial expansion; he was more of the opinion that the army – and to a lesser extent the navy – should aim for imperial conquest and antagonism with the European empires in the Far East. Yamagata's clashes with politicians in the 1900s focused on the powers of the Prime Minister and the Foreign Secretary and the cabinet to decide on foreign policy. There was no doubt that politicians of that period urged imperial conquest.

Yamagata served as prime minister from December 1889 to May 1891, then again from November 1898 to October 1900. He was president of the Privy Council from 1893 to 1894 and 1905 to 1922. He insisted that 'the key to military success is to know your enemy and yourself ... I cannot neglect intelligence for even a single day at the General Staff.'[7] He strongly believed that the cause of the First World War was the racial antagonism of Anglo-Saxons, Germanics, Slavs and Latins, and he assumed that Japan would confront the hostilities of the 'white races'. Imperial strategy, he hoped, should prevent the coming of the European threat and unite the 'yellow' races in China under Japanese control.[8] He mentored his prospective spymasters on his understanding of racial conflict.

During the Russo-Japanese war of 1904–05, Britain discouraged France from coming to the aid of its ally Russia, and the war ended with a Japanese victory. In 1905, Britain renewed its alliance treaty with Japan, fearing being left out in the cold if Japan claimed hegemony in the Far East. Admiration for Japanese military efficiency spread in a Britain traumatised by the failures of the Boer War. As early as July 1901, Foreign Secretary Arthur Balfour had concluded in 'rather gloomy tones':

> ... we were for all practical purposes at the present moment only a third-rate power; and we are a third-rate power with interests which are conflicting with and crossing those of the great powers of Europe. Put in this elementary form

the weakness of the British Empire, as it at present exists, is brought home to one. We have enormous strength, both effective and latent, if we can concentrate ... but the dispersion of our Imperial interests ... renders it almost impossible.[9]

In January 1905, Balfour entertained a fear that had started to grow in the elite. 'The idea of Japan heading an Eastern crusade on Western civilization seems to me altogether chimerical,' he wrote. He claimed that Japan did not have the fleet to challenge the 'fleets of the Christian world, who could therefore always cut her off from free communication with the mainland of Asia'.[10]

Gradually, British politicians realised that Japan was a true antagonist in strategy and an incompatible international diplomacy partner. After the Russo-Japanese War, the head of the Japanese embassy in Washington shared secret information concerning the Japanese tactical successes with US President Theodore Roosevelt, who confided to British ambassador Thomas Spring-Rice:

I wish to see our [US] navy constantly built up and each ship at the highest point of efficiency as a fighting unit. If we follow this course we shall have no trouble with the Japanese or any one else. But if we bluster; if we behave badly to other nations; if we show that we regard the Japanese as an inferior and alien race, and try to treat them as we have treated the Chinese; and if at the same time we fail to keep our navy at the highest point of efficiency and size – then we shall invite disaster.[11]

Roosevelt warned that 'if the menace [of Imperial Japan] comes I believe we [the United States] could be saved only by our own efforts and not by an alliance with any one else'.[12] The United States needed to defend its dominions in the Pacific and south-east Asia: Johnston Island, Midway, Samoa, Guam, Hawaii, the Philippines, and the Wake. Washington insisted on the freedom of the seas and commerce, ensuring an open door in China, antagonizing the European imperial powers.

In January 1905, the British envoy in Beijing wrote, 'The rise of Japan has as completely upset our equilibrium as a new planet the size of Mars would derange the solar system.'[13] Balfour accepted the renewal of the treaty with Japan, expanding the scope of Japanese forces to help Britain in case of a Russian invasion of India. Nevertheless, the General Staff emphasised that 150,000 Japanese troops in India could not be sent in case of war due to supply and transportation issues; and, most importantly, that it would show the world 'a clear proof of our national decadence'. Thus, Japanese troops should instead be used in Manchuria against the Russians.[14]

The imperial Japanese military during this period came into contact with a charismatic young man named Chiang Kai-shek, future leader of the Republic of China. The nineteen-year-old Chiang reached Japan in 1906 and attended military training at the Baoding military academy and at the Tokyo Shinbu Gakko, a preparatory military school for Chinese students run by the Imperial Japanese Army Academy. After his graduation, he served as an officer in the Japanese Army from 1909 to 1911. In spite of his Japanese education concerning the role of Japan in China, Chiang remained a nationalist, committed to the overthrow of the Qing dynasty and the establishment of a republic that would no longer be humiliated by foreign interventions, concessions and unequal treaties.

First to raise the alarm after the Russo-Japanese War were the British business communities in China and Manchuria. The Japanese military authorities unfairly promoted Japanese firms, blocking their competitors, treating occupation zones and concession areas as exclusive economic zones. Tariffs were issued and transports for foreign firms were not allowed to anchor; railway rates for non-Japanese companies skyrocketed. The Imperial Japanese Army brought with them settlers to populate the areas invaded. A merchant published an article in the *North China Herald*:

> True, the door of Newchwang is open, as the wily Japanese will smilingly point out to you ... But how much further can we get than the threshold of this open door? ... How long will the British merchants and the British government allow themselves to be so deceived and treated at the hands of their Allies, whose sailors they are banqueting with so much zest in England to-day?[15]

Alexander Hosie, the British commercial attaché in Beijing, reached Manchuria and reported on 'the game [of Japanese policies] which has proved so successful in Korea ... her object being to establish paramount interests and influence in these three provinces'. Francis Lindley, a vociferous pro-Japanese diplomat of the 1920s and 1930s, said that the British and Americans were 'more anti-Japanese' than the Russians and other Europeans. It is evident that his pro-Japanese bias started early on his career and guided his reporting. (Later, as British ambassador to Tokyo in 1931–34, Lindley would block the clear-headed interpretation of Japanese policy that was revealed by secret intelligence.)

Meanwhile Royal Navy officers of the China Squadron in Hong Kong, informed by the Merchant Navy of Japanese behaviour, grew suspicious and hostile to Japanese plans for China. It was widely shared in the public in Shanghai and other port cities that 'no Japanese can exist as a trader alongside a Chinese unless he have recourse to force and fraud. That seems to be the general impression.'[16] Those in the business community felt the British government did not care if they were mistreated by the Japanese. J. O. P. Bland, Shanghai correspondent for *The Times*, wrote in August 1910 that the British government accepted 'any political felony that our allies choose to commit'.[17] On 6 November 1909, US Secretary of State Philander Knox proposed the formation of an international syndicate to loan China the funds to purchase all railways in Manchuria; an international board of administrators would be established. The Russians did not agree. Foreign Minister Alexander Izvolsky argued, 'If we reject the American proposal, there may be a temporary cooling of relations with the U.S.A., but America will not declare war, nor will it send its navy to Harbin, whereas Japan in this regard is much more dangerous.' The Japanese ambassador in St Petersburg, Baron Motono Ichirō, suggested a Russo-Japanese alliance to Izvolsky. By January 1910, St Peterburg and Tokyo showed in public their intention to conclude an agreement not to accept American policy on China. Both Russia and Japan discounted the importance of British imperial colonies in the Far East.[18]

By the autumn of 1910, Everard Fraser, the British consul general in Hankou, concluded that the 'constitutional experiment; the opening of the parliament in Beijing would crumble and lead to the collapsing of the Qing authority in the provinces. A direct result would be revolution.' Dr G. E. Morrison, writing from

Beijing for *The Times*, wrote of Fraser's assessment in October 1910:

> Alert, ambitious, unscrupulous, [Japan] was on the spot and waiting for an opportunity. By bullying and cajolery, by corruption and fraud she was establishing 'interests' in every part of China ... Their only object can be to provide themselves with a plausible excuse for intervention when the smash comes ... The [Qing] dynasty would be saved from its merited fate by Japanese assistance, and the Japanese Minister in Peking would become a kind of Resident-General.[19]

Fraser's assessment was prophetic. In October 1911, a bomb plot in Wuchang was the pretext for a revolution that led to the fall of the Qing dynasty.[20]

Reacting to the emerging tensions, journalists in Canada, Australia and the United States warned against mass Japanese immigration. In December 1907, California Representative Everis Hayes claimed that war with Japan was 'inevitable' within the next five years. In his understanding there was no doubt:

> The Japanese immigrant is not an immigrant in the ordinary sense of the word ... They came to learn ... our weaknesses and defects so as to turn that knowledge to their own advantage. Before Japan went to war with China she had an army of spies and observers in Manchuria. The Japanese knew more about the Russian army than the Russians themselves.[21]

On 18 April 1906, San Francisco was devastated by a massive earthquake that caused three days of fires. In the ensuing chaos, with law and order broken down, Americans attacked Japanese immigrants. One Japanese business owner complained:

> Soon after the earthquake the persecutions became intolerable. My drivers were constantly attacked on the highway, my place of business defiled by rotten eggs and fruit; windows

were smashed several times. I was forced to hire ... two special policemen at great expense, and for fully two weeks was obliged to maintain the service ... Whenever newspapers attack the Japanese these roughs renew their misdeeds with redoubled energy.[22]

By November, American newspapers were publishing articles warning of a coming American–Japanese war; local politicians argued the same. The White House received letters from interested civilians, one making claims about a Japanese spy posing as a servant on a US warship. Roosevelt asked the Undersecretary of War for a contingency war plan. The Joint Army and Navy Board finished revising a redrafted war plan under the codename 'Orange'. Generals and admirals fretted about the security of the US-occupied Philippines. Roosevelt agreed with the recommendation to dispatch the US Atlantic Fleet into the Pacific as a show of force both to Japan and to an exasperated American public. He discounted the hypothesis of a war but felt insecure: 'There is enough uncertainty to make it evident that we should be very much on our guard and should be ready for anything that comes.'[23]

It was a formidable fleet that headed to the Pacific. Sixteen battleships steamed out of Virginia in mid-December 1907: the fleet flagship USS *Connecticut* (BB-18), the *Minnesota* (BB-22), the *Kansas* (BB-21), the *Vermont* (BB-20), the *Louisiana* (BB-19), the *Georgia* (BB-15), the *New Jersey* (BB-16), the *Virginia* (BB-13), the *Rhode Island* (BB-17), the *Maine* (BB-10), the *Missouri* (BB-11), the *Ohio* (BB-12), the *Alabama* (BB-8), the *Illinois* (BB-7), the *Kearsarge* (BB-5) and the *Kentucky* (BB-6).

Meanwhile, the Japanese ambassador in Madrid informed Tokyo that Spanish citizens, frustrated after their defeat in the Spanish–American War, were offering financial aid to Japan. The nervous Japanese naval staff and government considered deploying warships in large-scale exercises. The American warships were approaching; Japanese naval strategists deemed a war with the United States to be inevitable. The crisis was de-escalated when an influenza outbreak crippled the majority of the crews of the Imperial Japanese Navy. After this, the naval General Staff and then the government decided to postpone large-scale exercises. A major confrontation between the fleets was thus avoided.[24]

Diplomacy followed when the two governments reached the Root–Takahira Agreement. This was a joint statement signed on 30 November, but not an actual treaty. Both countries accepted the independence and the territorial integrity of China and free trade. Japan recognised the annexation of Hawaii to the United States and Washington recognised the Japanese protectorate of Korea and their role in Manchuria. Japan agreed to limit immigration to California. However, military strategists in Washington were insistent that the rise of Japan in the Far East was not inhibited by this agreement, which showed the United States effectively seeking a way to avoid confronting Japan. On 18 October 1908, the US Fleet reached Yokohama. The Japanese public welcomed the ships, waving American flags.

In 1907, Yamagata drafted a long-term plan covering the next twenty-five years. The Basic Plan of National Defence required the expansion of the army and navy to achieve a 'steady expansion' in Manchuria and Korea, while the Japanese commercial interests (to be protected by arms in case of emergency) should reach South Asia and 'the other shore of the Pacific ocean' (i.e. the United States, Mexico, Chile). The army should have twenty-five permanent divisions and the navy two battle fleets. Yamagata paid attention to the army and sidestepped the navy. In his war plan, the cabinet could not make decisions without the input of the *genrō*.[25] The 1907 plan envisioned confrontation with Russia, the United States, Germany and France, in that order – Britain was not included.

Edward Grey, the British Foreign Secretary, dismissed American capability to counter Japan. In July 1907, he wrote, 'The Americans talk angrily, but they have no means of getting at the Japanese unless they build a much larger fleet.'[26] In June 1908, Grey informed Sir C. Macdonald, the British ambassador in Tokyo, that 'the Americans have found out that there is a secret treaty between Japan and Russia'. Whitelaw Reid, the American ambassador, told Grey that 'the Russians were putting forward their extreme contention about Railway rights at Harbin because they had a Secret Treaty with the Japanese which bound the Japanese to support this contention'. Grey replied that he 'cannot discover that any Secret Treaty exists'. Indeed, it was American diplomats in St Petersburg who discovered the existence of the treaty.[27]

Perhaps as a result of the xenophobia arising from Japanese mass immigration to California, American officials and the press began to fear a Japanese invasion of Texas, with reports of National Guardsmen seeing 'Orientals' crossing from Mexico creating paranoia in 1908. One of the proponents of this panic was Captain Sidney Mashbir, who in the early 1920s would end up on assignment in Tokyo, tasked with organising an intelligence network.

In 1909, retired general Homer Lea, who had served with the Chinese army, echoed many of his colleagues in the US army by publishing a study, *The Valor of Ignorance*. In it, he warned of the coming war with Japan and laid a charge against the political culture of the United States: 'This Republic, drunk only with the vanity of its resources, will not differentiate between them and actual power. Japan, with infinitely less resources, is militarily forty times more powerful.'[28] Indeed, Japanese militarism, which seemed to inspire devotion and mobilise civilians and troops alike, was feared by the US military. Lea's book turned bestseller and was translated into Japanese. In London the Foreign Office took note of the study, which indicated American nervousness towards Japan.[29]

Lea wrote that over the last two decades, 'one nation after another, by one means or another, [Japan] has removed them from her way'. Tokyo was increasing defence spending after the victory over Russia; this proved that a war with the United States was inevitable. The American western coasts were in peril: Japanese troop transports could reach the Philippines in five days, Hawaii in fourteen, Alaska, Washington and Oregon in less than twenty and even California in twenty-two.[30] Balfour must have felt awkward when reading a Foreign Office note on Lea's claim that 'by Japan's alliance with Great Britain, the elimination of British power in the Pacific ... has been accomplished subtly'.[31]

A secret Russo-Japanese treaty was signed on 30 July 1907 between Ambassador Motono and Foreign Minister Izvolsky, the Foreign Minister. Japan conceded to Russian interests in Northern Manchuria and Outer Mongolia; Russia accepted Japanese concessions in the Korean Peninsula and South Mongolia. A second treaty would be signed on 4 July 1910; both parties agreed on shared interests in Manchuria, rejecting American proposals for the South Manchurian railway. A third treaty was signed on 8 July 1912 by which Inner Mongolia was divided into two spheres of influence: the western part for Russia and the eastern part for Japan. A fourth treaty was signed on 3 July 1916 whereby both parties agreed to protect their interests in Manchuria against China.[32]

In London, many members of Parliament voiced the fear of Australians that 'the white policy' was being altered by mass Japanese immigration – mainly for work in the pearl industry. The role of poor Japanese workers and divers in collecting pearls at this time was deemed 'indispensable'.[33]

A member of the Liberals described the stance of young Winston Churchill, then parliamentary undersecretary at the Colonial Office:

[Churchill] was very frank ... being in entire sympathy with Canada in the matter of keeping out Orientals and said that should there ever be any difficulty between Japan and the United States, Great Britain would certainly let the alliance go to the winds. He hated the Japanese, had never liked them, thought they were designing and crafty. He could not bear them.[34]

J. T. Hornsby, a member of the parliament of New Zealand, was frustrated:

We have been handed over to the Japs [*sic*]. The Pacific is deserted by the British fleet. We have a few tin cans floating in the Pacific which we call war-ships. There is not one of the first-class battleships of Japan that could not blow the whole lot of them out of the water in twenty minutes. You know perfectly well that is true, and I want to be prepared for the day, which for us will be the day of Armageddon.[35]

A November 1908 estimate from the Foreign Office concluded that in the Far East, the Imperial Japanese Navy ruled the waves: 'This superiority there is no reasonable prospect of England being able ever again to challenge.'[36] In June 1909, the Committee of Imperial Defence concluded that in case the alliance was terminated, the

Royal Navy should be ready to depart for the region 'in order to neutralize the danger from a preponderant Japanese Fleet in the China Seas'.[37] In February 1910, Balfour, after reading reports of American concerns about Japan and Lea's bestselling book, prophesied:

> It would, in my opinion, be folly for the Japanese to provoke a war which, however great their initial success, could only end in the richer and bigger country building a fleet superior to their own: and long before that position of superiority was reached the whole position of an island Power like Japan would be imperilled (*sic*) by the possibility of a coalition between the U.S.A. and some other European nation which has, or might have, ships in the Far East.[38]

In August 1910, Japan annexed Korea, a protectorate since 1905. Britain and the United States did not react. In July 1911, Yamagata informed the cabinet that war with the United States was

> ... at this point, almost unimaginable, the world will witness a sudden change in a few years. We do not know when and what type of transformation will occur, especially given that recent U.S. policy in the Pacific often carries points of friction with the Empire's interests and [in light of] the unavoidability of a mutual clash sooner or later if the present trends continue.[39]

Japan had been unable to raise tariffs under the 1905 Anglo-Japanese Treaty. In July 1910, a year before the Anglo-Japanese Treaty was due to lapse, Tokyo asked for a new commercial agreement that would include tariffs. The China Association, a mercantile organisation, put pressure on the Foreign Office upon learning this, claiming that tariffs would 'pave the way to that Japanese hegemony of the Far East'. *The Economist* warned that, if accepted, the Japanese policy amounted to the 'anti-foreign policy' and as a result would 'soon reduce the popularity of the Anglo-Japanese alliance to vanishing point'. Eventually the Japanese negotiators withdrew their proposals on tariffs.[40] In May 1911, at the Committee of Imperial Defence, Grey warned what would happen if the Anglo-Japanese Treaty was not renewed: 'Not only would the strategical situation be altered immediately by our having to count the Japanese fleet as it now exists as possible enemies, but Japan would at once set to work to build a fleet more powerful than she would have if the alliance did not exist.' Tokyo hesitantly agreed to renew the treaty, though it was made clear by London that it should not be interpreted as Britain siding with Japan in case of an American–Japanese conflict. The Japanese military deemed Britain weak. General Tanaka Giichi, a protégé of Yamagata, then the vice chief, warned that Japan would not gain much 'if we simply follow Britain, which has only the skeletal appearance [*keikotsu*] of an ally'.[41]

The diplomacy with Imperial Russia would aim at British interests, argued Prime Minister Katsura Tarō.[42] Katsura was a former samurai and general, a member of the *genrō*; he reached Moscow in July 1912 to begin secret negotiations with German representatives to form a German–Japanese alliance aiming to 'topple British [political and economic] hegemony' in Turkey, India and China.[43]

Australia, Canada and New Zealand feared the growing power and influence of Japan and were wary of London's futile attempts to reinvigorate the Anglo-Japanese alliance. By February 1912, Churchill, then First Lord of the Admiralty, assumed that there was an undisputed threat in the Far East, namely Japan. He remarked: 'If the power of Great Britain were shattered upon the sea, the only course open to the 5,000,000 white men in the Pacific [the populations of Australia and New Zealand] would be to seek the protection of the United States.'[44]

In the first months of 1914, British naval attachés in Washington and Tokyo concluded that Japan would defeat US naval forces in the first phase of a war, occupying Hawaii and the Philippines and thus posing a threat to the Californian coast.[45]

In May that year, Churchill, reassured the House of Commons that the Royal Navy 'would defend [Australia and New Zealand] from Japanese invasion'.[46] In the same month, General Tanaka, following Yamagata's thinking, sought an alliance with Germany.[47]

2

'THE EMPIRE IS THE MASTER'

As the crisis in Europe escalated after the assassination of Austro-Hungarian Grand Duke Franz Ferdinand in Sarajevo, the cabinet of Prime Minister Ōkuma Shigenobu consulted with the *genrō* on 8 August 1914. Yamagata Aritomo issued a warning that in spite of the Anglo-Japanese Treaty, the cabinet 'should not forget that Germany too is a friendly power'. He predicted that the German troops would win and 'capture the heart of France'. Later, Yamagata boasted that in the event of a French defeat he 'would like to see [British Foreign Secretary Edward] Grey's face'.[1] Yamagata argued that Japan should show that it merely served a treaty obligation in joining Britain and that Germany was still a 'friend'. Japanese forces would fight alongside the British in China so as to project Japanese imperial power and claim the spoils of war without offending Germany's status as a great power.[2]

Upon the outbreak of the war, Grey concluded that the Japanese had taken advantage of their alliance with Britain and claimed influence in China, elbowing British interests aside as well as antagonising Australia. Fearing that the Japanese regional strategy could result in invasion, he decided not to call on them for help against the German colonies in the Far East unless the Germans attacked. He was aware of American hostility towards Japan and did not want to provoke Washington. Imperial Japan was identified as an opponent; nonetheless, Churchill urged Grey to allow for Japanese actions against German colonies in China.

He sounded pro-Japanese: 'I think you are chilling indeed to these people. I can't see any half way house between having them in and keeping them out. If they are to come in, they may as well be welcomed as comrades.'[3]

Churchill won the argument and an Anglo-Japanese expedition against the German forces of Qingdao at Kiaochow Bay was launched in September 1914. The *Wakamiya*, one of the first Japanese flight tenders (predecessor of the aircraft carrier), was used. Japanese aviators flying French-made Farman planes carried out the first carrier-borne air raids in history, sinking a German minelayer.[4] Royal Navy officers aboard HMS *Triumph* present in the operations remarked:

> Daily reconnaissances [*sic*], weather permitting, were made by the Japanese seaplanes, working from the seaplane mother ship. They continued to bring valuable information throughout the siege [of the fortress] … During these reconnaissances [*sic*] they were constantly fired at by the German guns mostly with shrapnel, but were never hit. The Japanese airmen usually carried bombs for dropping on the enemy positions.[5]

The Imperial Japanese Navy believed in the aircraft carrier as a new strategic weapon that would project power in distant regions and islands. During the period of the Anglo-Japanese expedition, in which the British contributed 2,800 troops and the Japanese 29,000, Yamagata warned Prime Minister Ōkuma of 'Britain's oppression of our interests in southern China'.[6] Indeed, Japanese officers in the field did not work together with their British counterparts, sowing 'arrogance' as the Foreign Office was informed.[7]

Tanaka argued that the European war was an opportunity for Japan since all powers involved would be exhausted. Japan could expand to China and, 'if we cannot avoid a collision with the United States at some point, this is the best opportunity for the empire'. In his view, the Americans lacked adequate troops and the US fleet could not pass through the Panama Canal, which was yet to become operational.[8]

The logic of pre-emptive strikes at the United States was already in place in the mindset of Japanese military leaders. In February 1915, Yamagata insisted on further agreements with Russia to boost imperial Japanese policy in the Far East. He felt that the war in Europe weakened the Great Powers each month to the advantage of Japanese might. It was a war of Anglo-Saxon, Slavic and Germanic races which, he claimed, would disrupt the balance of power in the Far East and China in particular.[9]

Ironically, Yamagata – who always boasted of his intelligence-gathering talents – was not informed that in January 1915 the Japanese government surprised London by issuing a document known as the Twenty-one Demands to the weak Chinese government under President Field Marshal Yuan Shikai. The demands would essentially turn the country into a Japanese protectorate. Prime Minister Ōkuma and Foreign Minister Katō Takaaki kept Yamagata and the rest of the *genrō* in the dark. The overambitious foreign minister assumed that the ultimatum to the Chinese would be accepted. The British government discovered the full list of demands through the ever-informed Australian journalist G. E. Morrison, who had access to the full text of the demands and communicated them to the British ambassador in Beijing.

Ambassador William Conyngham Greene asked Katō about the demands, only to receive the reply that Katō 'had not communicated wishes to you, but neither had he invited your view on the memorandum ... He did not consider it incumbent upon the Imperial Government to acquaint His Majesty's Government with what concessions or rights they were seeking from China any more than His Majesty's Government consulted Japan in similar circumstances.'[10] Evidently, the Anglo-Japanese Treaty was yet again a dead letter. London was persuaded that Katō's policy was inimical to British interests in China, aiming to undermine them. Grey, taken by surprise, remarked:

> I am also most anxious that Japan should not put forward any demands which could fairly be held to impair the independence or integrity of China, as His Majesty's Government would be in difficult position if called upon to explain how such demands could be reconciled with the terms of the Anglo-Japanese Alliance.[11]

By April 1915, the Chinese were yet to reply; they procrastinated for as long as they could. Katō, under pressure from the *genrō*, the British and the French, decided to curtail the list of demands.[12] Grey, under pressure from the business communities in Britain and China, who feared the Japanese advance, sent a personal telegram to Tokyo. He warned that a war between Japan and China would break the Anglo-British treaty.[13] Katō was targeted by Yamagata, who sought improved relations with Russia and France against Britain, but for the time being did not want a crisis over China. In February 1915, Yamagata submitted a memorandum to the cabinet. He claimed that Japan should abandon Britain and side with Russia: 'To rely exclusively upon the Anglo-Japanese alliance to effect lasting peace in East Asia was not "sound policy".'[14]

Yamagata was panicked by the resolute stance of Grey. Eventually, the demands were modified, though they remained humiliating for the Chinese. Grey urged Shikai to accept the new terms from Tokyo. President Woodrow Wilson stated that the United States would not recognise any treaty changes that would impair the treaty rights of the United States and its citizens in China. On 25 May, the Chinese government agreed.[15]

One of the journalists who had helped to reveal the true nature of the Japanese demands was David Fraser of *The Times*, who warned that Japan ruling China and leading Chinese troops would be a menace to Hong Kong, Singapore and other dominions: 'It is not the comparatively small things that are at stake. It is the whole British position in Asia, which is at least half our Empire.'[16]

Ambassador Greene reported from Tokyo in December 1915 that 'malicious pleasure is taken in instances of humbled Britannic pride [in the battles in Gallipoli]'. The permanent undersecretary of the Foreign Office, Sir Arthur Nicolson, reached the conclusion that 'the Japanese are taking advantage of our preoccupations in a way hardly consistent with the alliance'.[17] By March 1916, Nicolson was deeply concerned: 'I regard with great misgivings the whole policy of Japan in regard to the Far East – and I much fear that we shall later have serious difficulties to confront – both in Tibet and elsewhere on our Indian frontier.'[18] In January that year, Ambassador Greene had judged that Japan was

... passing through a phase of mental exaltation arising from the fact that the Great War, which is exhausting the real combatants, has cost the sleeping partner little, and perhaps even brough her gain ... Shimada, Chairman of the House of Representatives ... said 'the continuation of the war in Europe, while regrettable from the point of view of the civilization, will be advantageous to Japan, whose power will be increased not by her own efforts, but by the exhaustion of the European powers'. This long war among the white races will mean removal of menace to the Orient.[19]

In January 1916, Yamagata explained to Hara Takashi, party president of the *Rikken Seiyūkai* (Association of Friends of Constitutional Government) and Prime Minister in 1918–21, in no uncertain terms that Japan should not 'depend upon the British way or on Britain'.[20] He and Vice Minister of War General Oshima and the Imperial General Staff were certain of a German victory in Europe. Boosting the relations with Russia, Yamagata felt, would compel the British to offer more to Japan.[21]

Meanwhile, Russian intelligence deciphered the exchange of telegrams between Japanese ambassador Motono and Foreign Minister Katō. The correspondence revealed that the German government had approached the Japanese in January 1915 to reach a separate peace agreement. In July 1915, Russian ambassador Nicholas Malevski-Malevich in Tokyo warned Foreign Minister Sergei Sazonov of the pro-German stance of the Tokyo elite and the public. Russian diplomacy worked towards approaching Tokyo once more to request Japanese-made arms and ammunition and to keep Berlin away from an alliance with Japan. Nevertheless, the Russians negotiated a convention (not a treaty) which did not hand over to the Japanese the Changchun–Harbin (Manchuria) railway north of the Sungari River. The Japanese assumed that this 1916 convention could be interpreted as an indirect guarantee for Russian support in case of a war between Japan and the United States. The conclusion of the agreement sponsored by Yamagata showed his power and influence in Tokyo.

Japan would not send troops to Europe. The government felt weak in parliament and did not want to give encouragement to 'ultranationalist' circles. Indeed, in this period it is difficult to distinguish 'imperialists' and 'ultranationalists' in Japan.

Ambassador Greene explained that the Japanese government felt that the public might assume that by sending troops to Europe, China would 'fall under American influences.' There were not enough supplies for the army, and besides 'there have been some rumours of scandals in the War Department similar to those which have recently occurred in the [Imperial Japanese] Admiralty, and one cannot help wondering whether the Government fear that a demand for the sudden dispatch of a vast foreign expedition might once more produce unpleasant revelations'.[22]

While Britain's minister to China, John Jordan, warned repeatedly of Japanese actions undermining British interests, the Admiralty scandal revealed corruption and imperial strategy working hand in hand. Colonel John Somerville, a British military attaché in Japan with a reputation of being a Japanophile, was furious:

Though any of these fellows [Japanese Naval staff officers] would *gladly* die fighting tomorrow for their country there's hardly one whose *moral* is proof against money. Is it that they are still too low on the evolutionary ladder, and that they will fight as a dog fights for his master though ten minutes beforehand he may have stolen his dinner? ... if these infernal scoundrels will sell their own country like this, how much more gladly will they sell ours.[23]

Japanese militarism was effectively blocking a true alliance with Britain and France. The ambassador explained:

... the Japanese Army has been built up on the German model; that the Officers of the Headquarters Staff have almost all been trained in Germany; that German strategy and tactics have been the groundwork of their studies, and that most details of the handling and drilling of the troops down to the famous 'goose step' have been copied from Berlin. This being so, it is easy to see how painful it must be to them to find that the Colossus whom they have looked up to, has feet of clay, and that their idol appears to be tottering to its fall. Moreover, another military link with Germany is the creed of blind devotion to a deified Warlord, which is of course present in both countries, only more so in Japan than in Germany, in as much as the Japanese Warlord is a real Godhead to his people, and not a claimant only like the German Emperor.[24]

Sir Jagadish Chandra Bose, a noted Indian polymath, informed Balfour of the conditions he encountered in Japan while there in 1914–15:

Being myself an Asiatic, I had better means of knowing the inner forces at work than those available to Europeans. I learnt that the Japanese believed their country to be destined at no distant future, to occupy the dominant position in the world; that in a very short time they will be Lords of the Orient. This is to them not a matter of aspiration, but of absolute certainty. They regard themselves as the best fighters, the Germans coming next ... All [political] parties were united in regarding China and India as their immediate objectives. It is within my knowledge that Japanese emissaries have been for the last 7 years or more under one guise or another, taking full stock of everything in India for some future object. Now our country is flooded with Japanese, who are not mere traders, but advanced guards. Their competition has already destroyed the hope of economic salvation of India. They boast that a battleship and fifty thousand soldiers would be quite enough to invade this country.[25]

At the end of 1916, Admiral John Jellicoe, commanding the Grand Fleet, voiced his suspicion of Japanese strategy to Admiral David Beatty. Tokyo was on a collision course with Britain and America as they had an idea 'of a greater Japan which will probably comprise parts of China and the Gateway to the East, the Dutch East Indies, Singapore and the Malay States'.[26] Nevertheless, at the Foreign Office a pro-Japanese bias was expanding, with memoranda commenting that 'Japan is barred from every other part of the world except the Far East and the Anglo–Japanese alliance cannot be maintained if she is to be barred from expansion there also'.[27] Indeed, it was myopic not to understand that Japan would expand at the expense of Britain's strategic position in the Far East.

Eventually, in April 1917, Japanese warships steamed to the Mediterranean, providing escorts for British and French transports moving soldiers to and from Europe and the Middle East and Africa. On several occasions the Japanese confronted German and Austrian submarines.[28]

After the entry of the United States into the war, the demands for US warship and escort patrols in the Atlantic made Washington agree a secret pact with a Japanese delegation for Japanese warships to steam around the islands of Hawaii on patrol against the improbable German naval threat.[29] Washington agreed with Japan to respect the independence and territorial integrity of China, while conceding on the subject of Japanese interests in Manchuria.

In 1917, the Japanese political and military leaders were thrown into disarray upon hearing that the Russian tsar had been deposed in the Bolshevik Revolution. The servants of the emperor had witnessed the fall of the Chinese dynasty of Qing in 1911, and the Japanese diplomatic representative in Berlin also informed them of an ongoing crisis in the Prussian House of Hohenzollern. In June 1917, King Constantine abdicated the throne of Greece. The Hohenzollerns and the Hapsburg dynasties would fall in short order, with Kaiser Wilhelm retiring to Holland.

The order of monarchy was collapsing worldwide. It seemed that the emperor's authority and throne could be in danger, too. Yamagata in his anger blamed the 'low, ignorant classes', claiming that the 'moral decline' of self-indulgence would 'bring doubt upon the monarchical system, malign militarism, and cause the destruction of the State'.[30]

Meanwhile, the British Foreign Office opined that royal diplomacy could sustain the Anglo-Japanese alliance and persuade Tokyo to join an expedition in Siberia. Francis Stewart Gilderoy Piggott was one of the Japanese-trained officers who proposed that George V's nephew Prince Arthur of Connaught should lead a British military mission to the Japanese capital and present the emperor with a field marshal's baton. Of course, it was not Piggott's gambit that led Japan to intervene in the Russian Civil War. Japan had invested resources in Russian regions of the Far East, and the 1917 revolution and the collapse of tsarist authority jeopardised investments and raw materials for the rapidly industrialising Japanese economy. The emperor and his entourage sought a limited intervention, whereas the army and the Ministry for Foreign Affairs aimed for a strong Japanese presence.

Piggott was born in England in 1883. His father was appointed legal adviser to the Japanese emperor and the family moved with him to Japan. The four-year-old Piggott learned his first words in Japanese. In 1891, the Japan Society of London was established and his father, who had been part of this endeavour, was considered a prominent lover of all things Japanese. Piggott junior joined the military in 1899, attending the Woolwich military academy, and in 1904 he volunteered in the first cohort of British military language officers in Japan. He quickly became a Japanese linguist, and an expert in the War Office. In 1917, during the First World War, Piggott served as staff officer in the 5th Army. At that time, the Anglo-Japanese alliance looked fragile. Piggott took the initiative to General Neill Malcolm at the War Office, proposing that George V name the Emperor of Japan an honorary field marshal in the British Army. It was hoped this would help persuade Tokyo to send troops to Siberia against the Bolsheviks under Lenin. General Malcolm sent Piggott's letter to his brother, Ian Malcolm, who was private secretary to the Foreign Secretary, Lord Balfour.[31]

This episode boosted Piggott's confidence that he could influence – at that time as a mere staff officer who spoke Japanese – British policy towards Japan. At the War Office he was considered an expert as few officers had his Japanese background, and he was assigned to attend major diplomatic conferences. In 1921–22 he was with the British delegation in Washington negotiating the naval treaty. Afterwards, he was named military attaché at the British embassy in Tokyo until 1926. In 1928, he gained more influence and was assigned to head the MI2 branch of the Directorate of Military Intelligence assessing Asian militaries. As Japan pursued a more aggressive policy in the Far East, Piggott failed to sound the alarm. To the contrary, he justified Japanese movements that would clash with British interests in the region. He was as committed to Japan as Kim Philby would be to the communist ideology and Moscow. Piggott was not a spy in the definition of a secret agent taking instructions as to what secrets to steal; instead he was a man obsessed with Japan who happened to be a high-ranking officer signing off reports reaching the Foreign Office, the Colonial Office and 10 Downing Street. He was committed to influencing British policy in favour of Japan at the highest levels. Indeed, Piggott admitted that his 'cause' was to work for the alliance of Britain and Japan – no matter what.[32]

There can be no doubt that during social occasions Piggott would tell Japanese officers and diplomats of British policy and his influence, as we will explore in great detail in following chapters. He was also insistent that the SIS should not develop a structure in Japan – in contrast to SIS chief Hugh Sinclair and the Admiralty, who warned of the growing Japanese threat that had to confronted in case of coming war.

In 1928, Piggott asserted that London had to set up an Anglo-Japanese alliance in the Far East. This did not materialise. Throughout the early 1930s, despite Japanese aggression and war crimes in Manchuria, Piggott insisted that Britain tolerate Tokyo's policy as a means to check China (then under civil war) and most importantly the influence of the Soviet Union in the Far East. In 1935, the War Office proposed to the Foreign Office that Major-General Piggott be reassigned as military attaché in Tokyo.[33]

He was never suspected on security grounds. In his memoirs, he boasts than in 1906 he met Captain Vernon Kell at the War Office: 'It was the beginning, too, of a life-long friendship with a man to become famous in the Intelligence Service.'[34] Kell was appointed director general of MI5 in 1909 and he, and the rest of MI5, believed that Piggott was 'one of us', a gentleman officer who would not be suspected of leaking secret information to anyone.

Military expediency necessitated Japan's participation in the intervention in Siberia against the Bolsheviks. At the War Office, however, it was feared that it would be difficult to persuade Tokyo to withdraw its forces in Siberia once they had secured Vladivostok. The Foreign Office deemed the Japanese 'practical and selfish' to the last degree. They cared nothing for the general purposes of the alliance, it was claimed, and if they took action it would be for their own ends and not to benefit Russia or the Allies. [35] Lord Milner, a member of the War Cabinet, did not share this suspicion and argued that 'the defence of the interests of the Alliance in that region of the globe is Japan's natural job'.[36] Lord Robert Cecil, parliamentary under-secretary at the Foreign Office, wondered 'if we are not over-suspicious of Japan'.[37] There was no doubt that a pro-Japanese bias was embedded at the War Office, the Foreign Office and the Cabinet, irrespective of the reports from British embassies in Beijing and Tokyo as well as the frustration of British authorities and the business community in Shanghai, Hong Kong, Manchuria and India.

Robert Hodgson, the British consul in Vladivostok, was trying to get some reliable information from local sources and spies, yet he could not communicate with London. Canadian Major Mackintosh Bell was working for the SIS and left for London. In December 1917, Bell reached Tokyo en route to London and asked to meet with Ambassador Greene, who was always willing to read intelligence reports, and informed him on the situation in Vladivostok. The ambassador promptly sent a cable to the Foreign Office, and shortly after Commander Cumming, chief of the SIS, got wind of the meeting and wrote angrily to the Foreign Office:

> I do not think you should place too high a value on this officer's opinion. He is a Canadian who was transferred to my Service and sent to Vladivostok as Military Control Officer. I ordered him to come home some time ago. He is the most determined conversationalist to have ever met but the opinions which he disburses upon every subject on the smallest provocation are much more remarkable for quantity that quality.[38]

In summer 1918, Britain and France called for the intervention of the United States in Siberia; Japan followed and eventually deployed a total of 72,000 troops. This large number of troops made Washington wary of real Japanese plans for the Far East.[39] Yamagata assumed that this was a strategic opportunity for Japan: 'With respect to the Far East, the Empire is the master and they [the Europeans and Americans] are the guests.'[40]

As he was celebrating the start of the campaign, Yamagata witnessed unparalleled public outcry and mass riots in Japan. He had been frustrated by basic economics. High inflation had hit rice, the national staple. Merchants and businesses speculated on the price of rice to be bought by the army for the troops in Siberia. Farmers and urban dwellers could not sustain themselves. In late July 1918, a riot in a small fishing town escalated into a national crisis that raged until September. Yamagata wrote, 'It is of unbearable regret that an incident like this was provoked at such a time as the expedition. To completely renew this public sympathy will not be an easy task.'⁴¹ Prime Minister Terauchi Masatake and his cabinet had no other option but to resign.

Intercepts of Japanese diplomatic and military communications supported British policy. Lord Hardinge, permanent under-secretary at the Foreign Office, commented on Siberia that 'we know from secret information that the Japanese have an entirely different scheme of intervention in their heads'. Soon, Major Bell returned to Vladivostok as a passport control officer to gather political intelligence, but once again 'his zeal outran his discretion' with the result that the military pushed successfully for his dismissal. By February 1919, the political intelligence department at the Foreign Office insisted that Japan's 'purpose ... is hegemony in the Far East and recognition of herself as the guardian of the Yellow Races together with acknowledgement of preferential rights in China'.⁴² British consuls were at the forefront of intelligence gathering in Siberia. In November 1919, Henry Sly, the consul at Harbin, reported that a Japanese business syndicate tried to purchase all the forests and mines between the Argun (Amur) River and Lake Baikal. Harry Steptoe, a young consul in China, discovered that the Japanese were selling weapons to Mongols, boosting White Russian General Ataman Semenov to reach Outer Mongolia. The pro-Japanese Semenov was a controversial figure, and has been called 'a strange and terrible man' in subsequent studies.⁴³

Steptoe would prove to be a celebrated SIS spymaster in cosmopolitan Shanghai. In December 1919, at a meeting of the Cabinet, Foreign Secretary Lord Curzon circulated a memorandum by an expert warning that the average Japanese was 'aggressively patriotic ... individually truculent, fundamentally deceitful, [and] imbued with the idea that he is under an obligation to impose his own particular form of culture on his neighbours'. Surprisingly, this memorandum reinforced a pro-Japanese bias, arguing that it was better for the Japanese to expand into the northern Far East than to the south.[44] As Antony Best put it, 'implicit in this reluctant compromise was the recognition that if Japan did decide to seek treasure elsewhere that this might well pose a substantial threat to British interests that the Empire would be ill-equipped to resist'.[45]

The GC&CS (Government Code and Cypher School) supplied the Foreign Office with intercepts of Japanese diplomatic cables which revealed the Japanese intention to withdraw troops from Siberia on the pretext of security arrangements. Reassured by this, British diplomacy was not focussed on pressuring Tokyo. In May 1921, the Japanese Foreign Minister informed the embassies in Paris and London:

A conference is now being held here [in Tokyo] of civilians and military officials … When a definitive decision has been reached, I will communicate again, till when I beg that you will keep this strictly secret. I hasten to make this communication wholly and solely for your own information; informal negotiations are to be opened with the government of the Far Eastern Republic in the shape of discussion of the question of trade. When the necessary conditions shall have been agreed upon for the removal of the menace to Manchuria and Korea and of the uneasiness respecting the security of the residents and communications which the Imperial Government have hitherto declared as their reasons for the stationing of troops, the (Japanese) forces are to be withdrawn from the Maritime Province and North Manchuria … When the evacuation of the troops along the Shantung Railway shall have been carried out, a suitable opportunity is further to be seized for attempting to effect an agreement on the [...] joint working of the Shantung line; and by this means a way is gradually to be devised for achieving a practical solution of the general Shantung question.[46]

In June, Tokyo informed their embassy in London that the Japanese forces would not support General Gelekoff: 'The [Japanese] authorities...decided not only-refrain from assisting him hereafter but even to afford him personal protection left him free to follow his own device ... '[47]

Meanwhile, the Americans were well aware of Japanese strategic plans in Siberia and had top-secret intelligence to verify it. General Uehara Yusaku, the chief of the Army General Staff, was an 'expansionist' against both Britain and the United States; he wanted to occupy Manchuria and the Russian Far East. Prime Minister Hara Takashi broadly agreed with the expansion strategy but preferred diplomacy. The Americans had been deciphering Japanese diplomatic communications and were aware of Japanese designs as the Russian Civil War raged. The American Cipher Bureau under Herbert O. Yardley provided President Wilson with key intelligence. In January 1920, Yardley cracked the Japanese codes. The Japanese wanted an intervention in the Far East against the Bolsheviks, but they needed to be 'invited' by the other powers.

In May 1918, along the Trans-Siberian Railway, Bolshevik forces clashed with the Czechoslovak Legion (former prisoners-of-war from Austria-Hungary who had been granted safe passage across Siberia after the Brest–Litovsk Pact). The Bolshevik defeat created the momentum for anti-Bolshevik nationalist generals, warlords and armies (the so-called White Russians) to unite. Wilson, assuming that anti-Bolsheviks had potential for victory as well as seeking to control a Japanese intervention, agreed to 'invite' Japanese forces – but no more than 12,000. Tokyo was provided with a unique opportunity. The first US troops landed in Vladivostok on 16 August 1918, and Japanese forces were already deployed there, taking key positions. The Japanese sought to control the Chinese Eastern railway in order to reach their strategic target: Manchuria. A special inter-Allied committee on the railways of Siberia and North China was established, called the Inter-Allied Railway Commission. By January 1920, American soldiers and the majority of the American engineers on the committee had returned home. In contrast, the Japanese made excuses and remained, increasing their troop numbers. A few American engineers, under seasoned railway engineer John Stevens, remained with the commission.

In early February, Iakov Triapitzin, anarchist leader of a band of pro-Bolshevik Russians, teamed up with Chinese and

Koreans and attacked the anti-Bolshevik and Japanese forces in Nikolaevsk, at the Amur River, across from Sakhalin. Alongside Japanese and anti-Bolshevik troops, many Japanese women and children were killed or burned before Japanese reinforcements arrived and Triapitzin's group fled. For the Japanese Army General Staff, this was an episode to be avenged and a pretext for the Japanese to remain.

Stevens recorded these episodes. At this time, he was approached by John Luebeck-Essensky, formerly with the Czech Legion and identified by Stevens as a 'Czecho-Slovak Secret Service Agent'. Luebeck-Essensky offered him secret Japanese army headquarters documents translated into Russian. He needed money to support himself and had a secret source inside the Japanese headquarters. He wrote to Stevens: 'I am obliged to pretend to be a man of means in order to get the information I receive from Japanese sources. I cannot help but have a great many expenditures and even endangering my health by frequent drinking with them.' Stevens was no spymaster and was sceptical of the offer. Nevertheless, a stream of documents in a period of months showed the real Japanese way of thinking, with talk of expansion and creating provocations to justify their presence in the region and stake their claim to Manchuria. Stevens had at his disposal cables from General Uchida himself; the general wrote that it would be made clear to the Western powers that Japan was fighting Bolshevism, especially in North Manchuria and along the border of Korea (then a Japanese colony). To a Japanese public struggling to put food on the table, it would be explained that the 'war in Siberia was for the sake of 'economic welfare'. These messages reached Washington.

The Americans were aware of the strategy of deception when on 3 December 1920 they received a secret communication between General Uchida and the commander of Japanese forces in Siberia, General Oi; he ordered the latter to facilitate Communist propaganda to 'pass through' stations west of Harbin in Manchuria, 'so that we could in time foresee the possible seizure by the Bolsheviks of certain regions of the Concession zone'. General Oi should block the Chinese warlords from attacking the Communists, 'thus assisting its penetration'. Meanwhile, the Japanese consul in Vladivostok believed that anti-Bolsheviks in the Maritime Province would 'provoke the Communists to opening [hostile] actions'. He claimed that the governments at Vladivostok and Beijing would feel that the Japanese were unwilling to stop Bolsheviks. General Uchida wrote that this would be 'a sign for the successful working out of our plan'. The Japanese would allow Bolsheviks into Vladivostok and other towns along the Trans-Siberian Railway where Europeans and Americans lived; after apparent massacres, they would intervene and establish their occupation with the blessing of the Western powers. Meanwhile, it was known through secret sources that the Japanese had dispatched forces into Mongolia to aid anti-Bolsheviks.

Eventually, the lack of clear Japanese victory and the strong diplomatic pressure by Washington compelled the Japanese government to back down and Prime Minister Tomosaburō Katō announced the unconditional withdrawal of all Japanese forces (with the exception of those on North Sakhalin) by October 1922, an announcement which was honoured.

The secret intelligence provided by Luebeck-Essensky's correspondence showed that the Japanese military, irrespective of the wishes of the civilian government, were following their strategy of expansionism by lying to everyone; they had the unshakable belief that Imperial Japan would soon be expanding in the Far East. Uchida wrote that the Russian Far East remained 'the most important economic base which – if the Imperial Government does not take advantage of its present strong position to strengthen its influence – will be taken advantage of by the American Government'. Katō was persuaded to sign the 1922 Washington Naval Treaty and was blamed by his compatriots for doing so; later he sided with the expansionists in the invasion of Manchuria and the creation of the puppet state of Manchukuo.[48]

By now, the United States had emerged as a leading power. London was not interested in maintaining close relations with Japan since the United States and Japan were deemed antagonists in the Pacific. Washington did not like the prospect of a formal

Anglo-Japanese alliance, which might help the Japanese achieve a dominant position in the Pacific market as well as in China.

The Versailles peace conference of 1919 worried the Japanese leadership, the *genrō* and the military. Lieutenant General Utsunomiya Tarō assumed that the Japanese Empire had become 'an object of the world's jealous gaze'. Japan was 'besieged' by Britain, the United States, China, Korea and the Bolsheviks. The country and people should be ready for war, but currently the public was tired and morale was 'exceedingly low'. A confident General Tanaka was certain that Britain and the United States would expand in China: 'The Empire has reached a point where it must act resolutely to carry out its own policies regardless of the reaction of the powers.'[49]

Yamagata, irritated and confused by the 'new diplomacy' declarations of Woodrow Wilson boosting peace and democracy, feared that the British had a plan of expansion in western China and the Americans for Manchuria. China, he felt, must be 'saved' by Japanese imperial strategy against the white races.[50]

Having noticed the rapid shipbuilding program underway in Japan, US naval intelligence warned about a coming war with Japan. In June 1919, Josephus Daniels, US Secretary of the Navy, agreed that the US fleet should be evenly distributed between the Atlantic and the Pacific so that it could easily blockade Japan. The top aide of the secretary was future president Franklin D. Roosevelt.

Secretary of State Charles Hughes aimed to nullify Japan's gains in the war, seeing this as the only option to preserve American interests in China. In this game of strategy, Washington was unwilling to tolerate Britain maintaining an official alliance with Japan, which it saw as a weak British Empire sanctioning the rising Japanese hegemony in the Far East.[51] Besides British officials, experts in commerce like E. M. Gull admitted that 'Great Britain ceased to be cock of the walk in China, falling commercially to third place behind the United States and Japan'.[52]

Tokyo was left with no official alliance. Moderate Prime Minister Hara Takashi was stabbed to death by an ultranationalist rail worker on the eve of the Washington Conference on naval armaments in the autumn of 1921. The Japanese government signed the Five-Power Treaty of 1921, assenting to restrictions on naval building: Britain and America were allowed to build battleships and battlecruisers each limited to a total tonnage of 525,000 tons, Japan to 315,000 tons, and France and Italy each to 175,000 tons; for aircraft carriers, Britain and America were each limited to a total tonnage of 135,000 tons, Japan to 81,000 tons, and France and Italy each to 60,000 tons. No single ship could exceed 35,000 tons, and no ship's gun calibre could exceed 16 inches. Japanese ambitions were frustrated by the treaty, leading ultranationalist officials and officers to gain more influence in an aggrieved Tokyo.[53]

However, the limitations imposed by the treaty saved the Japanese economy from crashing under the weight of the existing naval program. In secret, Katō had told the Vice Minister of the Navy, the Director of Military Affairs and the Director of the Technical Department from the Navy Ministry to the Prime Minister's office that the shipbuilding program could not be funded. The Washington treaty reoriented Japanese spending towards aircraft carriers and torpedoes as key platforms and weapons for a war against the US Navy in the Pacific. The 1923 Imperial Defence Policy moderated the Imperial Navy's demands and confirmed that the future enemy was the United States. Naval officers would focus on acquiring more information on the developing technology of torpedoes and aircraft carriers. Two battle cruisers under construction, the *Akagi* and the *Kaga*, were turned into aircraft carriers hosting sixty planes each; *Akagi* was operational by 1927 and *Kaga* by 1928.

Japan had entered the era of the large aircraft carriers. In parallel, the technology of torpedoes was improved. The Imperial Japanese Navy developed an oxygen-fuelled torpedo, known as the Type 93 or Long Lance. By 1933 it was operational, reaching speeds of 48 knots and boasting a range of 40,000 metres without a wake. Long Lance was Japan's secret weapon in the 1930s and in parallel the *Kaidai*-type submarine was developed, maintaining more than 20 knots on the surface. New submarine technology was a key intelligence-gathering focus for naval strategists and spymasters.[54]

Eventually, London decided to allow the 1902 Anglo-Japanese Treaty to lapse, to the surprise of the Japanese ambassador in

London. In 1921, twenty-year-old Crown Prince Hirohito – later to rule as Emperor – paid an official visit in Britain, making him the first crown prince ever to travel abroad. Yamagata and other officials in the imperial court and government were opposed, and indeed his journey demonstrated a more open, less imperialistic outlook in reformist circles in Tokyo. Even so, reformists still believed in the imperial future of Japan in the Far East. Hirohito showed a great deal of curiosity about the Royal Navy during his visit, and Piggott was only too happy to serve as his aide, keen to improve Anglo-Japanese relations.[55]

3

THE SPYMASTERS OF
THE EMPEROR

an Fleming, a wartime Royal Navy intelligence officer and
author of the James Bond novels, used the image of the
Japanese spymaster from samurai stock in *You Only Live
Twice* (book published in 1964; film released in 1967). This work
was believed to be based on real people using institutional memory
derived from the reports of liaison officers and co-operation with
Imperial Japanese Navy officers over the decades. By the late
1930s, Admiralty staff officers were worried by the Japanese:

> A cautious, thorough and methodical race ... Their plans are
> likely to be prepared with great case to meet a number of
> salutations and carried through with determination regardless of
> consequences. History shows that they thoroughly understand
> the importance of getting in the first blow. It is assumed that the
> elimination of the power of the British Empire to interfere with
> Japanese policy in the Far East will constitute the ultimate object
> of the Japanese Government. The presence of the British Fleet in
> the Far East is the dominating factor in the strategical situation.
> Hence the defeat of the British fleet is likely to be the governing
> consideration when Japan is formulating a course of action.[1]

By February 1939, the Admiralty was concerned about a possible
special action in the Suez Canal by the Japanese:

Japan was not a party to this agreement [the 1888 Suez Canal Convention], and may attempt to delay our fleet [steaming from the Mediterranean to the Far East] by blocking the canal, if she considers that the advantages to be gained will outweigh the risk of offending neutral powers. The most dangerous period of risk would be before the declaration of war, when a specially prepared merchant ship might make a successful attempt to scuttle herself in one of the rocky narrows of the canal.[2]

Black-and-white photos of Japanese generals in their late fifties, in full regalia and sporting inscrutable expressions, do not help us imagine them as youthful, zealous and unaccountable spymasters. In this chapter we explore their origins, from the 1880s to the 1920s, and the coups and practices that made them the overconfident, reckless agents of empire feared by British military intelligence.

Fleming's 'Tiger' Tanaka is the youthful, committed chief of the Japanese Secret Service[3] who knows martial arts well before he attends Oxford University. He spied in London as naval attaché before the war and was a *kamikaze* pilot who survived. He had under his auspices a school of highly disciplined special operatives, the ninja who have 'spiritual strength' and 'follow the art of concealment and surprise', as Tanaka tells Bond. These fighters employ their swords – the famous katanas – in a very different way to Western swordsmen. He also had the latest technology – Japanese-made pistols with 'rocket bullets'.

Scholar Nitobe Inazō believed in the imperial expansion of Japan, presented in English in *Bushido: The Soul of Japan* (1900). He presented an idealised story of the history and codes of the samurai, a class that was disbanded in 1872 upon the modernisation of Japanese society. British and American audiences assumed that the samurai had similarities to the knights of the Middle Ages. This was utterly wrong, and it would be the cause of constant serious misinterpretations of the Japanese, their attitudes and their policies by the British.

The ninja or *shinobi* were initially poor peasants who wanted to defend themselves against feudal lords. These fighters could not afford swords so they developed small weaponry like the *makibishi* (iron caltrops) and the *tekko-kagi* (hand claws) as well as employing tactics such as setting fires or poisoning. In later years they were employed as low-class mercenaries and bodyguards. By the second half of the nineteenth century, Japanese folklore legends about these invisible warriors were noted by Western observers, informing European views about the Japanese in a military context.

For Fleming, the Japanese spymaster who admires 'famous English stoicism' is suave, a man of the world, chauvinistic about the superiority of his culture and heritage, with sadistic tendencies and an implicitly threatening demeanour ('cruel, samurai face'). He is antagonistic but can be 'turned' by a charismatic British agent like Bond, as demonstrated in the following statement by Fleming's Tanaka:

Commander ... This morning I have betrayed a state secret to you. I was encouraged in my action by my friendship for Dikko [the Australian secret agent working with Bond]. I was also encouraged by the sincerity of your bearing and the honesty of your approach to the duty that has been laid upon you.[4]

On another occasion, Tanaka warns Bond about the effects of sake: 'It is the man who drinks the first flask of sake; then the second flask drinks the first; then it is the sake that drinks the man.' Indeed, the caustic humour of real-life spymasters is evident in Colonel Hikosaburo Hata, a military attaché in Moscow who provoked Soviet generals at a May 1936 reception:

After returning to Japan, I will give an order to provide cans of Japanese sake to every soldier on the border, thus the Soviet Army should do the same with vodka. If we have enough alcohol, there shall be no more border conflicts.[5]

It is claimed that Marshal Voroshilov and Marshal Budyonny were offended by this proposal, while Marshal Yegorov laughed.[6]

The psyche of the spy was portrayed in *School of Spies* (1966), a Japanese film directed Yasuzo Masumura and written by Seiji Hoshikawa. In contrast to mainstream Japanese cinema, the maverick director and screenwriter put emphasis on individualism and on personal dilemmas concerning duty and love. Jiro Shiina, the protagonist, is a cadet in an espionage school who breaks a British intelligence code and discovers that his fiancée is a spy. In contrast to *You Only Live Twice*, the portrayal of the spies' training is based on fact. The trainees are instructed: 'During espionage, assassination and sabotage are inevitable ... lethal gas and bacteria can be used to discreetly eliminate a target. Substances that kill slowly, such as arsenic and mercury chloride are recommended over fast-acting chemicals like strychnine and cyanide. The poisoning of a target must go undetected ... an expert magician will demonstrate the proper technique.' The cadets are warned that 'spies are eventually caught and arrested. When that day comes you cannot succumb to torture ... you must endure it and continue on your mission. Committing suicide by poisoning is the last resort – only when concrete evidence is presented against you.'

Eventually Jiro employs the tradecraft he learned. He spikes a glass of wine with poison and offers it to his fiancée, who upon feeling dizzy tries to show her love but soon loses strength and suffers an agonising death in front of him. In the last scene Jiro walks alone outside the barracks contemplating what he has done. He is approached by the unhappy head of the school; the rest of the students and staff are heard inside celebrating the end of the training. For the Japanese director, the spy is also a cold-blooded killer; this in contrast to the work of his contemporary John Le Carré, who is critical of the cynicism and incompetence that lead to immoral and fateful decisions.

The mentality exhibited by the fictional Tanaka and Jiro can be traced to real Japanese spymasters, naval and military attachés or councillors who are divided into two distinct categories: the suave spymasters in Europe, concerned with seeking the latest technology and recruiting Europeans; and the rough, unaccountable spymasters, the infamous 'agents of chaos' employing criminals in the Far East, orchestrating provocations and covert operations as well as pursuing information.[7]

A common characteristic of naval and military attachés before war with Japan broke out in 1941 is that they personally held meetings with their spies and agents to negotiate money, hand over task lists and receive intelligence. Trusting nobody, they eschewed intermediaries. They were not afraid of racial profiling, of standing out in the crowd in London or elsewhere. The approach of employing intermediaries from other nations was the least developed element of their spycraft, as will become clear in the following chapters.

Both the suave and the rough spymasters were mentored by Yamagata's underlings. Since he met with many middle-rank officers, businessmen and journalists, he would personally have advised spymasters on their missions. They were expected to show initiative and take matters into their own hands whenever it seemed expedient. Espionage was not a hierarchical activity.

For the Japanese spymaster, a foreigner's only motive when spying for Japan was money. As a result, they built their recruitment model on this premise alone. The Japanese naval attaché in London cabled the Director of Naval Intelligence of the Imperial Navy General Staff on 1 March 1933 concerning one European spy:

> I feel strongly that although his new requests etc are more or less small, that it reveals his real intention to draw out a large remuneration for himself. Though it can be expected to be the normal psychology of the sort of man who would engage in such work, one cannot be without misgivings as to where these requests will end.[8]

One intelligence organisation with police connections was the *Kempeitai*, established in 1881 as a military gendarmerie that drew from the civilian populace. Gradually, this service turned into a secret military police force. By 1907, its role in the occupation of Korea saw it identified with mass atrocities and sadism. The civilian secret police force was the *Tokkō* (*Tokubetsu Kōtō Keisatsu*, or Special Higher Police). The *Kempeitai* had its own *Tokkō* service.[9] The first official Japanese foreign intelligence organisation was established in 1890 as the Japan-China Trade Research Institute (*Nisshin Bōeki Kenkyūjo*), tasked with collecting information on the Chinese economy.

Fukushima Yasumasa is a strong example of the Japanese spy. Born in 1852 to a samurai family, he was a keen student of foreign languages. Initially, he was a civilian employee of the Ministry of Justice. He fought alongside the government forces in the Satsuma Rebellion of 1877 and afterwards was posted to the General Staff. From 1879 he travelled abroad and in 1887 was appointed military attaché in Berlin. When recalled, he returned by horse, riding all the way from Berlin to Vladivostok and recording his findings. Upon completing the 14,000-mile journey he was named a national hero, inspiring future rough riders and Japanese spymasters in China. But this hardly amounted to espionage as we define it today. His reports proved influential within the General Staff in terms of strategic intelligence, not tactical or operational military intelligence.[10]

In the Far East, killing was an option for the Japanese spymaster/officer, as in the assassination of Queen Min (posthumously named Empress Myeongseong), wife of Gojong, King of Korea: 'It was my role to enter ... Climbing up the wall ... finally reaching the rear private royal residence, we killed the queen ... We were stunned as it was unexpectedly easy,' wrote Kumaichi Horiguchi, the Japanese assistant consul in Korea, to his friend Teisho Takeishi on 9 October 1895.[11]

Tokyo had not sanctioned the murder of the empress, but she was an influential figure who was supposed to be in negotiations with the Russians to help them sidestep Japanese interests in the kingdom. Japanese spymasters needed deniability; this was a job for a civilian. A group of Japanese civilians stormed the palace in Seoul early on the morning of 8 October after palace guards had been withdrawn. The assassins entered unobstructed and hacked her to death with a sword, taken outside and burned. Her ladies-in-waiting were also murdered.

The murder of the queen was sanctioned by Lieutenant General Miura Gorō, who asserted, 'This was a matter which I decided in the space of three puffs on a cigarette ... whether my behaviour was right or wrong, only Heaven can judge.' For the lieutenant general – who was not punished due to 'insufficient evidence' – the queen was 'highly talented', the 'true monarch of Korea'. The assassination team comprised more than thirty young, educated Japanese immigrants with samurai backgrounds.[12] The Japanese spymasters in China would employ these reckless 'continental adventurers' (*tairiku rōnin*).

Japanese leaders did not see spycraft as a gentlemanly affair. A spymaster employs agents and has a clear understanding of the means and scope of deception. Prime Minister Itō Hirobumi and Foreign Minister Mutsu Munemitsu showed themselves ready for strategic deception. On the eve of the war with China over Korea in 1894, they deceived the Chinese in order to break a code by the Chinese Foreign Ministry leadership. This ploy was envisioned by Mutsu, who called on Sato Aimoro, chief of the Telegraphic Section of Japan's Foreign Ministry, an expert of Chinese codes.

War with China was declared on 1 August 1894 and the first major battle took place on 15–16 September with a Japanese victory in Pyongyang. On 24 October, the Japanese troops advanced into Manchuria. The last battle of the war took place on 5 March 1895 at Yinkou in Manchuria. In April 1895 the Chinese delegation accepted the treaty signed at Shimonoseki. Korea gained its independence (soon becoming a Japanese protectorate), and Japan won war reparations, trading concessions in China, and ownership of Taiwan (Formosa) and the Pescadores.

Almost a decade earlier, in August 1886 at the Nagasaki port, a quarrel took place between Chinese navy sailors, Japanese civilians and eventually the intervening police. A Chinese sailor lost an innocent-looking dictionary. This was taken to the police and then to the Ministry of Foreign Affairs. Cryptographers concluded that it was a supplement of a Chinese codebook. Nonetheless, not all characters could be decoded. By 1894, Foreign Minister Mutsu remembered the incident with the 'dictionary' and had the idea of sending a message to the Chinese delegation in Tokyo containing *real* information: Japan will not tolerate Chinese interference in Korea and will act unilaterally. The Japanese hope was that the Chinese delegation would send Beijing the message – in code – by telegraph. The Japanese would intercept the telegram and, knowing what it said, use it to decipher the code used. The message was sent on 22 June 1894; the war was declared on 1 August.

Indeed, the message was encrypted by the Chinese diplomatic mission in Tokyo and decrypted by the Japanese cryptographers of the Ministry of Foreign Affairs; they managed to draft the entire Chinese code employed by senior leaders. Throughout the war the

Japanese scored some coups in decrypting Chinese messages of generals and senior officials, among them of Viceroy Li.

Prior to the war, decrypts of the Chinese messages showed anxiety over Japanese actions in reaction to Chinese policies over Korea. The Chinese sounded worried about Japanese intervention. All this boosted the determination of the Japanese leadership: their enemy, China, seemed scared, meaning they were weak militarily despite appearances. Imperial Germany, meanwhile, expected a Chinese victory. Foreign governments, unaware that the Japanese had inside knowledge, assumed the Japanese were merely acting recklessly. Indeed, this could be a universal lesson: a reckless actor reading reports of a moderate opponent indicating its anxiety might lead the reckless actor to assume weakness on the part of the moderate opponent. The reporting of the moderate side could actually *invite* aggression.

At this time, Kamio Mitsuomi, the Japanese military attaché in Beijing, organised an espionage network based in Tientsin. It is claimed that he bribed officials from the imperial Chinese military council.[13]

During the peace negotiations at Shimonoseki, the Chinese delegation was compelled by Japan not to employ code in their communications with Beijing. The Japanese had broken many codes by now, so the prohibition was likely a ruse to prevent the Chinese from suspecting that their encrypted communications were insecure. Nonetheless, the Japanese held the military advantage and they did not discover any evidence of the Chinese acting in bad faith for the continuation of hostilities. [14]

At this point, negotiations were thrown into disarray. The head of the Chinese delegation, Viceroy Li, was shot by Koyama Toyotaro on 24 March 1895. A single bullet hit his left cheek. The pain was insufferable, but the Japanese physicians were afraid that anaesthetics would kill the elderly viceroy, so he decided not to take out the bullet. Instead he continued, stoically, with negotiations. Mutsuhito (known after his death as Emperor Meiji), as the host of peace talks, was most embarrassed. The government wanted to be accepted as a victorious new imperial power, but a single assassin had changed all the impressions of other imperial powers, including Britain. Viceroy Li recuperated and sent coded messages to Beijing which were decrypted by the Japanese: they revealed Li's impressions on the embarrassment felt by Japanese government. Eventually, the Japanese amended some of their demands and agreed to a ceasefire, as Li had wished.[15]

Mutsuhito issued a public apology to the Chinese government: 'It was of course incumbent on Us, in observance of international usage and on account of the credit of Our country to treat the Chinese Ambassador with proper courtesy and consideration … Most unfortunately, however, a fanatic has come forward and inflicted injury on the Chinese Ambassador.'[16] The then Field Marshal Yamagata Aritomo was furious: 'The scoundrel [the assassin] has undone the great achievements of the nation.' After the resumption of negotiations, Itō warned Li that should diplomacy fail, Japanese troops would attack Beijing and 'Japan would not be able to guarantee the safe return of the Chinese delegation'. Eventually China agreed to recognise the neutrality of Korea, but Japan did not recognise Korean independence. Japan agreed to reduce its territory in coastal Manchuria but kept the Liaodong Peninsula and Niuzhuang. As Japan was about to lead a diplomatic triumph with the Treaty of Shimonoseki, however, strong pressure came from Germany, Russia and France to hand over Liaodong to China. In the eyes of the Japanese this was a humiliation.[17]

On 23 April 1895, the diplomatic representatives of Germany, Russia and France called on the Japanese Minister of Foreign Affairs, offering some 'friendly advice': Japan should hand back Liaodong because the presence of Japanese armies there 'would be a constant menace to the capital of China, [and] would at the same time render illusory the independence of Korea, and would henceforth be a perpetual obstacle to the peace in the Far East'. This was a threat of intervention; at least it was taken that way by the Japanese, whose leaders were afraid that a combined naval operation of these European nations would annul all gains of the war with China, scrapping completely the Treaty of Shimonoseki. The Japanese government agreed to hand back Liaodong. Viceroy Li was involved in the consultations.[18]

In 1901, Li was the chief Chinese negotiator with the foreign powers that captured Beijing. On 7 September 1901, he signed the Boxer Protocol and achieved for the troops of the eight-nation alliance an exit from Beijing. He died the same year, exhausted from liver inflammation. Prime Minister Itō was shot by An Jung-geun, a Korean nationalist, at the Harbin railway station on 26 October 1909.

At the turn of the century, British officers concluded that the Japanese spymasters were military officers, professional, resourceful and merciless. It seemed that the Japanese intelligence officers blurred the lines between hatred and professional practice according to the evolving secret service ethics of the time. At that time, no secret intelligence service existed in Britain, SIS and MI6 being established in 1909. The Japanese spymasters were to be feared not least because Imperial Japan was turning against the weak British Empire in the Far East. In 1908, the Japanese General Staff established the Intelligence Department as a central hub of collection and analysis. This did not change the value of these *tairiku rōnin*. Officers of the Intelligence Department were dispatched to China to manage and direct espionage as well as the *rōnin*.[19]

At the turn of the century, British officers had concluded that the Japanese spymasters were military officers, professional, resourceful and merciless. It seemed that the Japanese blurred the lines between uncontrollable hatred and professional practice according to the evolving secret service ethics of the time. At that time, no secret intelligence service existed in Britain, the SIS and MI6 being established in 1909. The Japanese spymasters were to be feared, not least because Imperial Japan was turning against the weak British Empire in the Far East. In 1908, the Japanese General Staff established the Intelligence Department as a central hub of collection and analysis. This did not change the value of these *rōnin*. Officers of the Intelligence Department were dispatched to China to manage and direct espionage as well as the *rōnin*.[20] The aforementioned Fukushima Yasumasa was one of the first Japanese spymasters admitted in 1912: 'It is very bad to put active duty officers on the front ... they should operate on the backstage ... [and delegate the work] to merchants [*taiku rōnin*].'[21] The Japanese espionage machinery was constructed in such a way that accountability was non-existent because all the General Staff delegated spymasters on secret missions who either took matters into their own hands and initiated plots without informing Tokyo and waiting for authorisation or outsourced missions with broad directives to the overzealous *taiku rōnin* who sometimes formed large gangs with Chinese criminals and warlords.[22] This was not known to the British military, which admired Japanese discipline and samurai war ethics.

In April 1895, on the eve of the Triple Intervention, Admiral Beaumont, the Director of Naval Intelligence, feared a Japanese action; their navy had showed tremendous success employing torpedo boats against Chinese ships. The British legation in Tokyo warned that 'the incidents of the present war have conclusively shewn that the organization and efficiency of her Secret Service are perfect'.[23]

Admiration of Japanese espionage started to spread. In Seoul, British minister J. N. Jordan wrote that the Japanese had 'a large and fully trained Intelligence Staff at their disposal'. Their intelligence service was 'detailed, thorough and penetrating and their intelligence network the most accurate procurer of information which had operated these since 1900'.[24] Japanese spymasters excelled in recruiting retired officers. The case of Captain Fred T. Jane, a British naval attaché in Tokyo, is typical. His assessment of foreign navies was most valuable before the Russo-Japanese War.[25]

In 1901, the *Kokuryūkai* (the Amur River Society or Black Dragon Society) was formed, a paramilitary and espionage ultra-nationalist group operating in China in the following decades.[26] During the same period, Major Akashi Motojirō, after studying in Prussia, was assigned as military attaché in the Japanese embassies in Paris (1901) and St Petersburg (1902). Always under the eye of the Russian *Okhrana*, a secret police force infamous for elaborate surveillance methods, he made contact with Russian revolutionaries. Akashi was also a poet and a painter, though at the same time insensitive and cruel. He reported to the General Staff in 1906:

The European attitude of 'mistaken benevolence toward one's enemy' sometimes allows such things to happen. For example, an opposition member behaved in almost the same way when he tried to assassinate the Governor-General of Moscow [Grand Duke Sergei]. Though the murderer had a good chance of assassinating the Grand Duke, he abandoned the attempt, because in his opinion it was inhumane also to assassinate an innocent child who happened to be riding in the same carriage, even though it was Grand Duke Paul's child. I have heard of similar situations in which the life of an individual is placed above one's duty. I regard this attitude as little more than ridiculous.[27]

Akashi was the spymaster who facilitated covert arms support to Russian, Polish and Finnish revolutionaries. Whenever the military in Tokyo hesitated, he managed to persuade the General Staff to transfer arms and money to the revolutionaries. Akashi intrigued with the Japanese diplomatic representatives in Europe to help him with his scheme:

He also had Lieutenant Colonel Tanaka Hirotarō teach them how to sabotage railway lines. Later they [the Japanese-backer revolutionaries] tried to blow up a track in a few places, but the results were inadequate: they stopped trains for only one day even in the most effective instance. That was the reason why we finally gave up the venture.[28]

Arming revolutionaries was a managerial task for a spymaster. Akashi remarked:

In regard to buying arms, I decided to give the Poles money in advance and a free hand, but the other parties received money only after they had found arms for sale. It was hard to buy arms. This was particularly because each party wanted different kinds of arms. Parties composed mainly of workers, such as the Socialist Revolutionaries and the Polish Socialists, did not like rifles. In contrast, the Finns and Caucasians, who were mainly peasants, preferred rifles. Toward May, while Zilliacus set about buying revolvers and Mauser-action cavalry rifles in Hamburg, Germany, Dekanozi, Cherkezov, and the Swiss anarchist Baud purchased Vetterli rifles. The rifles and other equipment purchased in Switzerland amounted to 16,000 rifles and 3 million bullets to be sent to the Baltic regions and 8,500 rifles and 1.2 million bullets to be sent to regions of the Black Sea.[29]

Akashi was moving too fast, attending meetings with revolutionaries and drawing the attention of the *Okhrana* amidst the 1905 Russian Revolution. As early as July 1904, a special unit was established for counterintelligence on Japanese espionage in Scandinavia, western Europe, Britain and the Russian Empire. Russian intelligence officers reported on the arrival of Japanese officers/spies in Sweden; the Russians bribed Swedish police officials to report on Japanese and revolutionaries arriving or leaving the Stockholm port. In autumn 1904 the French cooperated with Russian espionage on a Japanese diplomatic mission. French intelligence assisted in the opening of Japanese diplomatic correspondence. French secret agents 'on loan' to *Okhrana* infiltrated the Japanese diplomatic missions in Brussels and in The Hague. The French offered the Russians intercepted diplomatic telegrams of Japanese missions across Europe. Japanese spymasters under Akashi and their spies, working with revolutionaries in central and northern Europe, were put under surveillance by *Okhrana* spymaster Arkadii Michailovich Harting. The Russians were bribing local police officers and customs officials.[30]

Meanwhile, Akashi reported how he learned that he was followed by the spies of the tsar:

> As I had business in Paris to discuss the arms transport to the Black Sea at that time, I decided to go there even though this letter was extraordinary. To locate my secret whereabouts was so strange that I thought, for better or worse, such a person could become useful, if circumstances permitted. So I was waiting for her at the meeting place at the appointed time. A lady in her forties approached me and later came to the hotel that I chose. She said, 'I am the French wife of an *Okhrana* agent. I am now separated from my husband. If you give me £ 400, I shall tell you about the *Okhrana's* secrets. I said, 'I spend money to obtain information. I only hope you will tell me as much as you know. [the mysterious lady replied:] 'Do you not know you have been closely watched by the *Okhrana*? They have never taken their eyes off you wherever you have been. Manuilov [I.F. Manasevich-Manuilov], Chief of the *Okhrana*, has already seen you walking near the Arc de Triomphe at eight o'clock this

morning, and reported that Akashi has come. You are cooperating with Nihilist leaders, such as Zilliacus and Dekanozi. The Russian government considers the *Nihilists* its most bitter enemy. As far as I know, you have been partly unsuccessful in buying arms from a person named Franck in Hamburg. Do you remember the person whom you met on the staircase of *Hotel Streit* where Zilliacus stayed, when you came from Berlin to Hamburg by a night train on a particular day? He was an agent named Springer and waited for your arrival there when you came to discuss matters with Zilliacus. After you came, Zilliacus hurriedly left the hotel with his luggage. I suppose your arrival at the hotel allowed Zilliacus to get away. Do you not know that the letter which you sent, under the pseudonym of George, to Dekanozi on a particular day was opened by the *Okhrana?* If you need, I can prove what was written in the letter. We know that you have been busily engaged in buying arms, but are now debating whether to buy them in Hamburg or elsewhere. It is so easy to follow a man on foot that I ask you not to walk. It is simpler to find you when you use your real name at a hotel. Will you use a false name there? Please stay at a big hotel, because it is easier for the secret police to keep track of a person staying at a small hotel than a big one. From now on I will warn you from time to time ... Though all of this was true, I said, for fear of her outwitting me, 'I am busy searching for agents who could smuggle themselves into Russia and collect information. If you know some suitable candidates, please introduce me. I am not so much interested in what the *Nihilist* parties (*sic*) do. Please give me information about conditions in the Russian army.'[31]

The lady warned Akashi, 'You must not forget to be extremely careful of the *Okhrana* during the arms purchase. What I would like to tell you is that the Japanese code has already been deciphered by the Russians.'[32] Meanwhile Colonel Manaki Takanobu, the military attaché at Japan's Berlin embassy, heading the special duty unit the *Manaki Kikan* (after his name as was the practice), recruited agents for Russian Empire dominions – Estonia, Finland, Lithuania, Poland – and Ottoman Turkey.

After the signing of the 1902 Anglo-Japanese Treaty, the War Office and the Japanese General Staff concluded an agreement for the sharing of military intelligence on imperial Russia. The Japanese proposed 'a joint system of secret service' between Britain and Japan. The War Office refused to go into this, but it was evident that the Japanese were going to take British advice.

British military assets based in Hong Kong shared military and naval intelligence with the assigned Japanese liaison. Sir William Nicholson discussed intelligence with General Fukushima in London in July 1902, and it was agreed that a Japanese Army liaison officer would be assigned to the Indian Army Intelligence Bureau at Simla in November 1903. Anglo-Japanese intelligence sharing on Russia expanded. In parallel, Japanese spymasters of the army and navy recruited British journalists and businessmen to watch for the Russian fleet in the Baltic.[33] In April 1902, Major Utsunomiya, a military attaché, consulted the War Office on intelligence sharing concerning Russia.[34]

A high-level conference took place in May at Yokosuka Naval Station. Admiral Gonbei Yamamoto, the Navy Minister, attended with War Minister General Masatake Terauchi and Vice Admiral Sir C. A. G. Bridge, Commander-in-Chief of the China Station, and Lieutenant-Colonel A. G. Churchill, the military attaché of the British embassy in Tokyo. In July, a new conference was organised in London with the attendance of naval intelligence (Admiralty) and military intelligence (War Office). It was agreed for the embassy attaché to exchange military and naval information on Russia.

In November 1903, Fukushima urged the General Staff to dispatch Captain Otohiko Azuma to India. The officer's mission was to spy on potential Russian activities in Afghanistan and Persia and report to the British government. General H. M. Kitchener, the Commander-in-Chief of the British forces in India, was happy with the Japanese aid, which seemed to appreciate British imperial sensitivities.

Meanwhile, in London, Captain Stuart Nicholson, the Deputy Chief of Naval Intelligence at the Admiralty, provided the Japanese naval attaché with copies of the Russian 'Confidential Order No. 102'; this was telegraphed from the Ministry of the Navy in St Petersburg to the Commander-in-Chief of the Black Sea Fleet on 21 April 1904. The Russian government dispatched both the Black Sea and the Baltic fleets to the Far East against Japan. Also, the British Admiralty provided the Japanese with a blueprint for the newest torpedo.[35]

In Odessa in 1903–04, Japanese consul Kametaro Iijima spied alongside Charles S. Smith, the British consul general, a retired Royal Navy lieutenant-commander. It was Smith who explained naval intelligence and technology to the Japanese diplomat, who was keen to learn. Kametaro recruited his own British spies, among them T. J. McKenna, correspondent for *The Times* in the city. On the eve of the Russo-Japanese War, Kametaro fled to Constantinople (Istanbul), where he asked for help from the British legation. He was interested in reporting on the Russian fleet passing through the Dardanelles. The Foreign Office, not wishing to jeopardise relations with the Ottoman Porte, did not allow diplomats to help the Japanese spymaster. Nevertheless, N. R. O'Conor, the British chargé d'affaires, offered naval intelligence about the passage of the Russian Volunteer Fleet through the Turkish Straits and of Russian activities in the Balkans.[36]

Meanwhile, Commander Kurakichi Tonami, a staff officer on the Imperial Japanese Naval General Staff, reached Port Said, Egypt, in early November 1904. Ostensibly, he was an employee of the Nihon Yusen Company, the biggest shipping company in Japan, and worked for Worms & Co., Yusen's shipping agent at the Suez Canal. Kurakichi's mission was to report on Russian warships passing through Suez into the Indian Ocean and the Far East. At the same time, Tokichi Tanaka, the Japanese consul in Singapore, collected information on Russian naval activities since Tokyo had concluded that the Russian warships would pass through the straits on their way to Manchuria. In January 1905, Tanaka recruited a British lawyer in Labuan, overlooking the Sunda Strait, to watch for Russian movements. William Graeme St Clare, the editor-in-chief of the *Singapore Free Press*, helped Japanese naval intelligence. The editor arranged for Tanaka to meet and recruit European secret agents in the region.

The Russian Baltic Fleet steamed through the Malacca Strait on 8 April 1905 and weighed anchor at Camranh Bay in French Indochina on 14 April. The fleet was ordered to wait for the Black Sea fleet before clashing with the Japanese navy. The French authorities did not help Japanese intelligence. In response, Seiichi Noma, the consul in Hong Kong, recruited Alfred Cunningham, the British editor-in-chief of the *China Morning Post*, to go to Camranh Bay. Cunningham reached the port, hiding in the bottom of a fishing boat, and observed the Russian fleet; nonetheless he could not telegraph his information as the French authorities prohibited this. He thus returned to Hong Kong and provided Noma with the information required. He published anti-French articles saying that France was violating its neutrality by providing anchorage to the Russian fleet. British diplomatic pressure persuaded the French government to urge Russia to remove its warship from Camranh Bay.

In Shanghai, Japan and Russia maintained consulates general who were gathering naval and political intelligence. Russian officials put strong pressure on the Great Northern Telegraph Company, a Danish company monopolising the China–Japan submarine cable, to intercept Japanese telegrams and hand them over. On 26 December 1903, the Japanese Ministry of Foreign Affairs directed Masunosuke Odagiri, the consul general in Shanghai, to find some European spies. Odagiri recruited J. O. P. Bland, correspondent for *The Times* and Secretary to the Municipality for the Foreign Settlements at Shanghai. Bland was a keen spy under the code name 'P.Q.R.' and, in addition to G. E. Morrison, *The Times* correspondent in Peking, proved himself an industrious informer for the Japanese war effort. Another keen spy was Frederic Bandinel, a British merchant and honorary Japanese consul in Niezhuang. He gathered information on Russian movements in Manchuria, sending messages to Hikokichi Ijuin, the consul general in Tientsin. F. P. Cooper, a British merchant living in Tientsin, carried his messages. In Vladivostok, Edgar J. Schwabe, the British commercial agent, offered to exchange information on Russian defence plans with Japanese diplomats. Ostensibly, a Russian officer was willing to sell classified information. In Tokyo, Lieutenant General Iyozo Tamura, the Deputy Chief of the General Staff, ordered Major Zenjiro Ishizaka, who was a spy in Vladivostok, to assess the offer. Ishizaka warned eventually that the Russians might be willing to deceive with fake defence plans; eventually this operation did not go further.[37]

At Port Arthur, the target of the surprise Japanese torpedo attack of 8 February 1904, Sidney Reilly, the future SIS master spy during the 1917 Bolshevik Revolution, worked as a commercial agent at Ginsburg & Co., having access to all information on merchants sailing from Yokohama, relaying rumours of the coming of war with Japan. Speculating on this was a job for all local merchants. It seemed that Admiral Togo had a clear view of Russian minefields and search-light locations. A Russian report of April 1904 concluded that Ho-Liang-Shung, a Chinese engineer under the Russian head marine architect, had accessed the harbour defence plans and offered them to the Japanese for money. The Russians noted that on 23 February, and again on 8 March, large sums of money were deposited into his bank account. On 10 April, Shung made a bid to flee Port Arthur without an exit permit and was detained by the port gendarme but eventually escaped.[38] Japanese spymasters had dozens of well-placed spies in Port Arthur doing various jobs, with Shung providing the most useful intelligence. Reilly most probably was not involved in the espionage, aiming instead to gain from speculating.

Ironically, in December 1903 a mysterious Briton had revealed to a Russian naval officer, Captain Lebedev, that the Japanese planned a 'surprise attack' at Port Arthur in the coming weeks. He had a total of three meetings with Lebedev and brought with him a map. Lebedev rushed to inform his superiors, who discounted the intelligence as rumour.[39]

By 1905, the Royal Navy officer serving with the China Squadron had concluded that the Japanese were 'highly secretive about their own naval matters'. Indeed, the ten-year naval plan demanded that all Japanese ships of all types be built in Japanese yards. By September 1909, the Japanese naval attaché in London was so interested in naval technology that the Admiralty issued special guidelines for restricting the information provided to Japanese naval officers: 'Cases having arisen which information has been asked from the Japanese which has led to embarrassing requests from them.' The Admiralty believed that, as the second Anglo-Japanese Treaty was due to expire, no information should be divulged, especially about fleet exercises and tactics, machinery, future warship construction and experiments.[40]

It is evident that Japan was considered a growing threat. Nevertheless, Japanese firms and the Imperial Naval General Staff were getting the best of British technology. By 1907, the navy had sent seventy-one Japanese Navy officers to visit Britain under the auspices of the alliance, gathering – openly – key technical information about warship constructions and armament. Until 1916, Britain boosted the sale of Dreadnought-class warships to Japan. The Imperial Japanese Navy nurtured its relationship with the Vickers shipbuilding company, with Hokkaido Tanko Kisen Co., Vickers and Armstrong & Whitworth forming Japan Steel Works. The British companies provided know-how to establish a plant in Muroran, constructing many types of naval armaments, armour and guns. Until that time, technical problems did not allow for the Japanese to construct large-calibre guns and as well as high-grade steel. In the period 1911–15, twenty-seven British technicians worked as supervisors in Muroran. In parallel, Japanese employees worked in British shipbuilding factories copying drawings and studying procedures.[41] By 1909, Colonel J. A. R. Haldane of military intelligence warned:

[Japanese] enterprise, ingenuity and evasion are equally displayed by them in peace time, while in acquiring information regarding inventions which foreigners desire to sell to their government, they are utterly unscrupulous ... On many occasions they invited tradesmen for drink while stealing the prototypes and their drawings to copy them. Indeed 'there are many well-authenticated cases of foreigners who have gone to Japan to sell new range-finders, telescopic sights and other military improved pattern.[42]

Admiral Kondo Motoki, heading the naval construction branch of the IJN (Imperial Japanese Navy), boasted in 1925 that British firms had 'given us the free run of their shipyards and workshops to our workmen, and enabled them to learn much in their trade which they could not have done otherwise'.[43] British research and construction know-how saved Tokyo's admirals and generals effort and money, and boosted the naval construction program, accelerating the rise of the Japanese threat already noted by

British military intelligence. British firms offered help, providing all the information needed to establish a plant in Muroran for many types of naval armaments, especially armour. Vickers was the key company that provided armour plates that the Japanese yards could not yet construct. The company's metallurgy data was invaluable.[44] Meanwhile, Colonel Samoilov, the Russian military attaché in Tokyo before and after the Russo-Japanese War, had reported:

> The habit of one spying on another, which has taken deep roots in the Japanese character, made them perfect secret police agents. They do not consider espionage to be something shameful. Gendarmes are usually trained to act as spies, and the military use them for secret intelligence in the war period. On the other hand, it is easier for police in Japan to keep an eye on any foreigner, a 'white man', therefore, can hardly escape from local authorities. They look upon every non-Japanese with prejudice, they suppose him to be a spy and control his life. His mail is being looked through secretly, every step is being watched and everybody he meets falls into the sphere of interest of the counter-espionage agency.[45]

Lieutenant General Spencer Ewart, Director of Military Operations at the War Office, stated he had 'always understood that the Japanese owed a great deal to the perfection of their pre-arranged system of secret service'. Colonel James Edmonds of the War Office Directorate of Military Operations authored a report about German espionage, remarking that 'the Japanese learnt the trick of using officers to perform menial duties as servants etc. to gain information from their masters in the art of war, the Germans'.[46]

Colonel J. A. L. Haldane, attached as military attaché to the Japanese forces during the Russo-Japanese War, praised Japanese military intelligence and espionage efficiency. A special lecture at the War Office in 1909 cemented his impressions of the Japanese, who were deemed careful and meticulous spymasters. The Japanese officers, fluent in Russian, did not hesitate to disguise themselves as barbers or other professions to penetrate the target cities and get intelligence in Manchuria.[47] The Japanese spymaster was interested in

> ... information, no matter how trivial it may be, is collected from every available source. Thus, besides such matters as the resources of a possible enemy, the personal feeling, friendship, jealously, dislike and so on between officers of the army in high positions and the existence of cliques are inquired to ... the characteristics of the army, which it is intended some day to overthrow, its state of discipline, patriotism, fighting spirit and power of endurance are examined ... [48]

The Japanese had an 'aptitude' for spying:

> This aptitude is an inheritance which was descended to the present generation from their forefathers of the Daimic period, when each chief or Daimic maintained a body of spies in the castle of his neighbor, white at the Court of the Shogun or Taicoon- who until 1868 was the actual ruler of Japan, the Mikados being mere puppets- these followers of, to us, an unsavory trade, swarmed in such numbers, that in Japan it was almost literally true that the paper walls of the houses had ears. Spies were themselves spied upon and no one holding a position of the least importance was safe from objectionable attentions of this nature. This general system of secret service prevails in Japan ... the Japanese is not ashamed to spy on his neighbor. While in Manchuria the Japanese interpreter of the 2nd Army to which I was attached, was employed to my knowledge, by the General Staff to watch the Japanese Colonel in charge of the foreign attachés, because this colonel was considered to be too friendly with one of the attachés- a French colonel ... the Japanese as a nation well-endowed with Oriental cunning, self-control that reticence which becomes less and less a distinguishing feature the further west in the world one travels.

In Manchuria, Japanese spies posed as Chinese to listen in on the Russians. Only Chinese working for the Russians could identify them, employing a crude method:

The Chinese, however, in Russian employment came to the rescue and showed that the Japanese and Chinese differed in three main things, viz: Gait, eyes and a habit which was described to me. It appears to be the habit of certain Chinese, probably dwellers in Manchuria, to eat after every meal the dry seeds of the melon. This they do not by using their teeth but by manipulating the seeds between their lips. The habit is one learnt in childhood and difficult if not impossible to acquire by an adult. The Japanese spies were put to the test. All failed and I believe that most of them lost their lives in consequence.

Women were employed as spies:

The Japanese women too are frequently employed to assist in collecting information, and in Port Arthur there were, before the war began, many *geisha* or prostitutes, who no doubt helped to worm information out of Russian officers and men. In fact it has been truly said that the Japanese army is preceded by *geisha* and spies, so if ever we hear of numbers of them landing in India or any of our colonies, we may be prepared for trouble... [49]

Haldane's reference here to a 'landing in India' is most important. He stated this in 1909, showing British fear of the Japanese threat.
A Japanese spy could be identified in the field:

Unless he has lived in England for some years he will have great difficulty in using correctly his *r*'s and *l*'s, there being no *l* in the Japanese language. Ask him to repeat after you a sentence such as 'A lump of red leather, a red leather lump' or say the world 'rough-rider' and you will find him using '*l*' for '*r*' and '*r*' for '*l*' quite unconsciously. [50]

Haldane concluded that '[concerning] the spread of false information in peace time, in order to mislead foreign armies, the Japanese do not, I think indulge in this practice'. [51] The colonel did not touch upon a key task of Japanese spymasters: subversion. No doubt the freedom of action for the restless Japanese military attachés-cum-spymasters surprises historians. Koichi Sugimura, the Japanese ambassador to Germany, wrote to Foreign Minister Kosai Uchida on 20 June 1912:

> An attaché's duties are not subject to any and all restrictions. Based on his own views, he carries out business that is extremely broad in scope. An attaché is responsible for reporting to the head of the respective military service (Chief of General Staff of the Army and Chief of the Naval General Staff) on military affairs, as well as domestic affairs, foreign policy, financial affairs, and all other matters relating to his country of assignment. Therefore, an attaché also has the freedom to report his opinions on foreign policy, which are at times the exact opposite of the Ambassador's, without notifying the Ambassador.[52]

Japanese spymasters employed torture in interrogation. First, they made a bid to extract information without pain. The spymaster should keep in mind that 'if the prisoner looks repeatedly and inquisitively at the interrogator's face and steals a glance at his eyes, this is a sign' that the man in question was 'concealing vital knowledge'.[53]

By 1915–16, Japanese spymasters in China were inciting revolt against the ailing President–Field Marshal Yuan Shikai. General Tanaka ordered the commander of Japanese forces at Port Arthur, Lieutenant-General Aoki Nobuzumi, to commence subversion in southern China. Aoki prompted revolutionary leaders Liang Qichao and Zai Ao to rebel. In Yunnan, Zai declared independence in December 1915. Soon Major Yamagata Hatsuo of the Army General Staff came to Zai's aid. Tanaka wrote of his European allies: 'It seems that Britain and the other powers have recently come to understand the international significance of our country. We are in the amiable situation that they finally follow our lead in foreign policy.' Nevertheless, by early January 1916, Shikai's armies had quashed the Japanese-backed revolution in Yunnan. He was aware of Japanese complicity in the mutiny and informed Sir John Jordan, the British ambassador in Beijing.[54] The Imperial Japanese General Staff began to fret, informing Aoki that his contacts with the rebels were known and were 'stirring up public opinion in our country. As a result, they have caused a rift, not only in Sino-Japanese relations, but between Japan and Britain.'[55]

Always keen to take the initiative, the Japanese spymaster was less interested in subtle espionage than in covert actions such as arms transfers, fomenting revolution and political sabotage. This attracted the attention of foreign counterintelligence. The level of Japanese subterfuge was evident to the extent that military intelligence in London, manned by pro-Japanese officers like Major Francis Piggott, noted by 1917 that there could be a prompt reaction to Japan threatening British interests as long as Britain invested in armaments and 'Japanese espionage ... under close observation, so that any marked increase of activity in any particular direction will come promptly to light'.[56]

It was evident that the Japanese tried to extract information from British officers in Japan. A common method was to get the target drunk. Captain Malcolm Kennedy wrote:

Last night [2 December 1919] I went to a dinner an account of which I think might interest you as bringing out in a very marked way 1) the attitude of the Japanese officer towards our Alliance, 2) The great dislike they have for America. I have been to a good many dinners in this Country at one time and another and I have at times heard pretty open statements made under the influence of drink; but I have never heard more open or more pronounced statements than were made last night -in fact, so much so was this the case that I could not help feeling that, even if those were the true sentiments of the Japanese officers, there was something behind it all, and that the whole thing was a more or less put up job to find out what I, as a British officer, thought about it. I got the impression from two things:

1. Colonel K[imura] came to my house on Sunday to see me, but as I was still in Tokyo, he came again next day when I happened to be out. Hearing I would be back again shortly, he came again about 5.30 and then asked me to dine with him with the ostensible purpose of meeting Major Yamanaka, the new commander of the 1st Battalion, who has just returned from England. He told

me to fix my own day. The point is "why should he have been so anxious to ask me as to trouble to come to see me 3 times within 2 days unless there was some special reason for it?" The dinner could apparently have taken place any day.

2. At the dinner, all present got very drunk except Captain K., Colonel K.'s adopted son. He remained sober and never joined in the conversation. They did their level best to get me in the same condition and then proceeded to "pump" me for all they were worth. I had to play up to the part by pretending to be as drunk as themselves and in fact I found some difficulty in keeping up mere presence as they plied ... I noticed that Captain K. kept his eyes fixed on me the whole time, and seemed to be taking in everything I said.[57]

Kennedy would become one of the most influential pro-Japanese voices in the British press during the 1920s and 1930s; he would also work as a linguist for the GC&CS.

By 1921, the Department of Overseas Trade decided it did not want the Japanese to visit yards and plants. They were the epitome of intelligence gathering, putting British interests in jeopardy with 'their unscrupulous methods of copying processes etc. when privileges are extended to them'.[58]

4

ON HIS MAJESTY'S
SECRET SERVICE

Japanese and Indian spies working for British intelligence turned up lots of information indicating continuous Japanese support for Indian revolutionaries. The spies attended private consultations and dinners where Japanese officials spoke freely of their intentions to confront Britain in the Far East. The Imperial General Staff, under the influence of Yamagata Aritomo and his protégés, were well aware that India was the jewel in the crown of the British Empire and did not block any secret unofficial, operation against British rule there. Indeed, until the Second World War, British intelligence remained unaware of the semi-autonomous nature of both the Japanese military and its intelligence operations. A semi-autonomous military can always surprise an opponent who assumes that the government of the day has to approve its actions.

Hassan Hatano, a self-declared Muslim Japanese, arrived at the British embassy in Tokyo on the evening of 27 April 1914 and asked to meet with an official. Parlett, the acting secretary, interviewed him. Hatano explained that he had secret intelligence of a plot by Indian revolutionaries to poison British officials in China. Parlett believed him, since in June 1913 the Government of India had telegraphed the embassy that one Hassan Hatano, described an editor, was implicated in revolutionary plots and anti-British propaganda. The same year, British criminal investigators in India revealed that Okakura Kakuzo, a leading traditionalist scholar propagating pan-Asianism, was providing advice to revolutionaries. In his book *The Awakening of Japan* (1904), he wrote that the glory of the West is the humiliation of Asia.

In addition, Count Otani, who was a descendant of the Imperial House and had been a Buddhist abbot, visited India in 1914 and 1916, supposedly to study Buddhist remains. Evidently, as the Indian Criminal Investigations Department reported, 'his interest in Buddhist research is more political than religious [as] he regards a Buddhist revival as an important step towards the political headship of Japan in Asia'.[1] The intrigue followed an assassination attempt on Lord Hardinge, Viceroy of India, led by Rash Behari Bose, going under the name Thakur. On 23 December 1912, at the ceremonial procession of the viceroy in Chandni Chowk, a suburb of Delhi, a revolutionary had thrown an improvised bomb filled with screws at the elephant carrying the viceroy. His servant was killed and he himself sustained several injuries to his shoulders and back. Investigations led to the arrest of four revolutionaries, but the leader fled India.

Hatano had reached the British embassy at a time when reports of Japanese involvement in India were multiplying. The British diplomat arranged to see Hatano and together with Lord Kilmarnock he interviewed the willing informer. Hatano gave them 500 names of revolutionary sympathizers and the name of the individual said to be in charge of the plot to poison British officials in Shanghai. He received £25 and would receive another £20 should he provide more information about the key revolutionary, Barakatullah, who was living in Japan. Hatano said that he no longer supported Barakatullah and the revolutionaries and offered to be a spy for the British on a permanent basis with 'regular payment'. He proposed to turn a paper, entitled 'The Islamic Unity', over to 'a secret organ' of British rule in India. Ambassador Greene telegraphed to the governor of Hong Kong and the consul general in Shanghai, warning them about the poison plot. Greene informed Lord Grey, asking for authorisation to pay the informer.[2] The British diplomats who interviewed the Japanese informer noted:

Hatano impressed upon us however that he had never at heart been a Mohamatan (*sic*); the hope of gain was he confessed one reason which had led him to adopt that creed and another though he did not tell us so, was probably the hope of acquiring notoriety. Whatever his reasons were for originally joining himself with Barakatullah he had long been desirous of severing that connection and he thought a convenient moment in which to do so had now arrived. Barakattulah and Bhagwar Singh [another leading revolutionary] were about to proceed to American to attend a general congress to be held presumably at Portland, Oregon of the sympathizers with the anti-British movement in India and Hatano hoped that HMG would take steps to see that the two never came back to Japan.

Hatano was certain that no revolutionary suspected him of working against them, otherwise they would have poisoned him. He wanted also to escape Japan and, on reaching Korea or Manchuria, to work as a secret agent:

> He seemed to fear that Barakatullah would do something which would force HMG [His Majesty's Government] to ask the Japanese government to intervene and that he [Hatano] would be involved in the consequences. He said count Ōkuma was a very good friend of the English and he did not want to come under the ban of his displeasure.[3]

A professor at the Tokyo School of Foreign Languages in Tokyo, Barakatullah was in receipt of monetary support from Ottoman Turkey and the Amir of Afghanistan. Hatano said that a wealthy Japanese named Umeya was 'very fond of revolutions' and was helping the Indians. Hatano said that he worked for Barakatullah for six years and was 'the sole channel of communication with the Japanese'. Prominent Japanese politicians like Tsuyoshi Inukai and Taisuke Itagaki, he said, 'smile upon the movement because they are naturally sympathetic with revolutionary ideas'. In addition:

> [There] are people like [the] Toyama Mitsuru type who see in it an opportunity for wire-pulling behind the scenes; there are megalomaniacs and visionaries who dream of an Asia, united under the leadership of Japan, defying the West; others still

there are who imagine sympathy with India means increased Japanese trade; and a few indulge in dreams of going to help and staying to conquer. [No doubt men like Toyama Mitsuru are] dangerous and mischievous in the highest degree because of their influence [in circles].[4]

Greene informed the Foreign Secretary that Barakatullah left for the United States on 6 May, being sacked by the Japanese government from the foreign languages school. After a second payment of £25, he terminated contact with Hatano, feeling that the poison plot was not 'very serious'.[5] In 1915 Barakatullah reached the Mesopotamia and, together with a German officer, *Oberstleutnant* Oskar von Niedermayer, reached Kabul by 2 October on a mission to persuade Habibullah, the Amir of Afghanistan, to side with Germany and Ottoman Turkey; their mission failed when the Afghan leader promptly informed the viceroy, stating that he sought for peace with Britain.[6]

Meanwhile, the British military attaché was in contact with a Kobe-based Japanese informer under the codename Shimada who consulted with Indian revolutionaries, among them one named Torabally. The Japanese spy divulged that a retired officer called Isomoko, together with Sayajirao Gaekwad III, Maharaja of Baroda, would go to India for commercial purposes. Shimada believed that their real task was to arrange plans for former Japanese military personnel to train revolutionaries. The maharaja was already in Switzerland to meet with Indian revolutionaries there. According to the spy, 'The most suitable [Japanese officer selected] is a major, graduate of the staff college, who has studied in France and speaks French, and has already been on a mission to Mongolia. He did not mention and professes not to know his name.'[7] Shimada proved himself greedy, demanding more money from the military attaché and threatening to break off contact with the British. The officer was firm: 'I have accordingly let him know that he is at liberty to do so, as nothing further can be forthcoming till instructions if any, are received from home.'[8]

Ambassador Greene missed a precious opportunity to employ Japanese informers to penetrate the Japanese elite backing Indian revolutionaries and thus report on real intentions and plans against the British Empire in the Far East. Later he showed great interest in spycraft and kept Grey and Balfour informed about details of the spying game in Japan and the Far East. The ambassador gradually educated the two Foreign Secretaries on recruiting, maintaining and rewarding spies who revealed the real Japanese government plans over the British interests in the Far East and India. Given Japanese boasts of an invasion of 50,000 that could cripple British rule in the Subcontinent while its troops were stalled in trench warfare in Europe and the Middle East, by October 1917 the ambassador believed that 'if an effective watch is to be kept upon these people [Japanese] it will be necessary to employ a number of minor agents, either of their own nationality or drawn from the natives of the country [of the Far East] in which they happen to be, since no European would be likely to succeed In living amongst them and in being trusted by them'.[9]

The British Vice Consul in Yokohama, Colin Davidson, was a mid-level official of the British government in India at the turn of the century. He would become the first spymaster expert on Japan, producing accurate reports of Japan's plans for strategic antagonism to the British Empire and introducing Arthur Balfour to spycraft. Born at Holkham in Norfolk in October 1878, he entered the consular service in Bangkok in 1900 as a promising interpreter keen to learn Thai. In 1903 he was posted to Japan, by which time he was fluent in Japanese. He was interested in understanding Japanese society and did not confine himself to the diplomatic corps' circles and their social contacts. Indeed, by 1907, Davidson had carried out an affair with a Japanese lady called Otomi; they had a child but did not marry. Davidson began to realise that Japan was rising into 'a position of such predominance in the Far East as will eventually enable her to impose her will upon those countries in which she is specially interested without fear of foreign intermediation or interference'.[10] Major Cardew in the Intelligence Bureau at Simla, India, played his own significant part in uncovering links between the Japanese Army and members of the Indian revolutionaries in 1915–16, alerting the Foreign Office and pushing for espionage in Japan; he now became closely involved in Davidson's plans.

In 1915, polymath Jagadish Chandra Bose had written to Balfour informing him that his amateur intelligence gathering in Japan had revealed Japanese infiltration of India and boasts of an attack that would end the Raj.[11] David Petrie of the Criminal Investigations Department in India, and later MI5 director general, concluded that the Japanese were 'invading' India. The Far Eastern Department of the Foreign Office agreed:

> Mr Petrie ... conclusively shows that Pan-Asia ... amounts to pure Pan-Japanism ... She is out for her own hand: her own aggrandizement comes first, and, so far as this can be enhanced by the expulsion of the white man from Asia, just so far and no further is she Pan-Asiatic at heart. That is to say, so far as the more jingoistic Japanese are concerned, and there are very many jingoists in Japan these days.[12]

Sir John Jordan, the ambassador in Beijing, assumed that the First World War was 'a temporary eclipse of western influence' in the region; he hoped post-war Anglo-American cooperation might 'represent the moral and material strength of the New World. Anglo-Saxon influence [would] dominate the East and China [would] turn to the people who will give her justice and fair play'.[13]

By April 1916, the Government of India was most anxious about the growing Japanese threat:

> It is known that Japanese espionage has been actively carried out in India, in Nepal, in Tibet and other neighbouring countries. Up to the present no proof has been obtained of any incitement of the sedition party in India by these agents ... but it is certain that these agents have made and are making a careful study of India's military strength, political questions and commercial possibilities.[14]

The Foreign Office did not follow the line of the India Office and the Government of India. They assumed it was merely Japanese nationals supporting Indian revolutionaries, not official policy from Tokyo, and that the Japanese press sounded hostile due to domestic politics. The SIS had intercepted letters from German diplomats in Asia; their writing revealed that only one attempt to charter a Japanese ship to carry arms to revolutionaries had been made, in autumn 1915. Germans had been trying to approach Japanese officials for some sort of a secret agreement, but the

Japanese Ministry of Foreign Affairs was apparently fearful of this getting back to the Entente powers, and even informed the Entente about these overtures. The Foreign Office judged that Japan remained loyal to the alliance.[15]

Captain William Hall, the Director of Naval Intelligence, remained pessimistic about Japanese policy towards Britain.[16] In Whitehall, debate about the true Japanese intentions lasted for almost eight months from autumn 1915 to May 1916. The Foreign Office assumed that since the intensity of arms transfers to Indian revolutionaries was minimal (there was only one case), essentially there was no threat. Indeed, constant warnings from the Royal Navy concerning the failure of the Japanese to help them regarding Germans in Asia indicated the growing strategic threat of Japanese policy towards Britain. Evidently, the Foreign Office was growing tired of Royal Navy complaints in Asia while war raged in Europe and the Middle East.

In August 1916, Davidson gathered all spies' reports and compiled his first full report on Toyama Mitsuru:

> [He is] one of the most sinister figures in Japanese political life. He is scarcely, if ever, seen in public and is hardly known except amongst his own followers, but is said nevertheless to possess a secret and menacing hold over certain influential members of the Government by means of his extraordinary personality which has attached to him a very large following of adventurers and ruffians of the worst description.[17]

The informers insisted that Toyama 'forced' the government to issue the Twenty-one Demands on China in 1915; he allegedly threated assassination and managed to persuade the government to look the other way and not implement the deportation of Thakur, the viceroy's would-be assassin, and fellow revolutionary Gupta. In January 1917, a spy of Davidson's reported that at a secret meeting of the Prime Minister, the Foreign Minister and Viscount Kiyoura (a former Justice Minister) it was decided to honour the Anglo-Japanese Treaty, avoid involvement in China and restrict the activities of Toyama and his loyalists.[18]

Davidson's spies established that the publishers of the *Asian Review* were subsidized both by the General Staff and the

Ministry of Foreign Affairs. The society members focused on topographic intelligence and, espionage in Manchuria, Mongolia and China. In India, the Criminal Investigations Department found Toyama's name in the supporters list for a revolutionary group. Allegedly there was a plot, Davidson's spies concluded, 'to secure some holy places in India connected with the traditions of Gautama Buddha, and to convert them apparently into places of pilgrimage for Japanese, but in reality into centres of anti-British activity in India'.[19]

Ryukwan Kimura worked at the Japanese consulate at Calcutta and was under surveillance by the CID. He disguised himself as a student of Sanskrit and visited Buddhist temples; all his activities were deemed suspect and subversive of British rule in India. In parallel, the Mitsui trading corporation was discovered to be involved in subversive activities. Davidson warned about a Japanese Buddhist monk, Eikai Kawaguchi, who organised the visit of seventeen Mongolian lamas to Tokyo under the auspices of the East Honganji temple at Asakusa and the Japanese–Mongolian Buddhist Association. Davidson's informers discovered that it was the Japanese General Staff under General Tanaka who sponsored the visit as means to expand influence in the Far East after the collapse of tsarist rule. Davidson insisted that the General Staff 'are very anxious to extend Japanese influence amongst the warlike lamas in the regions of Mongolia bordering on Siberia in order to give Japan *a pied a terre* in those districts in the event of future trouble with Russia'. Agent X reported that Kawaguchi, who was in Tibet and suspected there of subversion, told him upon his return to Tokyo that he 'strongly opposed continuing British rule in India'.[20]

Davidson's spies were informed that a Japanese named Okamoto was arrested by the police in October 1917 on charges of having attacked a fellow Japanese in the house of an Indian in Singapore. The British police suspected (and the spies were informed about it) that Okamoto was suspected of being 'something far better than the position of loafer which he assumed in Singapore'. Okamoto was deemed the organizer of smuggling out of Singapore of an Indian revolutionary called Abani Mukherji who was in secret contact with German officials. Okamoto had helped Santipada Mukerji, alias Niazullah Khan, a revolutionary who was afforded protection and taken to the house of the Japanese naval attaché in Singapore, 'who had supposedly encouraged him to pursue a revolution in India'. Nevertheless, Santipada was a spy, working for the CID and reporting on dozens of Japanese urging for revolution in India.[21]

The British authorities in Singapore were suspicious that a Japanese attempt to import fifty rifles and 15,000 cartridges for 'self protection' hid a clear intent to foment Indian rebellion. They called London to warn of 'an elaborate net of Japanese espionage' in Singapore and the Federated Malay States.[22]

Japanese officials were deemed persons of interest for British colonial counter-intelligence. In 1916, informers watched Mitsue Ishimura, a Japanese national, who reached the Dutch East Indies and met with Emil Helfferich, the German consul. Ishimura was reported as telling the German diplomat that he represented Japanese politicians who were anti-British and aimed for a secret treaty with Berlin and Moscow to divide British colonial territories in the Far East. The Government of India had trouble persuading London (preoccupied with the Western Front and the Mesopotamian campaign) that Japan's 'natural design is to dominate the East'.

In April 1915, Greene instructed Davidson to track down the source of Indian nationalist propaganda in Japan. Davidson recruited a Muslim Indian merchant, Rahim Baksh, to identify the printer of ultranationalist pamphlets. Baksh, moving freely in Indian and Japanese commercial circles, reported on the Japanese attitudes on India and the existence of secret ultranationalist organisations in Japan hostile to the British. Contrary to the scope and spirit of the 1902 Anglo-Japanese Treaty, Prime Minister Ōkuma had propagated pan-Asiatic positions for an 'Indo-Japanese Association'. Indeed, as far back as 1907 he had claimed that 'the 300,000,000 people of India are looking to Japan for protection'.

In August 1916, Baksh warned Davidson of a plan by Japanese nationalist groups to supply weapons to Indian nationalists. The arms came from the Kuhara Company and the shipment was secretly sanctioned by the Japanese government. In all, 14,500 rifles and 1,200 pistols were consigned to reach Burma via Siam.[23] The plan did not materialise, but secret intelligence proved the hostile intent. Ambassador Greene wrote to Lord Grey of Davidson's role:

> Davidson's conduct of these [secret] negotiations, which, it will be observed, lasted for several months, reflects great credit on his tact and ability, and I cannot speak too highly of this manner in which the loyal Indian [merchant] referred to as X, on this as on many previous occasions, has placed his services at the disposal of His Majesty's Government, neglecting for the purpose his private interests and not seldom risking exposure to the vengeance of his revolutionary fellow-countrymen.[24]

Davidson's spies soon found out that the ultranationalist pressure group the Black Dragon Society (initially formed before the Russo-Japanese War to force a confrontation the Russians in the Far East and take over Manchuria) had aligned with the Toyama's *Genyosha* (Black Ocean) and the *Shina* (China) *Rōnin* against British presence in India and the Far East. The societies had been receiving money and orders from the Japanese General Staff for their intelligence and mapping work in China. Greene did not accept this warning. In the diplomat's view, Japan was a 'frankly opportunist, not to say selfish country, of only moderate importance compared with the Giants of the Great War, but with a very exaggerated opinion of her role in the universe'. In December 1916, John Shuckburgh at the India Office sharply criticised the Foreign Office on a secret report from Greene on Japanese policy to India. Shuckburgh viewed the way the Japanese had been assessing British power. He laid a charge against the Foreign Office that they 'have in recent years shown such extreme complaisance towards Japan on every possible occasion'.

The future MI5 director-general David Petrie served with the Indian Police and was involved in the investigation on the attempted assassination of Viceroy Lord Hardinge by Indian nationalists. The main suspect was Rash Behari Bose who fled to Japan. The British embassy in Tokyo was asked to help secure his extradition. By spring 1916 it had become evident that the Japanese would protect Bose. In October, Petrie dispatched two secret agents to Tokyo to help Davidson to track Bose. Their codenames were 'P' and 'Q', and moved freely. 'P' was Professor Pandit Hari Prasad Shastri who knew and met Bose while in India. By late 1916, P and Q informed Davidson that Bose was living free, married to a Japanese with a son. The name of secret agent Q remained secret in the archives. Shastri was born in 1882 and was a Sanskrit scholar. He lived in Japan from 1916 to 1918 working as a lecturer of Indian philosophy at the universities of Tokyo and Waseda.

Davidson recruited a former Japanese policeman, Samejima. He worked with his informers and found out where Bose was staying. The British embassy was informed and asked again for Bose to be extradited; the Japanese government refused. Davidson recruited yet another Japanese to put Bose under surveillance. The Indian nationalist consulted regularly with the *Rikken Seiyūkai* party, and in particular Sennosuke Yokota, a prominent member.

Secret agent Q found out to what extent the Japanese government did not want to deport Thakur and his ally Gupta at the beginning of December 1915. Greene thought that the information of Q 'afforded additional proof of the weakness and duplicity shown by the Japanese government then in power'. Most importantly, secret agent P moved freely in Japanese circles and was frequently invited to dinners hosted by officials and officers. P confirmed that Thakur was the wanted man Rash Behari Bose. Greene put emphasis to his cable to Balfour: 'Japanese sympathisers are especially anxious to keep secret [the name of Bose].' Davidson's spies put the house under close surveillance and questioned many people and soon concluded that Bose had left for Kobe. Davidson cabled the British consuls in Kobe, Shimonoseki and Nagasaki to direct their informers to look for Thakur. The general officer commanding in Singapore was also informed about Bose.

Davidson, who was looking for a Hindustani teacher called Pandit Hariharnath Thulal Atal at the time, took the security of his agents seriously, so P was not informed that Q worked for them; and eventually they suspected each other of working for the revolutionaries. Balfour must have smiled on reading Greene's report:

A somewhat farcical though embarrassing situation was produced by the simultaneous presence in Tokyo of agents P and Q. By Mr Petrie's express wishes the fact that each of these men is a servant of the Government has been concealed from the other with the result that they vehemently suspect each other of revolutionary tendencies and denounces each other to Mr Davidson. The climax was reached by the action of Q who, under the name Singha, took up his abode with P. in order to gain his confidence and discover his true opinions. Q has however now left Japan for Tientsin. Atal, in the course of a recent visit to this Embassy, betrayed great curiosity about both these men.[25]

Atal visited the British Embassy on several occasions 'ostensibly to ask advice and has always appeared ready to give information about Indians whom he suspected or revolutionary tendencies, though he has never been asked to do so. His statements about the members of my staff are gratuitous and mischievous lies,' Greene wrote.

The ambassador was disappointed for some time because the intercepted letters of Indian revolutionaries (intercepted and photographed by the Japanese postal services) did not reveal much; the letters were addressed to Japanese recipients.

An official of the Ministry of Foreign Affairs suggested that this effort should be abandoned. Greene initially agreed but later, upon receiving two batches of the last intercepted letters, he changed his mind to the dismay of the Japanese who wanted to hide the involvement of their nationals in Indian revolutionary plots. After the letters were translated, Davidson was tasked to 'discover the names and addresses of the Japanese who receive seditious letters on behalf of Indians.' He was immensely helped by secret agent X who had to live with the danger of the stronger suspicion of his compatriots.[26]

Agent Q was moving among Indian revolutionaries and learned that Thakur and Gupta stayed with one Sisir Kumar Mojundar. Once the official deportation note was issued, Thakur went to see the infamous Toyama with a translator named Coorey. Toyama 'expressed great sympathy for both of them and sheltered them in his house until a safe hiding place had been found for them'. Mojundar confided to Q that 'the Japanese Government authorities knew all along what was being done to shelter these men, and the place where they were in hiding, but having no real wish to see them deported, they pretended to the British authorities that no trace of their whereabouts could be found'. In Q's eyes, Mojundar was 'a very cunning fellow [who] complained bitterly of the unmerited suspicion of being a British spy which had fallen upon him, and asserted that he had always done what he could to further the nationalist movement, and had even himself secretly sent arms to India'.

Meanwhile, agent P was invited to the home of radical pan-Asianist Shumei Okawa. There, Okawa showed him a silver pocket watch; P noticed the inscription on the back – 'From Rash Behari Bose, Japan'. Okawa, a close associate of Toyama, remarked to P that only two people in Japan besides himself had seen this inscription. P also saw in the house a map of Central Asia issued by the Japanese General Staff and marked with possible invasion routes into India from Afghanistan and Tibet.

P was later invited to dinner at Toyama's house as a guest of honour. There he saw 'many motor cars parked outside'. In the house he noted a photo of a man 'who had murdered the foreign ministers twenty years ago'. Indeed he was told this man 'was a beloved discipline of Toyama'. 'The vulnerable looking old man' then asked P about 'the revolution in India'. P replied that he did not have current information. Dr Nagase, head of the diplomatic department of the War Office, was also present at the dinner.[27]

Elsewhere, the German legation in Mexico City operated a secret apparatus for working with Indian revolutionaries. This bureau was headed by a Japanese named Ujda, who arranged for at least one agent to go to Japan. Eventually Ujda made a secret contact with British intelligence in the city. The report of the officer who met with the Japanese read:

> I had secret interview with Ujda tonight. It is difficult as he is closely watched not so much by German Legation as by his own agents who are dangerous. I took notes ... Briefly he says: two messages sent from Berlin. A Japanese Government official tentatively approached by Germans declared definitely that Japan cannot break treaties ... Asia is of no interest at present, for submarine action.[28]

The Germans did not have the resources to fund smuggling of arms into India. Ujda was afraid of disclosing the means of communication with Berlin 'because only four persons know it and disclosure would be traced to him'. In any case, Ujda said that the German cypher no. 5950 was used, and he could offer the British a translation used by the legation. He reassured them that 'no attempt will be made to send arms to India … very few [Indian] revolutionary agents [were] in El Paso for moving on border'. The Indians, he said, were suffering low morale because they felt the Germans would not help them with money and arms. In Ujda's eyes, 'Berlin does not seem to order efforts to cause trouble between United States and Mexico.' The British officer asked what Ujda wanted from him. The Japanese replied that 'he had not yet been able render any service that merited pay', adding that submarine patrols close to Mexican coasts had been 'abandoned'.[29]

Hideo Nakao was another Japanese who worked for the German secret service in Mexico. A trial of Indian revolutionaries in San Francisco exposed him and he fled to Japan. Davidson's spies noted him and kept him under surveillance. The British embassy asked for his deportation, but the Japanese government delayed action and eventually he disappeared. He was found later in Vladivostok. As a result, the Government of India was wary of Japanese intrigue and espionage.[30]

Police officers are street-smart. In addition, having served in a bureaucracy, they can interpret policy and methods employed as well as gleaning information and valuable gossip from their former comrades. Samejima, one of Davidson's spies, was an example. The former policeman and his associate started looking for Bose and mingled easily in the crowd, developing sources. Intelligence from Samejima was crucial because he provided an authoritative interpretation to reveal the Japanese government's complicity in aiding Indian revolutionaries.

The British government put strong pressure on Tokyo for Bose and Gupta to be deported. Once they received the order for deportation, Bose went to Toyama, who told him to go and hide with a baker at Nakamura-ya. The baker was Aizo Soma, a known pan-Asianist. Bose and Gupta stayed with him for three months.

It seems that the ever-present Japanese police decided not to raid the house of Aizo in Shinjuku and arrest them. Surprisingly, Aizo allowed Bose to marry his daughter and thus secure the right to remain in Japan legally. According to Samijima's reporting, the marriage was Toyama's idea. Throughout this period, Samejima and his associates kept the bakery and the house under surveillance. Indeed, he spoke with unsuspecting customers who told him the daughter of Aizo was 'spending her time with "the black man"', meaning Bose.

The police kept Samejima under tight surveillance and eventually he and his associate were summoned to the police station. They had been asked to refrain from their activities. Samejima was told this by Ikariyama, the inspector general of the Kagacho police station, who told him that 'Mr Oshima had again telephoned to inquire whether he had been able to persuade the two British agents to give up their pursuit of Thakur. Mr N.Oshima's real position appears to be that of Director of the Secretariat in the Metropolitan Police, Tokyo, a position I am told of very high rank.'[31]

Samejima was defiant, replying to Ikariyama that 'unless he were given good reason showing that what he was doing was injuring the interests of Japan, he would continue his work, and that if he continued to meet with obstruction from the Police, he would report the whole circumstances to the British authorities'. To Samejima, Bose/Thakur was not a political offender but 'a dangerous criminal and a German spy whose protection by the Authorities could not be to the interests of Japan'. The police inspector 'promised' to get a reply from Tokyo as soon as possible and assumed that Oshima was in Osaka. Ikariyama reassured Samejima that the police 'were in no way interfering with his work and begged him not to report in that sense to the British authorities'. The inspector general had concluded that the interference in Samejima's surveillance was 'undoubtedly caused by members of the China Roni (*sic*) who were known to be protection (*sic*) Thakur'.

An angry Samejima continued his approach. He was a policeman 'for so many years' and 'was well acquitted with the methods adopted by them, and that he had not the slightest doubt that it was the Police and not the Shina Rōnin who were rendering his task almost impossible'.[32] Indeed, he was too confrontational for a secret agent, betraying the keenness of British intelligence to find

Bose and the rest of the Indian revolutionaries harboured by the Japanese.

In early 1917, Davidson's spies provided him with invaluable secret intelligence: minutes of a cabinet meeting showed that the Japanese government decided to honour the 1902 treaty and not to confront Britain in China, to the dismay of the increasingly influential ultranationalists. Nevertheless, Davidson reported that with reference to India, Japanese leaders believed that 'an upheaval in India if properly utilised might prove highly beneficial to Japan'. The Japanese government 'would not perhaps be displeased to find their hand forced by such societies as the *Shina Ronin'*.[33]

Davidson read the reports of secret agent 'X' about Toyama and informed Greene:

From my informant's account of his secret activities, Toyama Mitsuru appears as one of the most sinister figures in Japanese political life. He is scarcely, if ever, seen in public and is hardly known except amongst his own followers, but is said nevertheless to possess a secret and menacing held over certain influential members of the Government by means of his extraordinary personality which has attached to him a very large following of adventurers and ruffians of the worst description who are ready and willing to obey his smallest behest, even to assassination. He counts also amongst his henchmen a number of prominent business men, bankers and politicians. Of late he has mixed very little with domestic politics and has devoted himself principally to affairs in India and China in which latter country he takes a special interest ... [he] is credited with being largely responsible for the exorbitant demands presented by Japan to China last year contrary to the more moderate views held by Viscount Katō and some other members of the cabinet. He is represented by his followers as practically holding Marquis Ōkuma in the hollow of his hands and it is said that the latter is in genuine fear of his life should he incur Toyama's active displeasure ... Terauchi and Viscount Katō are, however, so my informant tells me, free from the malign influence of this redoubtable person and refuse to be controlled by him in their actions. Such a condition of affairs may seem almost incredible at the present day, and one would be inclined to regard it as pure exaggeration on the part of Toyama's followers were it not to come extent borne out by certain events which have recently taken place, such as the case of the two men, Thakur and Gupta, whose evasion of the deportation order was obviously effected by assistance received from some influential quarter. From the same source I have ascertained that, when the deportation order in question was issued by the Government, the two men hastened to the house of Mr Inukai, a member of the Diet and a staunch follower of Toyama's and implored his assistance saying that it meant death to both of them should they fall into the hands of the British authorities. Inukai replied that there was only one thing which could save them, namely, an appeal to Toyama Mitsuru. This he did on their behalf and Toyama, after considering their case, decided that they should be rescued. That his words were no idle boast is evident from what occurred subsequently.[34]

The account about Katō and the twenty-one demands on China was wrong; as elaborated in a previous chapter, Katō presented excessive demands and Yamagata Aritomo tried to soften them. Evidently Davidson mistakenly assumed that a liberal politician like Katō was not an imperialist like Yamagata. Nevertheless, the influence and threats of Toyama could not be discounted. Davidson decided to make the mysterious Toyama talk. 'My informant X was able to secure an interview with this person ... Hatano, whose name will be familiar to you as the person who supplied certain information to the embassy regarding Bhagwan Sinh acted as an interpreter.'[35] The spies were directed by Davidson:

Acting on my advice, X. adopted the role of a sympathizer with the Indian seditionary movement and thanks Toyama warmly for the aid he had given to two compatriots in their hour of need. Toyama replied that what he had done was merely an act of humanity, and inquired of X whether he was acquainted with Thakur and Gupta. To this X replied he was not acquainted with Gupta but that Thakur had come to his house on several occasions. Hatano was anxious that X should ask Toyama regarding the present whereabouts of the two men, but X fearing, and I think rightly, that to put such a question after so short an acquaintanceship might arouse Toyama's suspicions, merely replied that there was no necessity to do so as he knew that both were safe. Toyama's reply, however, sufficiently confirms my conviction that he was mainly instrumental in enabling Thakur and Gupta to evade the deportation order.[36]

Secret agent X complained to Toyama that 'things were going very badly with the Indians just now that all their movements were closely watched by the British Authorities so that they were in constant danger'. Toyama advised patience since Japan's official policy would change soon. X told Toyama that the infamous Barakatullah was in Constantinople and send him greetings. Toyama 'assured X that he would be very pleased to see him at any time.'[37] Greene, believing in the value of espionage as well as of published sources (a magazine article on Toyama), informed Grey:

Dr Toyama appears chiefly to have enforced his influence through the agency of a numerous band of *soshi* or hired bravoes such as in earlier days were freely used by politicians and these were prepared to decide elections by violence in Japan, to stir up riots in Korea, or to organize revolutions in China, as he might require. In spite however of the resemblance of his methods to those of a medieval *condottiere* and of his share in organizing in 1890 an attempt on the life of the present Prime Minister which was very nearly successful, there is no doubt that he wields very great influence and is in his way, a patriot, even though one of an unscrupulous and chauvinistic type.[38]

Toyama represented the sabre-rattling mentality in Japanese politics, foreign and domestic. He confronted Yamagata, calling for the elder statesman's assassination because Yamagata had expressed strong reservations on the impending marriage of Crown Prince Hirohito; he assumed that the bride had familial colour-blindness which could pass to her children. Indeed, police guards were placed at Yamagata's home because it was feared that Toyama's henchmen would attack the statesman.[39]

Arthur Balfour, who had succeeded Grey as Foreign Secretary, was convinced that Japan's stance did not constitute a threat to British concessions in Asia. Only after the end of the war would Britain negotiate any changes with Japan, taking into consideration the occasional unhelpful stance of Japan during the war.[40]

In March 1916, the Japanese Ministry of Foreign Affairs requested their consul in Yunnan, China be allowed to use a British-owned telegram cable to send reports to Tokyo. The Foreign Office agreed and the India Office rushed to dispatch cryptographers. In December 1917, Davidson informed his superiors in India that one of his agents, a British subject, was in contact with a retired official named Okuda, until the previous summer the Director of the Bureau of Information at the Japanese Ministry of Foreign Affairs. The retired diplomat admitted in conversation that it was Prime Minister Ōkuma who, in 1914, under pressure from secret societies, ordered Japanese authorities to offer the Indian nationalists clandestine support. Greene had reported to London that the contemporary Japanese press promulgated the idea that 'the entire Indian population has no thought but to throw off the British yoke'.[41]

Captain Godfrey Scott-Pearse of the SIS was dispatched to Tokyo in 1917 to report on the Japanese attitude towards the October Revolution in Russia and the fall of the tsar. The head of legation in Tokyo praised Scott-Pearse as being 'of great service to this Embassy and consulates'. [42] In 1917, a British officer remarked, 'It must be remembered that scrupulousness is not a characteristic of the Japanese, while espionage and secret propaganda are arts in which they excel.'[43]

Lord Curzon, Balfour's successor, stated that Japanese activities close to the British colonies in Asia were 'wrapped in a mist of doubt and suspicion which was creating very general alarm'.[44] By summer 1917, Frank Ashton-Gwatkin, a former consular officer in Japan, was assigned an espionage mission against Japanese businessmen and diplomats in Singapore. His cover role was to be assistant director of the Imports and Exports Office, and his appointment indicated that London did not discount Japanese designs in the Far East.

Meanwhile, in Yokohama, Davidson controlled a spy, an Indian working at the Tokyo School of Foreign Languages.

In December 1917, he reported that his superiors asked him to organise examinations in Hindustani for unnamed students who did not attend the school. Evidently, Japanese military intelligence officers were trained in Hindustani and dispatched to survey British defences on the North-West Frontier. Meanwhile, military intelligence in London reported in July 1917:

> Japanese espionage has to be kept under close observation so that any marked increase of activity in any particular direction will come promptly to light. Failing an opportunity elsewhere, Japanese expansion may be expected to make progress in China. Provided such expansion is strictly limited to North China and Manchuria, it cannot be said that the interests of Great Britain are seriously threatened.[45]

Ronald Campbell of the Foreign Office noted to Colonel French of MI (Military Intelligence) 1a in January 1918: 'The question [of spying on Japan] is of such vast political importance and of such extraordinary delicacy that after the war it should not ... be handled by an intelligence centre, or any other local official body. It must be entirely and absolutely subterranean.'[46]

This fear of expanding espionage would make the intelligence gathering lose momentum until Piggott took over and blocked espionage operations in Japan on various false pretences. In a memorandum on Anglo-Japanese relations submitted to the Imperial Conference held in March 1917, the Foreign Office claimed that Japan's encouragement of 'the use of its territory as a focus of intrigue on the part of the most active and dangerous Indian seditionists ... Japan has failed the Allies'. Tokyo was 'bent on pursuing a *realpolitik* as evil as Prussia's'.[47] In March 1918, one Kraft, a German double agent working for British intelligence, with a Lieutenant Oelsner reached Japan to meet with Indian revolutionaries. Greene, like a seasoned spymaster, aimed to employ Kraft to unveil the Japanese government's intentions towards Britain. Nevertheless, the Director of Naval Intelligence, Admiral Hall, and the Director of Military Intelligence, General Macdonogh, made a fatal mistake. On the grounds that Japan was officially an ally, they thought the British government ought to inform the Japanese government about the secret German mission and 'hostile' activities in Japan. The news of the secret mission was leaked by the Japanese. Greene read in Tokyo newspapers that there was a plan for German secret agents to arrive in Japan. He remarked, 'I was hardly prepared for so drastic a breach of confidence by the Japanese Foreign Office.'[48]

In May 1918, Professor Kazunobu Kanokogi of Tokyo's Keio University visited India to study Sanskrit and Hindu philosophy. CID agents kept him under constant surveillance, reporting on 'an enthusiastic promoter of the Pan-Asiatic Movement'. In November 1918, Calcutta police arrested Kanokogi and found documents which proved his connection with the Indian revolutionary movement. Members of the Mitsui trading corporation had agreed to take correspondence written on behalf of Bengali terrorists to Japan. The DCI concluded that 'the case of Kanokogi shows ... that certain Japanese in India have behaved in a most improper and outrageous manner and that a great deal of suspicion was more than justified'.[49]

Davidson proved that as long as a spymaster worked hard, reliable spies would always be available, even in a secretive society. He recruited a Japanese hotelier, a visiting Chinese agent, and most importantly an official inside the Japanese Ministry of Foreign Affairs.[50] In 1919, Davidson was promoted to consul and was transferred to Tokyo. The Foreign Office – effectively the SIS under Mansfield Cumming – praised him:

> Davidson's services have been invaluable and there appears to be no one else capable of taking up his special work. All the information we have here indicates that Japan is likely to be a centre of sedition for some time to come and it is therefore very desirable that Mr Davidson's services should be retained, for the present at any rate.[51]

Davidson would serve as consul in Tokyo until 1927. He was then moved to Seoul but in 1929 returned to the British legation in Tokyo to work in intelligence and analysing Japanese politics. He died in 1930 at the age of fifty-one, having completed seventeen years of service as a spymaster covering Japan. The spy networks in Japan would thereafter be left to dust. The Indian revolutionaries were the unique secret agents who could go into circles of officials and officers where their intentions towards Britain could be revealed.

The Foreign Office and the War Office were willing to scuttle spy networks but the chief of the SIS showed indisputable foresight when he continuously warned of the rise of Japanese hegemony particularly against the British Empire in the Far East. The Admiralty sided with the SIS warnings; nonetheless, limited budgets as well as hostility from the War Office and the RAF did not allow for an efficient espionage organisation to be built. The Foreign Office would prove indifferent until the 1930s. Throughout this period, military intelligence at the War Office was under the influence of Piggott's views, promoting a pro-Japanese interpretation of events and a policy that suited Tokyo.

In 1918 Cumming sought to appoint a spymaster in the Far East with one mission: the 'observation of Japanese designs' deemed antagonistic to the British Empire.[52] Scott-Pearse remained in Tokyo until 1920. He was replaced by Colonel David Drummond Gunn, who would be the first station chief. Gunn was surprised by the attitude of the head of legation, who wanted to curtail the activities of the SIS and divert funding to the spies under Davidson. In any case, the SIS station in Shanghai was tasked with gathering foreign intelligence on Japan.[53] Gunn was appointed first as a passport control officer at the British consulate in Yokohama and later moved to Tokyo. In January 1920, Cumming warned Neville Bland, private secretary to the Foreign Secretary, that intercepted correspondence between the Japanese diplomatic missions in Bern and Rome proved the gradual work of Japan, Italy and Germany to form an alliance that was 'possibly only commercial'.[54] Wild rumours spread in Italy that there was indeed a German–Japanese wartime agreement.[55]

Sir Victor Wellesley in the Far Eastern department of the Foreign Office insisted that 'a militaristic and immoral' Japan could not be a post-war ally of Britain.[56] The First Sea Lord, Sir Rosslyn Wemyss, argued prophetically that Japan would be 'the enemy in any war in the Far East'. Lord Jellicoe emphasised that Japan was 'the Germany of the Far East'. This country claimed China and India; it was 'almost inevitable that the interests of Japan and of the British Empire will eventually clash'.[57] Major General Dudley Ridout, the general commanding the Straits, had followed Japanese espionage since 1917 and by 1919 claimed that Japan was 'our only possible enemy' in the Far East.[58]

In an attempt to make obvious Japan's disloyalty, Churchill showed the cabinet members a Japanese-issued map of Gibraltar retrieved by MI5. He urged them to let the Anglo-Japanese Alliance lapse, insisting that 'Japan was the only real danger to Imperial interests in the Pacific ... Getting Japan to protect you against Japan is like drinking salt water to slake thirst.' Surprisingly, however, he did not actually subscribe to theories about the Japanese menace, as we will explore in later chapters.[59]

In December 1922, First Lord of the Admiralty Leo Amery proposed the establishment of an SIS station in the Far East that would be able to warn of any imminent Japanese attack within twenty-four hours of a threat developing. The Committee of Imperial Defence agreed, ruling that this secret intelligence organisation should be fully operational by 1928.[60]

5

HELPING THE IMPERIAL NAVY

In 1920, the Japanese ambassador in London filed an urgent request for a British official naval aviation mission to be dispatched to Japan to instruct their counterparts in modern combat flying and navigation, torpedo launching, and landing and taking off from aircraft carriers. The Japanese offered to cover the costs; the ambassador was explicit that his government needed advice to build modern aircraft carriers.[1]

After hesitation, the Foreign Office and the Admiralty, concerned that an official mission would irritate Washington, encouraged the British government to grant the Japanese request to send a mission of thirty civilian instructors and support staff to advise the Japanese. Despite the cooling of Anglo-Japanese relations with the lapse of the 1902 treaty, London hoped this mission might persuade Tokyo to buy British-made aircraft among other technologies.

The Japanese proved themselves astute hosts. They commissioned their instructors into the IJN, with the mission leader, aviation pioneer William Forbes-Sempill, later Lord Sempill, being given the rank of naval captain. At that time, eight types of RAF aircraft had been bought and employed by the Japanese and Sempill and his associates advised about their use and technology. The British-made aircraft operated by the Japanese were the Gloster Sparrowhawk, the Avro 504K trainer, the Parnal Panther carrier reconnaissance aircraft, the Short Type 184 reconnaissance seaplane, the Blackburn Swift and

Sopwith Cuckoo (both torpedo bombers) and the Supermarine Channel and Felixstowe F.5 (both flying boats). Sempill showed the Japanese construction plans for British aircraft carriers HMS *Argus* and HMS *Hermes*.

At that time the Japanese operated the carrier *Hōshō*.[2] It borrowed features of HMS *Hermes* and HMS *Campania* with a forward flying-off deck, thirty-two aircraft, four low-angle 14-cm (5.5-in) guns, and four anti-aircraft guns. HMS *Furious* and HMS *Argus* were also models for the *Hōshō*, which hosted nine Mitsubishi 1MF (Type 10) fighters and three to six Mitsubishi B1M3 (Type 13) torpedo bombers. By 1931, the carrier air group would consist of Nakajima A2N (Type 90) fighters and Mitsubishi B2M (Type 89) torpedo bombers. *Hōshō* would play a key role in the battle of Shanghai in 1933 – the first employment of aircraft carrier in offensive operations.

Flight Officer R. Vaughan-Fowler, an associate of Sempill on the mission, concluded that the Japanese pilots were 'slow thinking' and lacked technical knowledge. Nevertheless, they were brave and keen to learn, thus having the prospects of turning into good airmen.[3]

British aircraft and technicians had reached Japan and instructed the Japanese before Sempill and his unofficial mission had arrived. The Japanese Embassy in London had approached engineers and technicians made redundant by the folding of the Sopwith Aircraft Company. Keen for work, they arrived in Japan and worked at Mitsubishi factories in Nagoya. The Japanese officials who recruited the British engineers instructed them that if asked by a journalist or anyone else why were they going to Japan they should 'politely tell him it was our business'.[4]

Tokyo had attempted cooperation with France in 1919 by inviting an aviation mission to advise the air service of the Imperial Japanese Army (IJA). Approaching companies paid dividends in 1920 when the Kure Naval Arsenal secured the assistance of a British company, Short Brothers Co., to produce flying boats. In 1928 Kawanishi, an aeroplane manufacturer, also agreed with the Short Brothers to produce flying boats under contract with the IJN. Meanwhile, Aichi industries, another aircraft manufacturer, collaborated with the Heinkel Company in Germany.[5]

The ex-Sopwith workers, meanwhile, helped the Mitsubishi Internal Combustion Engine Company develop aircraft engines. Sempill and the British embassy in Tokyo were aware of this group of British engineers; he may have tried to bring them under his aegis, but this did not happen. In fact, they stayed longer than the Sempill mission.

Herbert Smith, a leading aircraft designer with Sopwith, was the head of this group of engineers and technicians. He was visited by a boastful admiral who excitedly told him that he would order 100 planes of his design. A year after the arrival of the mission, the first fighter prototype was complete: the Mitsubishi No. 1. Captain William Jordan, formerly of the Royal Navy Air Service, was the test pilot and concluded that it flew well. The British embassy in Tokyo reported to London about this development but the ambassador was dismissive. The Mitsubishi No. 1 was a one-seater scout, of 300hp, capable of 145 mph and armed with two guns. Subsequently, the British engineers developed a two-seater bomber. Smith and his associates designed four aeroplanes: the Mitsubishi 1MT, a single-seat triplane torpedo bomber operated by the IJN aboard the *Hōshō*; the Mitsubishi B1M (Navy Type 13 carrier-borne attack aircraft), a torpedo bomber employed by the navy and army in operations in China; the Mitsubishi 1MF (Navy Type 10 Carrier Fighter); and the Mitsubishi 2MR (Navy Type 10 Carrier Reconnaissance Aircraft). The British team had to respond to the growing obsession with aerial torpedoes, fine-tuning the instruments and devices for launching these weapons. In trials in 1923 they employed dummy torpedoes made of wood. In front of an audience of high-ranking officers, Captain Jordan took off and successfully dropped the torpedo. The weapon was to follow a route parallel to the place where the officials sat, but the torpedo struck something and changed course, heading at full speed towards the audience which dispersed in fear. In any case, the Japanese deemed the trials success, and the incident a mere joke.[6]

On 24 February 1923, Captain Jordan landed with his Mitsubishi No.1 on the aircraft carrier *Hōshō*; the landing and taking-off trials were a success. In spring 1924, the Japanese requested the prolonging of the Smith mission for another two years. Engineer Bert Venn agreed to stay at the Mitsubishi factory at Nagoya, which had turned into the largest centre for aircraft manufacturing in Japan.[7]

Key aircraft manufacturers Mitsubishi, Aichi, Nakajima and Kawanishi developed designs and prototypes to compete for navy contracts, while IJN research and development focused on modifications. In 1927, the Naval Aviation Department was established as a separate service to undertake the development of airframes, engines, ordnance and equipment relating to naval aviation. Nine years later the Naval Air Arsenal was founded to put under single control the construction of prototypes, the aircraft design and the flight testing.[8] During the Shōwa financial crisis, General Tanaka (the protégé of Yamagata) took over as prime minister. Fluent in Russian and commended many times for his war planning, he was in favour of Japan taking over Manchuria and Inner Mongolia, separating them from China. Nevertheless, he did not have control of the Japanese army officers in Manchuria who plotted to kill Zhang Zuolin, a powerful warlord of the province. He held office until 1929, and during his tenure rearming and the development of new weaponry accelerated.

Meanwhile, in Britain, Commander S. Oyagi worked at the Whitehead factory – from which Japan had purchased torpedoes before – gathering information on technical problems in producing torpedoes. There he heard rumours that the Royal Navy was developing oxygen-fuelled 24.5-inch torpedoes for warships HMS *Nelson* and HMS *Rodney*, which were each armed with nine 16-inch guns.

Throughout the 1920s and 1930s, Japanese pilots were instructed by their countrymen and by the British missions to fly at low altitudes and slowly on torpedo missions, careful that the torpedo, once released, should not be damaged on impact. The Japanese Nakajima B5N monoplane could not fly smoothly at lower altitudes, however, so the Japanese chose to modify the available torpedo, the Type 91. The torpedo was fitted with reinforced lower nose section and wooden stabilising fins to control the glide angle so it could be launched from higher altitudes and at speed.[9]

Once back in Japan, Oyagi and his team developed a 24-inch torpedo with 100 per cent oxygen fuel. It was finalised in 1934 and named Type 93, from the year 2593 (1934) in the Japanese calendar; its maximum speed was 49 knots and it could carry a 490 kg warhead. It was the best torpedo of its year and the blueprint for the Japanese arsenal in the coming war, with pure oxygen fuel allowing greater speed than compressed air and a range above 10 miles. This was bad news for American admirals, who, like their Royal Navy counterparts, incorrectly assumed that the torpedo remained a short-range weapon and that powerful guns could neutralise the approaching threat by sea while heavy anti-aircraft guns could make it impossible for fighters to approach close enough to launch from the air.

6

NO WAR WITH JAPAN

By the end of 1922, Royal Navy strategists concluded that Britain was weak, Japan was a clear threat and the United States would not come to the aid of Britain. At the meeting of the Imperial Defence Committee, First Sea Lord Leo Amery was emphatic:

... since the Washington Conference the situation from the naval point of view had altered in the Pacific. The United States were now incapable of naval action in the Western Pacific, thus leaving the British Empire the sole Power to counter with naval forces any aggressive tendencies of the part of Japan. This had already been pointed out to the Committee of Imperial Defence, and a decision had been taken that the naval base at Singapore should be proceeded with. Without Singapore we should be swept out of the Western Pacific and have no means of countering a naval offensive by Japan. There was reason to believe that if the war had taken a definite turn against us, Japan would have thrown over the Allies and associated herself with Germany, and that even during the war Japanese agents were in touch with Indian agitators. Japan might fall to a similar temptation in the future, when, by encouraging a revolt in India and raising the banner of Asia for the Asiatics, it would be no exaggeration to say that Japan would be able to wrest from us our position in India.[1]

As Imperial Japanese strategists accelerated the development of naval and aviation armaments to challenge British and American supremacy in the Far East, in London the Foreign Office insisted that there could be no war with Japan. At the Imperial Defence Committee meeting held on 5 January 1925, Foreign Secretary Austin Chamberlain was bullish:

> I regard the prospect of war in the Far East as very remote. I cannot conceive any circumstances in which, singlehanded, we are likely to go to war with Japan. I cannot conceive it possible that Japan, singlehanded, should seek a conflict with us. The only case in which I think Japan (which is an uneasy and rather restless Power, whose actions is not always easy to predicate) might become dangerous is after a new regrouping of the European Powers ... unless we see signs of a German-Russo-Japanese Alliance or agreement, such a new regrouping of the Powers as being a danger signal which would at once call out attention to the situation and would require that we should review it afresh ... I should regard the danger of war between ourselves and Japan as being as remote as the danger of war with any other Great Power. Japan has ambitions in China. I am quite certain that she is not seeking an occasion to make war for the sake of China, and would be very reluctant to do so ... As long as Japan is isolated, as she will be if she should seek a quarrel or get into a position in which she cannot avoid a quarrel with America and ourselves ... But in any case, that we should have Singapore as a necessary link in our line of Imperial communications I consider sound policy and in itself something of a guarantee for peace, because it is never a guarantee for peace that you should have great territories open without defence to possible attack, but I repeat that I regard the possibilities of such attack as being very remote ... It [Japan] has suffered tremendously by the earthquake. Its finances have been- I was going to say ruined- at any rate, profoundly upset, and that again strengthens my argument that there is no conceivable danger at the present time. Japan is much more inclined to fear aggression by others than to contemplate aggression on other at the present moment.[2]

Lord Curzon, the lord president of the council, agreed:

> ... all our evidence from Japan – and some of us have friends who write to us from there apart from the official statements which we read – tends to show that while Japan feels sore and sorry and rather sick at the loss of the British Alliance, she is anxious to replace it ... so far I can judge, to conceive of any state of affairs in which the general trend of Japanese policy would for many years to come be anti-British.[3]

Winston Churchill had commenced his tenure as Chancellor of the Exchequer in November 1924; he would remain in this post until April 1929. Post-war reparations and deflation due to the return to the gold standard were key issues of domestic economic policy, as were unemployment and strikes. Churchill sought to maintain British imperial hegemony, but he assumed that this could be achieved by improving the economy and limiting defence spending. He sided with Chamberlain, writing to Prime Minister Stanley Baldwin, 'Why should there be a war with Japan? I do not believe there is the slightest chance of it in our lifetime.'[4]

Churchill assumed, wrongly, that Anglo-Japanese relations would enjoy a 'long peace, such as follows in the wake of great wars'.[5] The reasoning shared by Chamberlain, Curzon and Churchill boosted pro-Japanese bias in the War Office and Foreign Office corridors, informed by the views of Piggott and Lindley, who influenced this Japan-appeasing strategy in the Far East for a decade.

In contrast, the Admiralty feared that the Japanese shipbuilding program (despite announced cutbacks due to struggling finances after the Great Kantō earthquake in 1923)[6] could change the balance of power in the Far East and establish Japanese power over British dominions and commercial interests. Admiral of the Fleet Earl Beatty threatened to resign in protest against proposed cuts and delays in warship construction. 'That extraordinary fellow Winston [Churchill] has gone mad, economically mad, and no sacrifice is too great to achieve what in his short-sightedness is the panacea for all evils, to take 1/- [one shilling] off the Income Tax. Nobody outside a lunatic asylum expects a shilling off the Income Tax this Budget,' he fumed.[7]

Beatty and his fellow admirals insisted that demography, industrialisation and commerce would lead Japan to act in a dominant and reckless way: 'The need of outlets for the population and for increased commerce and markets, especially new sources of self-supply, will probably be among the most compelling reasons for Japan to push a policy of penetration, expansion and aggression.' Indeed, Beatty emphasised that 'by encouraging a revolt in India and raising the banner of Asia for the Asiatics, it would be no exaggeration to say that Japan would be able to wrest from us our position in India'.[8] Admiral Sir Roger Keyes, the deputy chief of naval staff, warned that Britain must deter Japan by building more warships; if it did not, Tokyo would 'remorselessly push forward her policy of expansion and domination in the Pacific, and always at the cost of the European races'.[9]

Undeterred, Tokyo continued with the build-up of warships and aircraft. The Japanese opted to arm their new cruisers with 8-inch guns. The contemporary British cruisers were armed with 5.5 and 6-inch guns. Admiral Beatty warned:

An 8-inch [gun] ship is in a position to crush a 7.5-inch ship without laying herself open to be crushed in return, and obviously equally so with the 6-inch ship or the 5.5-inch ship. The advent of the 8-inch gun ship has made not only the 6-inch ship, but also the 7½-inch ship out of date, and if you pit a 7½-inch gun ship against an 8-inch ship you are courting disaster.[10]

Across the 1920s, rearmament would see the cruisers *Furutaka* and *Kako* commissioned in 1926, *Aoba* and *Kinugasa* in 1927, and four cruisers of the Nachi-class – *Nachi*, *Myōkō*, *Haguro* and *Ashigara* – ready by 1929.[11]

In December 1924, Churchill hit back at the Admiralty. He wrote to Baldwin:

It seems to me that the Admiralty imagine themselves confronted with the same sort of situation in regard Japan as we faced against Germany in the ten years before the war … There is absolutely no resemblance between our relations with Japan and those we had with Germany before the war.[12]

His argument was that 'Japan is on the other end of the world. She cannot menace our vital security [NB: clearly Churchill refers to England, not the British Empire] ... the only war it would be worth our while to fight with Japan would be to prevent an invasion of Australia.' By March 1925, Churchill was confident that any Japanese aggression would trigger an American response, causing the formation of an Anglo-American alliance against Tokyo.[13]

Despite his dismissals, the Admiralty put on strong pressure for a program to build more warships and explicitly warned of the coming Japanese threat in the Far East. Admiral Sir Dudley Pound (later First Sea Lord) said that Churchill was a 'bully' in conferences examining naval strategy and naval construction programs, 'absolutely unreliable' and 'quite unscrupulous' in dealing with the Admiralty generally.[14]

Since 1919, increased consumer demand had caused inflation. In December that year, the Cunliffe Committee on Currency and Foreign Exchange Rates had recommended an early return to the gold standard; the pound sterling had to be stabilised against the pre-war dollar, and this required equilibrium in the balance of payments and a reduction in the money in circulation. In February 1925, the Chamberlain–Bradbury Committee had once again recommended a return to the gold standard. Churchill was warned against it by John Maynard Keynes, who predicted heavy deflation and mass unemployment, but the Chancellor was fascinated with the concept of a 'drastic' policy to heal post-war British economics. In April 1925, he made the fateful decision to return to the gold standard. Severe cutbacks in government spending (among them in the shipbuilding programs of the Admiralty) followed, and strikes were widespread.

Meanwhile, Britain's ambassador in Tokyo, Sir Charles Eliot, supported Churchill:

> The Japanese Treasury are determined to carry out the policy of retrenchment which was announced when the present Government came into office. That they regard this policy as essential in the present financial condition of Japan is clear from the fact that the Finance Minister has been able to enforce his views upon the two great spending Departments; for not only has he been able to resist the demands of the

navy, but also he succeeded last year in obliging the army to agree to a reduction in the number of divisions.'

At the Foreign Office, Ashton-Gwatkin noted on the ambassador's report that 'this reduction in expenditure on Armaments must mean a decline of bellicosity on the part of Japan, and an increasing reluctance to a sharp policy in China'. The conclusion was clear:

It seems therefore both unreasonable and unfriendly to regard Japan as an active enemy and deliberately to commence a competitive programme of ship-building against her ... and if they [that is, the Japanese] now became aware that we were deliberately building up our Navy against them the result would not only be deplorable in its effect on Anglo-Japanese relations, but would give other nations to suspect us of militaristic designs.

Victor Wellesley, the deputy under-secretary of state, underscored this view:

I feel strongly that to embark upon a policy of building against Japan at the present moment is both provocative and dangerous...What [Japan] is really aiming at is military & naval predominance in the Far East, not for aggressive purposes, but to be able to say to all comers 'hands off'.[15]

First Lord of the Admiralty William Clive Bridgeman warned that Churchill's assessment of Japan 'ignores history, real facts and the psychology of the people', but Churchill was relaxed, stating that 'in three or four years we could certainly sweep the Japanese from the seas and force them to make peace'.[16] He assumed that a Japanese victory even in Singapore would see the Royal Navy withdraw to the Indian Ocean 'without being drawn into decisive action at an inferiority', awaiting reinforcements. He added:

Great as are the injuries which Japan, if she 'ran amok', could inflict upon our trade in the Northern Pacific, lamentable as would be the initial insults which she might offer to the British flag, I submit that it is beyond the power of Japan, in any period which we might foresee, to take any action which would prevent the whole might of the British Empire being eventually brought to bear upon her.[17]

In December 1920, Cumming arranged with the India Office for Godfrey Denham, the deputy director of the Delhi Intelligence Bureau, to be chief spymaster for the Far East with responsibilities including Japan and China. In 1921, Denham reached the cosmopolitan Shanghai 'with a mandate to be in charge of all our work in Japan, China, Tibet and Siberia and Southern Asia'. In April 1923, Cumming had sent out a representative, 'CT/60', posing as a businessman, to report on Japanese naval and air intelligence; sadly, two months later, on 14 June 1923, Cumming died aged sixty-four.

Cumming's successor, fifty-year-old Rear Admiral Sir Hugh Sinclair, was also worried by Japanese strategy in Asia. By 1925, against dwindling SIS presence due to the Great Kantō earthquake of 1923, dozens of contacts were listed as informers in Tokyo, Kobe and Nagasaki and other commercial and industrial cities. Recruitment and information gathering was inhibited, as the spymaster noted, due to Japanese class system: 'There was complete mistrust that these people (from the highest to the lowest) have of their fellow beings.'[18] The same year, the Committee of Imperial Defence concluded that no war would occur with Japan for the following ten years; thus the call to establish a fully operational early-warning organisation was left underfunded.[19]

To the surprise of the British embassy in Tokyo, Denham informed the SIS in London that anarchism was a serious threat on the island. He claimed that some 57,000 Japanese were members of revolutionary societies, while the embassy maintained that the number was limited to 7,000.[20] The Japanese communist party had been established in 1922, but collapsed the same year. Some anarchist factions had merged with communists, creating anarcho-communist groups. Terrorist activities were noted as anarchist societies like the *Girochinsha* (Guillotine Society), established in Osaka, instigated the murder of government officials in revenge for repressive policies. Osugi Sakae, the recognised leader in the anarchist movement, was captured by the police along with his wife and six-year-old child. All were executed without trial in what is known as the Amakasu Incident of 1923, ushering in further chaos.

Staff officers at the War Office and the military attachés in Tokyo concluded the IJA was backward in doctrine as well as in weaponry, though they acknowledged its high morale. In the war games of 1926, tanks participated for the first time. It was felt that the traditionalist mindset of the Japanese army officer corps did not allow for innovation and speedy modernisation; they still trained their officers using the experience of the triumphant Russo-Japanese War rather than the tactics and operations of the First World War. Based on the Japanese training and equipment, British military intelligence wrongly believed that the Japanese had no intention to challenge Britain but rather wished to project their imperial power over north-east Asia, confronting the fractured Republic of China and the weak Soviet Union.[21]

By 1927, naval attaché Captain Cloudesley Robinson confirmed that the Japanese navy's aviation capacity was 'progressive and efficient'. In contrast, the army pilots were deemed to be of poor calibre by RAF flight lieutenants serving in language schools in Japan. Failed trials in 1928 led to the conclusion that 'this miserable fiasco shows how weak the Japanese air arm still is, and tends to show that the Japanese are still far behind the West in technical matters'.[22] Generally, the Japanese were credited with blind obedience ('complete suppression of one's real feelings'), 'slow mental adaptability', 'lack of initiative' and an inability to understand technology.[23]

Throughout the 1920s, the Japanophile Francis Piggott persuaded the War Office in London to view the Japanese as allies in the confrontation with Russia in the Far East and not as a future enemy. Some intelligence on the Comintern was exchanged until 1929, when London concluded that the Japanese would not offer anything useful without real strategic concessions in the Far East, such as access to Singapore and the provision of new military technologies.[24]

Piggott insisted that the development of an SIS structure in Japan was unnecessary. In effect, he blocked British espionage in the country. In February 1928, he wrote to SIS that 'military intelligence was best left to above-board methods. The position of trust and confidence built up during the days of the Alliance, and continued since 1922 by successive Military Attachés and language officers, was a far more valuable potential source of information than anything which could possibly be obtained by S.I.S.'[25]

In 1924, Paymaster-Commander E. P. Jones was appointed Japanese specialist in the GC&CS station in Hong Kong. The station had been flooded with intercepts of the Imperial Japanese Navy. By the following year, Paymaster-Lieutenant Eric Nave of the Royal Australian Navy, a fluent Japanese speaker, headed the signals intelligence operations of the station. The Admiralty at this time complained that deciphering of radio communications was an issue, and in January 1926 the Admiralty demanded the station speed up its interception of Japanese navy signals alongside making warships function as intercept stations. By December that year, the Admiralty was happy with the effort and the result:

> Over 1,000 Japanese W/T messages are being intercepted per month and in addition to interception a large amount of information has been collected concerning the Japanese naval W/T organization. Lines of traffic have been observed, methods of procedure, call signs and many signals elucidated and at the same time a number of previously unknown stations have been identified.[26]

Such were the numbers of intercepts that Paymaster Lieutenant-Commander Shaw complained that he needed an additional interpreters, and thus funds for training more specialist personnel. Sinclair, the chief of SIS, complained that too few staff knew Japanese.

In March 1928, Sinclair wrote to the Foreign Office and military intelligence branches at the War Office that the 'primary intelligence' foreign target in the Far East was Japan. The next month, he requested more funds to maintain espionage in Japan; the Admiralty refused, and the RAF and the Army concurred. In difficult fiscal times, the Foreign Office sided with the Admiralty, killing off any effort for boosting espionage in Japan. The Foreign Office ruled that 'valuable information' was already provided from time to time from a 'Japanese source'. Ostensibly they hinted at the deciphering of Japanese diplomatic codes by the GC&CS, thus no spies were needed.[27]

Davidson, Cumming and Sinclair, citing reliable secret intelligence, had been warning the British government of the Japanese strategic threat to the British Empire in the Far East. Beatty's assessment was most valuable, pointing to the many factors that made the Japanese likely to expand at the expense of the British interests in the Far East. Churchill's assessment of Japanese policy and strategy shifted one way or the other at this time; he supported the lapse of the Anglo-Japanese agreement only because of the hostile American stance. Rightfully, Britain could not side with a 'militaristic' country that had been deemed a threat since 1909.

By January 1928, as the Japanese arms industry was *upgrading* its naval and air armaments, Churchill boasted that 'Beatty's Japanese bogey has completely collapsed'.[28] He could not have been more wrong.

Evidently the warnings of the spymasters of SIS and MI5 as well as of the Admiralty were ignored as their services were stripped of funding. In effect, it was a pro-Japanese stance of Churchill and the rest of the Cabinet members ignoring the warnings, allowing for more time to Japan to gear up for war. The gradual pro-Japanese stance of Churchill in the 1920s, the crisis with the gold standard – weakening Royal Navy's shipbuilding program – facilitated other pro-Japanese voices in Whitehall (like Lindley, Piggott and Kennedy) to condone Japanese policy.

A naval conference concluded in London on 22 April 1930 with the signing of the Treaty for the Limitation and Reduction of Naval Armament, whereby representatives of Britain, the United States, Japan, France and Italy agreed on limitations to naval shipbuilding and regulation of submarine warfare.

Meanwhile, at the War Office, Piggott and his followers asserted that a Japanese advance in Manchuria would *help* British interests by checking Russian influence in the region, establishing a 'powerful barrier against the extension of Soviet influence in the Far East and the Pacific'.[29]

'No war with Japan' meant the diminishment of espionage in Japan shadowing the Japanese strategic elite. Davidson's hard work to penetrate the elite with the help of Indian secret agents was scrapped. The Foreign Office's reliance on signals intelligence was damaging the prospect of a reliable espionage network that could cope with Japanese counterintelligence.

Piggott's blocking of espionage in Japan – with the ambassador's tacit approval – was almost criminal, crippling Britain's intelligence gathering in the interwar period. In October 1935, a memorandum submitted to the committee under Sir Warren Fisher concluded:

In the Far East, an unsatisfactory position exists, especially in regard to Japan. As long as 1928, it was pointed out that if it was desired to obtain S[ecret].S[ervice]. information in this very difficult country it would be necessary to guarantee large sums, and the establishment of a good Secret Service would probably take some years. The proposal was turned down, however, and not raised again until the end of 1932, when SIS was directed to establish a Service in Japan, but without the provision of funds necessary to enable this to be done. In consequence money had to be found by diverting sums being spent, with valuable results, on other countries. The amount so found is wholly insufficient, and only suffices to maintain a skeleton organization. It must be borne in mind that even when adequate funds are available, it takes at least 2-3 years under the most favourable circumstances to establish a satisfactory S.S. in any country ... it is plainly apparent that, in the future, Germany, Japan and Italy will have to be regarded as potential enemies from without, as well as Soviet Russia from within...[30]

7

THE AVIATOR AND THE SUBMARINER

'[There is] no question that Squadron Leader Rutland is perfectly well aware that in going over to the Japanese Government he is, in effect, selling to a Foreign Power valuable and secret information which he has acquired solely by reason of his official position.' This was the position of MI5 intelligence officer Desmond Ball, later a key intelligence advisor to Churchill, when writing to SIS counter-espionage head and future wartime chief Stewart Menzies.[1] Rutland was described as an officer 'with unique knowledge of aircraft carriers and deck-landings',[2] and Ball further warned that 'this individual has been heavily bribed to betray his secret knowledge to the Foreign Power whose service is now entering'.[3]

Frederick Rutland was born in 1886. In 1901 he joined the Royal Navy as a boy seaman, and thirteen years later in December 1914 he became a flight sub-lieutenant in the Royal Naval Air Service. In early 1915 he completed his flight training and by January 1916 he was commissioned as a lieutenant. Rutland was hailed as a hero during the naval battle of Jutland. He flew a Short Type 184 on the seaplane tender HMS *Engadine*, and on 30 May 1916, at 1500 hours, he observed three German cruisers and five destroyers; naval historians argued that this was the first real wartime air-naval reconnaissance. He was awarded the Distinguished Service Cross for 'his gallantry and persistence in flying within close distance of the enemy light cruisers'. In the following days, during the battle of Jutland, he dived overboard to save a sailor and was awarded the Albert Medal in Gold. Here was an officer who would act beyond the call of duty.

In 1917, flying a Sopwith Pup, 'Rutland of Jutland' was awarded a Bar to his DSC for 'services on patrol duties and submarine searching in home waters'. On 18 June 1917, now Flight Commander Rutland experimented by taking off on a platform on a gun turret of the cruiser HMS *Yarmouth*. It was a successful launch, another 'first' by Rutland for naval historians. In April 1918, he was transferred to the RAF. During the last years of his service, he experimented with technology enabling safe take-off from ships' platforms.

In December 1922, an excited Admiral Seizo Kobayashi, the Japanese naval attaché in London, cabled the Imperial Navy General Staff. Rutland was interested in providing the Japanese with top-secret intelligence on aircraft technology. It was 'an offer of service' to spy. Kobayashi urged the Naval General Staff to authorise Rutland's recruitment. They certainly made no objection; he was a precious source of information on technologies that could be used to upgrade the navy, particularly aircraft carriers. Negotiations were opened by Captain Gorō Hara, described by Japanese assets as 'very sly … not a naval officer but a politician'.[4]

In early 1923, Rutland asked for permission to retire, and 'after considerable discussion in the Air Ministry, it was decided that he should be allowed to do so. He retired in October 1923.'[5] At that time he was serving aboard HMS *Eagle*, a converted aircraft carrier. *Eagle* was considered the largest carrier in the world, hosting twenty-four aircraft, among them Fairey Flycatchers, Blackburn reconnaissance aircraft, Blackburn torpedo bombers and Supermarine Seagull flying boats. In February 1924, HMS *Eagle* was operational and assigned to the Mediterranean fleet.

Rutland's retirement came about because he had somehow learned that the Air Ministry, informed by MI5, knew that he had met Japanese officers in London and suspected him of disclosing confidential information.[6] Nevertheless, under the existing regulations there was no order banning him from serving with foreign powers.[7]

In early March 1924, Rutland and his new wife moved to France. SIS took a strong interest in his case when he moved to a large house, the Villa Georges on Avenue Andrew Guillaume in Garches near Versailles. The SIS station chief in Paris was instructed to arrange for a watch to be kept on Rutland, who flaunted his wealth; the source, they suspected, was the Japanese military.

Rutland's servants disclosed that he had only a few friends, but 'two or three times a week he was visited by various Japanese gentlemen with whom he sometimes returned to Paris by motor car ... on one occasion the Rutland's had party at which all the guests were Japanese ... Rutland did not appear to have any regular business, although he went to Paris fairly often. At home he busied himself with matters relating to wireless, on which subject he seemed to be very interested.'[8]

The Rutlands were heard boasting that they would be moving to work in Japan for four years and that the salary paid would be considerable.[9] The source was not British secret operatives but the local French police.[10] Eventually, the SIS station chief informed his superiors:

> ... we have now received a reply to our further enquiry as to why the statement was made that it was known that R. [Rutland] was in touch with Japanese circles in Paris, and it is to the effect that the agent who undertook the enquiry stated off his own bat that R. was constantly visited [at his villa] by individuals of Japanese nationality.'[11]

Surveillance in Paris by SIS and their French police liaisons revealed that Rutland was meeting the Japanese naval attaché of the embassy in France.[12]

On 9 March 1925, Menzies, then SIS assistant director for special intelligence, reported on Japanese espionage in Paris: 'From what I believe to be a very reliable source I have heard that the centre of Japanese Naval Espionage in Paris [...] is directed by *Capitaine de Corvette* IZAWA, the Assistant Naval Attaché at the Japanese Embassy ... One of the principal agents is a certain MUNEYUKI whom I fancy you [Robert Laney, a French liaison intelligence head in Paris] will have no difficulty in identifying.'

Menzies wanted French intelligence to put surveillance on Muneyuki (eventually identified as Muneshige): 'If we could find out with whom he (Rutland) associates we could learn much about the Japanese espionage system.' Menzies further mentioned a certain Margoulisse who was supposed to be advisor on aviation to the Japanese ambassador in Paris. He was also aware that two Japanese officers had been caught taking photographs within the fortified area in Calais and wanted the French to provide their names 'in case they ever attempt the same thing in this country'. On 31 December 1926, Menzies wrote to a contact:

> Information has reached me from the Far East that a Japanese named AKAMINE should reach France in January. It is reported that he is engaged on aviation espionage, so you may care to conduct investigations particularly as my source is reliable. I have not received any further particulars regarding his status. Should he be a diplomat I fear that investigations will be exceedingly difficult. Perhaps you will be kind and let me know the result of anything you discover.[13]

On 25 July 1924, Rutland, his wife and his two children had boarded the *Kaiser-i-Hind* for Yokohama. Once there he came into contact with Captain Royle, a British naval attaché, who wrote to the Admiralty that Rutland wanted to get a job in aircraft manufacturing and to act as a spy for the Admiralty:

> He [Rutland] has apparently just completed designs for 3 Oleo undercarriages big, medium and small. These carriages are used at home [the RAF] but he has made his own modification and is getting out a patent. The trials of these carriages took place at Kasumigama a few days ago and were apparently a great success. They are to be given another trial at Yokosuka in a few days. This job will apparently complete his contract with the Mitsubishi firm- however he expects to continue for another year and I think they are offering him a higher salary if he will 'given

them advice on Naval flying, particularly with reference to aircraft carriers'. He was quite open about it and said that up till now they had particularly refrained from asking him questions outside his particular job of designing Oleo carriages ... he [Rutland] wanted to know what I thought about this new proposal because as he said and I quite agreed with him that if he took it on he would feel bound to give away everything he knew i.e. he would give them the best advice at his disposal ... if he does [get the job], then he will be able, to a certain extent, as he said, *keep us informed of progress made.* My personal advice to him was to accept the new proposal.[14]

The oleo strut was a pneumatic air-oil hydraulic shock absorber, part of the landing gear of models used on aircraft carriers, employed to manage the impact of vertical oscillations on landing. In 1915, the Vickers Armstrong Company patented the first oleo-pneumatic shock absorbing strut. In the mid-1930s, the introduction of retractable landing gear compelled aviation industries to upgrade the models of oleo struts. The leaders in this key naval aviation technology were Britain, France and the United States. Rutland started working with Mitsubishi on landing gear, and also trained Japanese aviators in how to land on aircraft carriers.[15] Occasionally he met with a British naval attaché who reported about him to the Admiralty and SIS. The War Office was reassured by the naval attaché:

I shall keep myself well informed as to his movements but I feel very inclined to put a spoke in his wheel as he must be giving most valuable information away to the Japanese. There are rumours in business circles that Yokosuka is to be made the great Naval Air Base ... Rutland is probably going to take a big part in the whole scheme and I shall try to find out from him what he knows about it. Rutland talks a lot and is sure to give himself away pretty soon. The Consul General (Davidson) here told me that Colonel Piggott's suspicions of Rutland had been aroused and I told him in absolute confidence, that I knew something about the man and that if Piggott wanted a few particulars I could give them to him. I don't know what Piggott knows if he intends to have the man watched I might as well help him.[16]

This is a unique reference to Piggott, at that time a military attaché in Tokyo, knowing about Rutland. In any case, Piggott did not suspect that the Japanese might be interested in recruiting a spy.[17]

In 1927, Rutland left Japan to visit Chile, Argentina and Brazil and returned to Britain in 1928, becoming a board member of a firm of motor engineers in London. It seemed SIS and MI5 had lost interest in the former officer. More fool them, as in truth the Japanese naval attaché in London, Captain Shiro Takasu, had recruited Rutland back in 1922. He had insisted on Rutland going to the United States in response to his request to join the Imperial Japanese Navy, and he was clear on his intentions: there would be a war with the United States, and Rutland should be in Los Angeles ready to gather secret intelligence.[18]

In November 1932, MI5 opened Rutland's correspondence and learned that he had met with Takasu. His successor, Captain Arata Oka, meanwhile reached an agreement for Rutland to be paid £2,000 per year plus travelling expenses.[19]

Rutland compiled a report in June 1933. He had a meeting with Eugene Dooman, the first secretary of the US embassy in London, who had served for twenty years in the US embassy in Tokyo and was 'an expert in the Japanese language'. Rutland reported that Dooman told him in confidence:

> … in the matter of China, until the state of affairs in America is stabilized [the recession], America will not at present interfere. As long as Japan does not attack America, America will not for the present take positive action [meaning aggression]. He [Dooman] could not guarantee that after 5 years (or when a change of President takes place) America would not proceed to take positive action.[20]

This intelligence about US passivity while war raged in China was most welcome to the Japanese naval and military leadership.

SIS intercepted and decoded the report, but at that time did not know that the author was Rutland.[21] An angry Sinclair was now convinced that there would come a day when the SIS would have to inform the US Department of War and the FBI about a British spy working for the Japanese against the United States.

In July 1933, a Metropolitan Police constable discovered a dispatch case in the street. Upon examination it was found to contain money and documents in Japanese, and it belonged to naval attaché Captain Oka, who was the Japanese spymaster in London. Police informed Naval Intelligence, and they in turn told the MI5 and SIS. One instruction note in Japanese read, 'Discuss with R. most suitable place for him to reside in USA and method of communication.' Agents quickly began checking passenger lists, and it was spotted that on 31 August Rutland and his wife, two children and their governess were due to set off for Yokohama via New York, the Panama Canal, San Francisco and Vancouver on board the SS *Olympic*.

The SIS took the lead; two secret agents were instructed to board as passengers and befriend Rutland. One was ordered to encourage Rutland into a business partnership and task him with contacting retired US naval officers interested in these fictitious business plans. During the voyage, intercepted communications revealed that Rutland received instructions from the Japanese, the naval attaché in London and a Mitsubishi employee.[22]

The social chatter aboard the SS *Olympic* saw many boast about business schemes in the United States, and Rutland told an agent that he planned to open an importing business in the United States and indicated 'extreme interest in US Navy yards on the East coast'. He felt that importing technologies related to warships was a niche area with serious profit potential. The secret agent performed his task well, and 'subsequent meetings resulted in our man being requested to act as Rutland's business agent in New York such employment to commence with [not declassified] liquidating (selling) certain opals for Rutland while the latter was en route to Japan.'

Eventually, Rutland settled with his family in Los Angeles. He kept correspondence with the SIS agent who had won him over, giving him 'vague hints of probable business dealings'. In 1934,

Rutland arrived in New York to sail for Britain. He informed the agent that he had returned from Japan and left his family in Los Angeles. When the agent complained of a 'lack of business', Rutland replied that 'he was in touch with a T. Omori of Yokohama and that they might sell Japanese captured pearls in the United States'. Nevertheless, Rutland did not follow up.[23]

In the meantime, the intercepted communications between the Japanese naval attaché in London and the head of naval intelligence at the Imperial Navy General Staff confirmed that Rutland was a spy. On 19 July 1933, the head of naval intelligence cabled the naval attaché to decide some reliable method by which Rutland might communicate with an intermediary in Britain. He decided to change Rutland's codename from Furuyama to Shinkawa.[24] Another missive raised concerns about using what was called the 'White' cipher in communications with Rutland:

> There are numerous objections to the White cipher, and if he [Rutland] were in possession of this and the worst happened, there would be a grave risk of his connection with our Navy being exposed, so it is not be used ... it is our intention later to instruct Shinkawa [Rutland] to construct a code for intelligence reports emanating from him.[25]

The naval attaché reported to the head of naval intelligence that Rutland was trying to set up a cipher for secure communications in March 1934. An intercepted cable dated 8 March from the naval attaché to the head of naval intelligence in Tokyo stated, 'We have no intention of asking him to participate in the collection of intelligence concerning Britain.'[26]

On 21 July 1934, the Japanese naval attaché in London cabled the head of naval intelligence that Rutland had established a business office 'according to plan, and had left a woman as Branch Manageress and typist'.[27] This cable was intercepted and deciphered, and the manageress identified as one Mrs MacDougall. In August, MI5 surveillance operatives 'pick her up at 74a Regent Street where observation is rather difficult'. Correspondence between Rutland and MacDougall was opened regularly and examined.[28]

Rutland's activities in the United States prompted officials to ask whether it would be appropriate to inform the FBI that he was working for Japanese espionage. Sinclair was against any briefing of the Americans:

I have seen the DNI (Director of Naval Intelligence) and have informed him that I do not propose to tell the Americans anything about R[utland] ... if we did so we should be completely blind in the future as to what was happening. In my opinion, the letters which R. writes to Miss MacDougal most certainly contain a code, but up to the present we have been unable to completely solve it. This however, definitely links up Miss MacDougal as being part and parcel of the (espionage) organization (of Rutland).[29]

One letter from Rutland to MacDougall, dated 1 November 1934, was examined by the SIS 'for an exact system of ciphering':

There is little doubt that it does contain some such system; for example 'Kikuchi must be' reads Mitsubishi, O.K. Malham O.E. reads 'Oklahoma etc.' There is therefore, little doubt that Mrs M. is in the picture and my suggestion was that we want to find out how she passes letters or messages to Oka. There is also a possibility that she may receive letters from R. (Rutland) at other addresses than Regent Street.[30]

On 3 March 1935, 'an absolutely certain source' claimed that Rutland 'is to be employed in the collection of intelligence concerning Britain'. SIS was aware that in June 1933 Rutland had proposed 'to work in England, which was turned down'.[31] Eventually, in April 1935, Rutland closed his London office and MacDougall left for another business.[32]

Rutland and the naval attaché relied on letters for their communication. On 24 March 1934 Rutland was told that Tokyo and the Japanese naval attaché in Washington, D.C. could be reached by embassy telegraph. Soon the naval attaché in London cabled the head of naval intelligence that in case of emergency he would not cable the naval attaché in Washington but would go to France and cable from there. The Washington naval attaché would meanwhile request that Mexico cable either Tokyo or the naval attaché in London.[33] By the end of March, Tokyo had received a special cipher that Rutland had drafted. A 'reliable source' noted that that the Japanese naval attaché entrusted a cipher to the captain of the transport *Hakone Maru*, due to reach Yokohama on 16 July 1934.[34]

Meanwhile on 15 March an SIS report stated: 'Information from an absolutely certain source is to the effect that Rutland is to be employed in the collection of intelligence concerning Britain.' It was reported on 3 April that he received $2,000 in bonds from an indefinite source in France payable through a Canadian bank. Rutland then decided to return to the United States, travelling under the title of Squadron Leader. He reached New York on 16 April 1934 and contacted his old friend, the SIS secret agent, promising a 'sketchy' future business relationship and providing the names and addresses of his associate commercial agents in Peking (Lionell H. Howells), Honolulu (H. Reilly) and Sydney (D. Price). By November 1934, Rutland, now in Los Angles, set up a stock exchange office and continued his correspondence with the SIS agent. The agent managed to secure an invitation to Rutland's house in Los Angeles and stayed with him from February to April 1935. Rutland explained that he was planning to open an investment bureau in London; in fact, he had already opened an office and it was under MI5 surveillance. Eventually, in May 1935, Rutland and his family returned to London. He told the agent, who remained in the USA, that he had made preparations to start a wine agency with William Ellis, an Australian living in Surrey.

That month, Rutland wrote to the Japanese Director of Naval Intelligence. The naval attaché forwarded the message on his behalf, and it was duly intercepted by the GC&CS:

Everyone I have met in America thinks war with Japan is inevitable, many even say it will be their way our of depression. They say that their action of taking the profit out of armaments and many other schemes are part of a general scheme. The Army and Navy want war and in my view this might be put off for a few years. I feel sure that there is a distinct possibility of the administration being forced into using their method to get out of their difficulties either during the Presidential term or the middle of the next term…Businesses are subject to all kinds of enquiries in the ordinary way of business and you must know that in the case of an alien these enquiries are made also by the secret service as a regular routine.[35]

The MI5 tracked Rutland and reported that on 30 July 1935 he had a meeting with Captain Oka, the Japanese naval attaché in London.[36] During June and July 1935, Japanese officers had some seven meetings with Rutland in which he asked for more money.[37] Evidently the Japanese spymaster was not cautious enough and did not employ an intermediary.

On 25 November 1936, Rutland sailed again for Japan. An SIS agent in New York was directed 'to make overtures to Rutland with a view to becoming confidante in respects of his activities in Japan'. Rutland went back to Britain in April 1937 aboard the *Queen Mary*, travelling in tourist class, ostensibly for the coronation of King George VI. A year later, while back in the United States, Rutland established the Security Aircraft Corporation and sold three civilian aircraft to Japan.

A few months later, in October 1938, the secret agent who had for so long been acting as Rutland's friend was directed by London 'to refrain from too much association with Rutland as US authorities must now be aware of his activities'. The following month he met with Rutland and was informed that 'when the China war is over' he would arrange to purchase American-made planes for the Japanese. On 22 April 1939, the agent reported that Rutland told him he was friends with a Squadron Leader Adams of the RAF who worked as a test pilot for the Lockheed company in California. On 3 June Rutland met two Japanese employees of the Mitsubishi Trading Company, and in August he 'took [a] hurried' trip to Japan; he returned in October. From May to June 1940, Rutland, representing an inventor, attempted to persuade the Canadian government to buy 'a machine capable of disintegrating certain metal substances at various distances'.[38]

Until 1939, the FBI was unaware of Rutland's activities in the United States. In September of that year, the FBI Los Angeles field office received a phone tip from an unknown man who warned that Rutland was a spy of the Japanese and 'his activities had been under the scrutiny of the British intelligence for some time'.[39]

The FBI commenced surveillance of Rutland, but 'no facts were secured definitely establishing that he was in fact engaged in Japanese espionage at that time'. The surveillance continued.[40]

Almost a year later, in August 1940, Captain Ellis Zacharias of the US Navy Office of Naval Intelligence told the FBI that Rutland was his informant on an intelligence scheme in Japan. Rutland supposedly told Zacharias:

When in Japan he (Rutland) had agreed to operate in the United States as an espionage agent in the event of war between the United States and Japan, but that he had accepted this assignment only to facilitate the payment of certain money which was owed to him in connection with a business he at one time had financed in Japan. [the development of an Oleo strut with a Japanese engineer] It was further determined [by the FBI] that Rutland had suggested a plan whereby certain inconsequential information would be furnished to him got transmittal to Japan in order that he could not only establish channels of communication but could thereby display to the Japanese that he was in fact fulfilling his mission. He was reportedly of the opinion that if such an arrangement could be worked out, his value as any informant in the United States would be greatly enhanced.[41]

By that time, US naval intelligence assets tracking Rutland had informed the SIS liaison that they were 'definitely of the opinion that Rutland is "utterly worthless"'.

In July 1941, Rutland approached the British intelligence representative in New York offering to 're-establish' contact with Japanese officials so that he might become a double agent. Rutland met Lieutenant Commander Ringle in Los Angeles 'on neutral ground' and presented a file detailing his connections with the Japanese. He claimed that his income currently derived from the Japanese as he had sold Mitsubishi the patent for a 'device for improving the taking off and landing of aircraft on carriers'.

On 16 September 1941, Rutland reported that he no longer had a point of contact with the Japanese after the deportation of Itaru Tachibana, the naval attaché in Washington who had visited Rutland in his Los Angeles house.[42]

In a bid to persuade them to employ him, Rutland told British intelligence that he had been 'instructed' by the Japanese to go to Mexico and meet Japanese officers there. He asked the British for any information he could disclose to them to convince them of his value, but the SIS under Sinclair was not playing any games and his request 'was refused ... in a manner calculated not to arouse his suspicions'. Sinclair instructed SIS agents in New York to convince Rutland to return to Britain; the FBI was after him, and 'an anticipated accusation initiated by the FBI against an ex-British officer was extremely undesirable' at a time when Churchill was pleading for American military aid against Nazi Germany. For their part, the US government did not want to charge a British former officer with espionage so they 'suggested to Rutland to contact the British Mission in Washington'. The mission was soon informed that Rutland was an advisor to Lord Sempill's Japan mission and 'a very competent aviator' who did 'considerable work in teaching the Japanese how to use aircraft carriers (from technical and mechanical point of view)'.[43]

Eventually, in October 1941, Rutland flew to Britain. Despite his subterfuge there was no concrete evidence that he worked against Britain or violated the Official Secrets Act, so internment was not an option. This was a concern for the SIS liaison in Washington, who feared that a failure to detain him might lead US naval intelligence to conclude that he was a British secret agent who had been conveniently extracted from the United States.[44]

When Rutland reached London he was not arrested. Instead he made a courageous bid to meet with officers – a former RAF air marshal, a squadron leader, and officials of the Ministry of Aircraft Production – to discuss his plan to feed false information to Japanese contacts in Mexico. On 8 December 1941, after the attack on Pearl Harbor, MI5 persuaded the Home Office that Rutland should be interned; he remained locked up until 1943.[45]

In 1946, with the Allied occupation of Japan underway, MI5 suggested that the SIS take advantage of Rutland's report on his friendships with Japanese officers in the 1920s and 1930s. Kim Philby, an SIS officer who was later dramatically revealed to be a Soviet spy, replied rather emphatically to Courtenay Young, the MI5 officer following the Rutland case:

As I told you at our last meeting, our representative in Singapore (SIS station chief) has telegraphed us to the effect that he does not consider that your comprehensive study of the Rutland case could profitably be exploited in view of the extreme difficulty of conditions in Tokyo.[46]

A year later, Rutland, his reputation in tatters, committed suicide.

Returning to the inter-war period, in 1926 Sinclair met with the Director of Naval Intelligence at the Admiralty and was told that intercepts of communications between the Japanese naval attaché in London and the IJN General Staff revealed one Lieutenant Commander Colin Mayers, a noted submariner, had offered his services to Japanese intelligence.

Mayers was born in 1891 in British Guinea. In 1907, he joined the Royal Navy. In 1912 he was promoted to lieutenant of the submarine service and eight years later he was made lieutenant commander. Two years later, he was assigned the command of the M. Group submarines until 1926. An officer of 'brilliant knowledge of the secret and constructional parts of the whole of submarine-service',[47] during the First World War he commanded submarines of various classes while also becoming well versed in French, German, Italian and American submarine practice. Fluent in Dutch and German, after the Armistice he was a member of the Allied commission for the surrender of German submarines.

In the meeting discussing Mayers, Sinclair was notably troubled:

[He] seemed very agitated regarding the potential danger of Mayers, not only placing his present knowledge at the disposal of the Japanese but also, in view of his position in Vickers, the considerable facilities which he would obtain for keeping himself posted on all the latest naval information ... the DNI also takes a serious view of the case and is anxious that he should do everything possible to keep in touch with Mayers' activities. The DNI considered the question whether it has anyone in Vickers whom he could take into his confidence, but decided that he would not trust anyone there from top to bottom.[48]

Sinclair had taken the matter personally because he knew Mayers. In September 1926, he invited his acquaintance for a discussion. Mayers did not know that he was speaking to the chief of SIS, only that Sinclair was a vice admiral. Sinclair asked Mayers about rumours that he was thinking of resigning as he had been passed over for promotion, to which Mayers replied that he was in contact with some British firms. Sinclair then asked directly whether 'he intended to offer himself to the Japanese'. Mayers answered 'with an emphatic negative'. Mayers was lying and Sinclair knew it.

At this time, Mayers was serving aboard the submarine HMS *Dolphin*, based at the Royal Navy's Fort Blockhouse in Gasport. On 12 September 1926, he wrote to Captain Toyoda, the Japanese naval attaché in London, stating that he would be happy to offer his services upon his resignation from the Royal Navy. To prove his qualifications, he included three service references: Vice Admiral (Submarines) Wilmot Nicholson, Captain Max Horton and Captain C. G. Brodie.[49] These men did not know that Mayers would use their references to work for the IJN. Nicholson remarked:

> I consider him (Mayers) one of the best submarine captains in the Navy, most capable and reliable in every way and possessed of great determination ... Possesses exceptional knowledge of wireless telegraphy and under-water sound signalling, and an inventive mind, several of his suggestions having proved of considerable practical value.[50]

Horton wrote in his reference that Mayers

> in submerged communications (w/t and sonic) is recognised as being almost solely responsible for modern progress. He has also had much to do with the recent advances in submarine tactics. The new types of submarines which are now being proceeded with by the Admiralty are largely the result of this officer's association with myself, for although the proposals and sketches were sent in under my signature, yet he and one other were the chief contributers (*sic*) to the plans. From the above it will be realised why I consider Lieutenant Commander Mayer's qualifications and capacity

as a submarine officer unique. He is that rare combination of an inventive genius and a thoroughly practical man.[51]

The third referee, Captain C. G. Brodie, commanding officer of the 5th Submarine Flotilla, wrote of Mayers:

His technical knowledge is altogether remarkable in a branch of the service where most officers take a thorough and detailed interest in the engineering and electrical side of the work. Very few of the technical improvements in all types of submarines during the past two or three years have not been initiated or improved by him/ his grasp of principles has not been obscured by his mastery of detail and his work in preparing the training manual could hardly have been done by anyone else. He has an inventive mind both mechanically and electrically, and also as regards tactical and strategic problems.[52]

Mayers was impatient. On 20 September 1926, he wrote to Commander Gorō at the Japanese naval offices in Broadway Court Westminster, arranging a lunch with him. Mayers met Toyoda too. In November 1926, he was informed by the Admiralty that his resignation would be accepted without delay should he take up employment with a British firm. By now the Home Office had given MI5 permission to open Mayers' correspondence, and they concluded that he was about to commence work for Vickers at their naval construction works in Barrow-in-Furness.[53]

Intercepts of Japanese communications revealed the Japanese were slow in understanding the value of their would-be spy. On 11 January 1927, Toyoda informed the vice minister of the Marine and Naval Technical Department in Tokyo that on 10 January 1927 Gorō had again interviewed 'the person reported on in British Naval No. 61' who would commence working for the Vickers submarines department on 1 February 1927. Gorō 'at the interview' gave Mayers 'a list of the information required', meaning a list of subjects that interested them: the construction of vessels; trade war; warfare against fleets; tactics for attacks on bays and harbours; the firing practice of submarines; reconnaissance; landing operations; and armaments for use by submarines against submarines. Mayers and Gorō reached some sort of agreement that a full report would take up to four months to be drafted; the Japanese would offer £300.[54] On 10 February 1927, the IJN General Staff cabled further instructions to Toyoda on Mayers' assignment, putting emphasis on the upper limit of the payment available after confirmation of the supplied secret intelligence.[55]

While working for Vickers, on 10 March 1927, Mayers wrote to the outgoing Toyoda to announce that he was coming to London on 15 March and would like to have a farewell dinner with the naval attaché. On 12 March, an investigation was launched when it was discovered that eight technical plans had gone missing at Fort Blockhouse.[56]

The investigation at Fort Blockhouse revealed that Mayers had been given the eight technical drawings for teaching purposes in March 1926. They were listed: Submarine X.L. General arrangement; Submarine X.I. Telemoto System; Submarine X1 Watertight compartments; Submarine O Class General arrangement; Submarine O.1 Watertight compartments; Submarine O.1 Projector Binnacle; Submarine O.1. Stern tubes; Submarine O.1. Bow tubes.

MI5 and the SIS agreed that Mayers should be brought in, and the public prosecutor ordered his arrest for breaching the Official Secrets Act. He was quickly detained and a frantic search in the Vickers offices revealed the drawings. On 15 March, the company returned them to Fort Blockhouse.[57] Commander Arthur William Johns, the assistant director of naval construction at the Admiralty, stated in court that he had examined the drawings, which were the sole property of the Admiralty: 'The information contained in these drawing is calculated to be directly or indirectly useful to an enemy ... The information these drawings has never been communicated by the Admiralty to Messrs Vickers.'[58]

Vickers was embarrassed enough. Retired commander Craven, who worked for Vickers, told an MI5 officer he was 'very concerned as to the position of his firm in this case and said that it had already been suggested that Vickers had engaged Mayers with the idea of making use of secret and confidential Admiralty information ... he understood from [Admiral] Lord Beatty that a further and more serious charge against Mayers was under consideration and he was anxious to know whether this was so

... He (Craven) was very anxious to avoid any mention of the Japanese in his statement as he felt this might prejudice a *large* contract which Vickers negotiating with Japan.'[59]

Fortunately for Mayers, the SIS was aware from intercepting Japanese embassy communications that a retired commander named Thurston was being paid by the Japanese naval attaché and was 'the sole source of shipbuilding information'.[60] As a result, Mayers was eventually convicted under section 2 of the Official Secrets Act, which referred to wrongful communication of information (the sketches) to Vickers and *not* to Japanese intelligence. At that time, he had not received any money from the Japanese nor commenced writing the secret report they had requested. Vickers recovered from this debacle, but a year later the Admiralty was informed about further irregular practices by the company.

Lieutenant Firth of HMS *Osiris* reported to the Admiralty that he had witnessed a discussion at the office of Lieutenant Commander Spurgeon of HMS *Headway* – at that time being built in Barrow – with a man called Sedgwick who was head of the electrical department at Vickers, and who narrated the story of Mayers, who upon retirement had brought to Vickers eight drawings from his service: 'These were distributed among certain departments [of Vickers] with a view to enabling Vickers to prepare a commercial patent on their own in this connection.' Sedgwick had panicked upon being informed that Mayers was arrested and said he had burned all of the sketches. After his conviction, Mayer returned to Barrow, telephoned Sedgwick and asked about the drawings. Sedgwick feared the phone line might be monitored and denied any knowledge. Eventually they met that night and Sedgwick admitted that he destroyed them, to which Mayers 'expressed the greatest possible relief'.[61] These sketches must have been copies of the original eight sketches, which were retrieved from the Vickers offices.

In 1930, after he officially pledged that he would not disclose any information from his service to a foreign power, Mayers was granted a passport by the Foreign Office and emigrated to Los Angeles, where he worked in the film industry. At the same time, he made a bid to re-approach the Japanese but they were suspicious. An intercepted cable from the IJN General Staff to the naval attaché in London warned that Mayers, who was interested in teaching at the naval college in Tokyo, 'was unsuitable for reasons of character'.[62] By 1943 he was working as an electrician for Metro-Goldwyn-Mayer in Los Angeles, and, despite their proximity, after inquiries by the SIS there 'was no evidence that he was ever connected with Rutland'.[63]

It is clear that the Japanese spymasters – who generally did not hesitate to meet prospective spies and seemed unconcerned about surveillance – were slow to appreciate the value of Mayers' expertise; he could provide precious technical intelligence, but not information on tactics and strategies.

Meanwhile, the embarrassing investigation into Vickers had revealed to Sinclair and MI5 a parallel plot whereby commercial businesses sought to gain classified Admiralty intelligence for financial gain.

Most importantly, however, decorated British officers – veterans of the First World War – were clearly willing to work for Japan. Troubled by this, Sinclair urged action.

8

THE MEMORANDUM OF WAR

In May 1927, civil war had broken out in China. As a result, Prime Minister Tanaka Giichi convened a 'Far East Conference'. Running from 27 June to 7 July 1927, it was attended by ministers and officials from the Foreign Ministry, the Army Ministry, the Navy Ministry and the Finance Ministry, including General Mutō Nobuyoshi, commander of the Kwantung Army; Hideo Kodoma, governor of the Kwantung Leased Territory; Yoshizawa Kenkichi, minister to Peking; and Yoshida Shigeru, the consul in Mukden, along with those from Shanghai and Hankow.

The conclusion reached by this conference was that Japan would support the Chinese nationalists of the Republic of China, led by Field Marshal Chiang Kai-shek, against the Chinese communists. The key precondition of this backing was for Manchuria to be turned into a buffer state, effectively a Japanese colony. Tanaka authored a memorandum addressed to the Emperor, opining that Japan should first dominate in Mongolia and Manchuria before taking on the rest of China and the Far East.

Manchuria's ruler, General Zhang Zuolin, posed a challenge to Japanese strategic interests, but he was killed when his train was bombed near Shenyang on 4 June 1928, the culmination of a plan organised by the maverick Colonel Daisaku Kōmoto, an officer in the Kwantung Army. Captain Kaneo Tōmiya was in charge of executing the plan, while the bomb was planted on the bridge by Sapper First Lieutenant Sadatoshi Fujii. Neither the Japanese government nor the General Staff had sanctioned this assassination, and in their embarrassment Tanaka and his cabinet were forced to resign en masse.

The Japanophile Colonel Francis Piggott was then serving in the War Office, but between 1936 and 1940 he would return to his role as British military attaché at the Tokyo embassy. He distorted the story of Zuolin's assassination, causing a misinterpretation of Japanese policy:

> ... the death ... in a railway accident details of which were shrouded in obscurity. The Japanese admired his [Zhang's] ability to keep order, even when his policies ran counter to their own.[1]

Meanwhile, a Japanese-born Taiwanese businessman, Tsai Chih-Kan, claimed that he had personally copied the Tanaka memorial on Far Eastern domination after obtaining it from the Imperial Library on the night of 20 June 1928 with the assistance of disaffected Japanese officials. Perhaps this was further copied; in any case, it gradually became clear, first through Chinese sources, that Tanaka and his cabinet and officials at the June 1927 conference had agreed to an imperial plan. (It would take the SIS until 1931 to report on the existence of the memorandum.)

On 16 September 1929, the Japanese consul in Peking reported that pamphlets in English and Chinese concerning the Tanaka memorial were circulating in the city. On 9 September, an employee of the South Manchurian Railway Company notified Japanese consular authorities in Mukden that Chinese delegates then in the city on their way to attend the Kyoto Conference of the Institute of Pacific Relations (to be held from 28 October to 9 November) had purchased such a 'document from a friend in Tokyo' for a sizeable sum.

The Chinese delegation would use the document to prove Japanese hostility towards China. A Nanking-based magazine representing the Chinese nationalists, *Shihshih Yiiehpao* (*Monthly Report of Current Events*), published a lengthy article in its December 1929 issue entitled 'Shocking Policy of Japan in Manchuria and Mongolia: Tanaka Giichi's Memorial to the Japanese Emperor'. In 1930, the Japanese Foreign Ministry issued a formal note of protest to the Nationalist government. Despite their efforts, the Chinese press published the Tanaka note in Chinese. On 24 September 1931, a Shanghai-based English-language weekly, *The China Critic*, published a translation of the memorandum. This was only days after the infamous Mukden Incident, in which the Japanese detonated explosives on a Manchurian railway line and blamed it on Chinese dissidents as a *casus belli*. By the early 1930s, the memorandum was available in China, Japan, the United States, Canada, Britain and continental Europe.[2]

In July 1931, the SIS forwarded the English translation of the memorial to the Foreign Office Far Eastern department with the title 'Japan's Positive Policy in Manchuria'. A representative of the SIS in China had 'recently' obtained the document in Mukden, it was said, and the accompanying report estimated – wrongly – that the paper was authored by Tanaka before his death in September 1929, during the first half of that year. 'Its origin is obscure,' the report read, 'and one theory is that it was obtained by a Chinese military student at one of the Japanese military colleges in Japan, who handed it to the authorities in Mukden, where it was first translated into Chinese and later into English.'

However, officials from both the SIS and the Foreign Office suspected the Tanaka memorial was in fact a forgery, the work of anti-Japanese propagandists in the Chinese nationalist camp:

> Our representative has ascertained that certain portions of it have appeared in a Chinese paper published in Mukden named *Shin Min Pao*, but that owing to a protest to the Mukden authorities by the Japanese consul general, the whole pamphlet was never published in Chinese. Our representative has also ascertained that the English text was printed by the so called 'Public Association for Foreign Affairs' in Mukden, which is largely anti-Japanese, and that its distribution was undertaken with the full knowledge and approval of Mukden authorities. Whatever may be the origin of the pamphlet, and even if contains some statements of fact which are disputable, it seems that a good deal of it can be taken as a fair guide to what Japanese policy in Manchuria.[3]

For the SIS, the document represented 'very faithfully the trend of mind of one important, viz. the imperialistic, school of thought in

Japan. Imperialism is a strong force in Japan and open and avowed imperialism directed Japanese policy towards China until quite lately: But in 1922 Japan agreed with the rest of us to abandon imperialistic aims in China.'

It was observed that another approach prevailed in Japan, whereby trade and not force was employed to build a presence in China. Nevertheless:

> This only holds good up to a certain point: even the adherents of the trade theory and the anti-imperialists are only prepared to be conciliatory and friendly to China so long as the ark of the covenant is not touched: and I think it is a pretty clear that the ark of the covenant is the South Manchurian Railway. That is the scaffolding round which any future Japanese expansion in Manchuria must be built, and, if it fails, Japan will no longer be able to choose between the two theories: the Imperialist plan will be ruled out for generations or for ever.

The South Manchurian Railway was of strategic importance to Japan, and the possibility that the Chinese might build a rival railway threatened to jeopardise their interests. For the SIS, 'China's growth as a nation can only continue up to the point at which it becomes a serious nuisance to Japan or Russia or both, when the necessary steps will be taken'.[4]

The British military attaché in Tokyo at this time, Lieutenant Colonel Hugh James Simson, was given a copy of the Tanaka memorial. He opted for vitriolic comments, calling it along 'the kind of thing which [First World War German field marshal] Ludendorf might write nowadays assisted by a bout of indigestion. If it is the production of the late Premier [Tanaka], it is thoroughly bad ... because it is a dyspeptic rumination totally lacking in definition'. For him, 'it reads like the production of a man of "the very old school undoubtedly suffering himself from fixed ideas"'. The military attaché was dismissive, insisting that the ideas and plans of the Japanese military did not have an influence on Japanese foreign policy. He admitted that the 'wish eventually to control more that is at present possessed certainly exists in Japan', but presumed the Japanese would not 'repeat the mistake of the Germans in 1914' and 'risk bringing into the fields enemies beyond their ability to tackle'. The Tanaka memorial represented to him 'a kind of Japanese mind, and not the kind that is responsible at present'. The document was 'of value, as it enables us to note overt pieces of evidence in regard to possible events in Japan, whilst focusing our attention of the more probable'.[5]

In truth, the memorial never existed as one unified work; most possibly it was a collection of service papers from various commands. The documents were translated and re-translated to the extent that verbs and phrases changed scope and meaning. For example, with reference to the phrase 'to conquer even Europe' it is arguable that 'conquer' was used metaphorically or that the original word used didn't even translate to 'conquer'. Indeed, the document is rich in 'stylistic discrepancies, factual errors, and internal contradictions ... The memorial's rough, even earthy style has no parallel in the annals of imperial petitions in which precisely prescribed formal usages are *de rigueur*.' It did not read like an address to the Emperor,[6] but British diplomats had no previous examples to which they could compare the memorial.

According to the memorial, Tanaka brought the Emperor into the loop on intelligence activities:

Since Manchuria and Mongolia are still in the hands of the former princes, in the future we must recognize them as the ruling power and given them support. For this reason, the daughter of General Fukushima, Governor of Kwantung, risked her life among the barbarous Mongolian people of Tushiyeh to become adviser to their prince in order that she might serve the imperial government. As the wife of the prince ruler is the niece of Manchu Prince Su, the relationship between our Government and the Mongolian Prince became very intimate. The princesses of Outer and Inner Mongolia have all showed sincere respect for us, especially after we allured them with special benefits and protection. Now there are 19 Japanese retired military officers in the house of the Tushiyeh ... hereafter we shall send secretly more retired officers among them. They should wear Chinese clothes in order to escape the attention of the Mukden Government. Scattered in the territory of the Prince, they may engage themselves in farming, herding or dealing in wool. As to the other principalities, we can employ the same methods as in Tushiyeh. Everywhere we should station our retired military officers to dominate in the Prince's affairs ... Once the opportunity comes, Outer and Inner Mongolia will be ours outright. While the sovereign rights are not clearly defined and while the Chinese and the Soviet Governments are engaging their attention elsewhere, it is our opportunity quietly to build our influence. Once we have purchased most of the land there, there will be no room for dispute as to whether Mongolia belongs to the Japanese or the Mongolians. Aided by our military prowess, we shall realized our positive policy. In order to carry out this plans, we should appropriate 1,000,000 [Yen] from the 'secret funds' of the Army Department's budget so that four hundred retired officers disguised as teachers and Chinese citizens may be sent to Outer and Inner Mongolia to mix with the people, to gain the confidence of the Mongolian princes.[7]

In fact, despite the claims at the opening of the above extract, the daughter of General Fukushima Yasumasa, born in 1898, never married a Mongol nobleman. When the Tanaka memorial was printed, she was attending school in Tokyo.[8]

General Suzuki Tei'ichi, who had attended the 1927 Far East Conference with Tanaka, recalled that a document with similar content to that in the memorial was drafted by Mori Kaku, a *Rikken Seiyūkai* official, and sent to Chiang Kai-shek by an enemy of Tanaka in the *Kenseikai* (Constutional Politics Association). In the final analysis, there is the strong possibility of the memorial being drafted by a *tairiku rōnin*, a Kwantung army officer or a pro-Japanese Chinese.[9] Nevertheless, the probably spurious Tanaka memorial was vital in helping to raise the alarm at Whitehall concerning Japanese strategic plans during a time of complacency.

Fukushima Yasumasa, a national hero for his epic journey from Berlin to Vladivostok, during which he made observations as military attaché.

Kenji Doihara, dubbed 'Lawrence of Manchuria'.

Prime Minister Kodama
Gentarō.

Prime Minister Hideki Tojo.

Above: Baron Motono Ichirō, Ambassador to Russia. (Library of Congress)

Right: Kanji Ishiwara, a maverick major general who made his name in Manchuria and derided officers/analysts as 'completely worthless, [not doing] real work, just sit[ting] on your butts and theorizing'.

Prime Minister Kōsai Uchida.

Prime Minister Masatake Terauchi.

Lieutenant General Miura Gorō, architect of the assassination of Korean Empress Myeongseong. He asserted, 'This was a matter which I decided in the space of three puffs on a cigarette … whether my behaviour was right or wrong, only Heaven can judge.'

Foreign Minister Mutsu Munemitsu, who plotted strategic deception against the Chinese government in 1894–95.

Prime Minister Kōki Hirota.

Prime Minister Katō Takaaki.

Prime Minister Katsura
Tarō.

Prime Minister Keisuke
Okada.

Foreign Minister Yōsuke Matsuoka.

William Forbes-Sempill, later Lord
Sempill, showing Admiral Tōgō
Heihachirō the latest naval aviation
technology.

Above left: Prime Minister
Tanaka Giichi.

Above right: Zhang Zuolin,
warlord ruler of Manchuria
from 1916 to 1928. (Library
of Congress)

Right: Admiral Tōgō
Heihachirō, the 'Nelson of the
East'.

Admirals Inoue Yoshika, Togo Heihachiro and Okada Keisuke in 1927. (Library of Congress)

Prime Minister Tsuyoshi Inukai (far left) with ultranationalist Mitsuru Toyama (centre) and Chinese leader Chiang Kai-Shek (right).

Right: Foreign Minister Teijiro Toyoda.

Below: Emperor Hirohito inspecting the troops in 1938.

Prime Minister Yamagata Aritomo, arguably the father of Japanese imperial strategy. He dons the Order of Merit (Military) yet he wanted Imperial Japan to elbow the British Empire out of the Far East; he mentored dozen officers who would become key leaders in the 1930s and during the Second World War.

Hōshō, the first commissioned ship to be built as an aircraft carrier. It would play a key role in the Battle for Shanghai. (SDASM)

The oxygen-fuelled Type 93 torpedo, or Long Lance, Japan's secret weapon in the 1930s. (Naval History and Heritage Command)

Above: Robert Craigie (left), Ambassador to Japan 1937–41, at a farewell party hosted by the deputy minister of the IJN.

Left: Hugh Sinclair, chief of the SIS. He never stopped warning of the Imperial Japanese threat, citing secret intelligence.

Lieutenant Commander Colin Mayers, an experts' expert in submarine technology and warfare, convicted under the Official Secrets Act after being suspected of working for the Japanese. (Courtesy TNA)

Retired Squadron Leader Frederick Rutland, a hero of the Battle of Jutland and a pioneer in aviation technology who was interned by the British authorities for working on behalf of the Japanese. (Courtesy TNA)

Le Journal illustré

L'ASSASSINAT DE LA REINE DE CORÉE

Right: Le Journal Illustré's cover depicting the assassination of Empress Myeongseong of Korea by Japanese 'continental adventurers' (*tairiku rōnin*) encouraged by Miura Gorō.

Below: Frontispiece of *Broken Thread*, the published memoirs of Japanophile Francis Piggott.

AUTHOR
on retirement from the Army

Broken Thread

By

MAJOR-GENERAL F. S. G. PIGGOTT, C.B., D.S.O.
COLONEL COMMANDANT, ROYAL ENGINEERS
Sometime His Majesty's Military Attaché at Tokyo

An Autobiography

"LOOK HOW WIDE ALSO THE EAST IS FROM THE WEST . . . "
(Psalm ciii, v. 12)

With Preface by
THE LATE FIELD-MARSHAL THE
LORD MILNE OF SALONIKA AND RUBISLAW
G.C.B., G.C.M.G., D.S.O.
(MASTER-GUNNER, ST. JAMES'S PARK, 1929–1946)

and Foreword by
COLONEL THE RT. HON. LORD HANKEY
P.C., G.C.B., G.C.M.G., G.C.V.O.

ALDERSHOT
GALE & POLDEN LIMITED
1950

9

THE AMBASSADOR

In late August 1931, the SIS reported that the Japanese looked likely to intervene in Manchuria. The following month the Mukden Incident occurred, and the Kwantung Army exploited this false flag operation to capture Mukden and other cities, expanding their occupation zone to the south. The Foreign Office and War Office did not protest; indeed, General William Bartholomew, director of military operations and intelligence at the War Office, was cheerful: 'I am glad there are some people [i.e. the Japanese] left who kick back when their nationals are ill-treated or even murdered.' The War Office also assumed that the Japanese incursions would drive the Chinese into Western arms, compelling them to accept the interests of foreign powers over their provinces. At the same time, Sir Francis Lindley, British ambassador to Tokyo, was growing in influence and urged London to condone Japanese practices.

In early 1932, a local crisis in Shanghai escalated into armed conflict. On 28 January, in the Shanghai International Settlement, Japanese Army officers provoked a disturbance with the result that a mob attacked Japanese Buddhist priests calling for Japanese rule in Asia, killing one and wounding two. In retaliation, the Japanese burned down a nearby factory, killing two Chinese. Heavy firefights ensued, with casualties on both sides. Chiang Kai-shek pleaded for support in the League of Nations, but to no avail.

The Japanese deployed forty planes, thirty warships and about 7,000 troops around the shoreline of Shanghai. The *Hōshō* aircraft carrier launched bombers that targeted civilians in greater Shanghai, beyond the International Settlement. Another carrier, the *Kaga*, participated in the operations. This was history in the making: the bombing of Shanghai was the first time an aircraft carrier had been used as a launch pad for bombers, showing the evolution of naval aviation and the progress made by the Japanese.

The Japanese employed mainly Yokosuka E1Y Type 14 reconnaissance seaplanes, Nakajima Type 3 (1928 model) carrier-based fighter planes and the Mitsubishi Type 13 (1924 model) carrier-borne attack aircrafts from *Kaga*. The Chinese air force, meanwhile, deployed German Junkers K-47s, British Blackburn Lincock IIIs, American Vought O2U Corsairs and Corsair V-65Cs, and American Douglas O-2MCs. Since the invasion of Manchuria, Washington had been selling aircraft to the Chinese government to counterbalance the Japanese presence.[1]

On 19 February 1932, US Reserve 2nd Lieutenant Robert McCawley Short, acting as an advisor to the Chinese air force, flew an armed experimental fighter plane, the Boeing XP925A, to Nanking from the Hongqiao airport after the plane was quickly set up and armed for delivery to the Chinese government as a test offering. Near Nanxiang, Short engaged three Japanese fighters. Three days later, Short engaged again in a dogfight attacking the formation of six Japanese naval aircraft from *Kaga*. He shot down one Type 13 Mitsubishi, killing Lieutenant Kotani Susumu. Subsequently three Japanese fighters shot down Short's plane, killing him.[2]

Sir Miles Lampson, the British ambassador in China, urged negotiations. US Secretary of State Stimson and his British counterpart Sir John Simons considered an armistice, even as the Japanese demands aimed at Tokyo's further advance into China. Chiang Kai-shek was put under considerable pressure to withdraw his forces so as to not 'hand the Japanese any pretext to expand the war from Shanghai'. Indeed, by February Lindley was urging retired Captain Kennedy, a Japanese expert and journalist, to continue to present a pro-Japanese line:

> You must do your best to emphasise the Japanese viewpoint as favourably as possible in your cables in order to remove the possibility of the British public demanding further pressure

on Japan, as it is more than ever essential now to avoid any action that might arouse national sentiment in Japan to the extent of challenging the world. They would simply have our people at Shanghai at their mercy if that happened.

Lindley, Kennedy and Piggott were key experts who would influence the War Office and the Foreign Office on Japan.[3] Lindley always condoned Japanese aggression, influencing British foreign policy to accept the rise of Japanese power in the Far East. He was the one who blocked the clear-headed interpretation of Japanese policy which has since been revealed in secret intelligence. On 1 February, Captain Kennedy wrote of a meeting with Captain Montague Legge, the naval attaché covering both Peking and Tokyo, revealing further pro-Japanese sympathies in the forces:

Had a visit from Legge to enquire about the latest developments at Shanghai. His sympathies are plainly with the Japanese whose main mistake, he considers, is failure to use sufficient force to teach the Chinese a lesson! 'I fired 300 rounds at the Chinese myself in 1927,' he remarked, adding, 'My only regret is that I didn't loose off 3,000 at the b____rs!' The good old Nelson touch! I asked him if the rest of the Embassy held similar views, but he replied 'Simson, I think, does; but the diplomats seem rather upset at the measures adopted!'[4]

On 4 February, at a special meeting convened to discuss the conflict, Lindley, Simson and Kennedy agreed to give the Japanese a week before calling for a diplomatic intervention by Britain and the other Western powers. Nevertheless, Miles Lampson, the British representative in Peking, insisted on the morality of confronting the Japanese invasion and condemned the failure to intervene in Manchuria. Kennedy hit back:

Which is the more immoral? To refrain from interference while Japan slays a few hundred Chinese in order to restore peace, or to bring pressure to bear on Japan and thereby risk precipitating a world war, in which millions may be killed and civilization dealt a blow far greater than in 1914-18?[5]

Lindley later sent a cable to the Foreign Office arguing that the sound policy was not to sanction Japan at all. Meanwhile, at the War Office, Piggott and his pro-Japanese colleagues orchestrated support for Lindley's position. A few years later, H. G. W. Woodhead, a British correspondent in China, wrote:

> In 1925, and again in 1927, British subjects and officials in China were the victims of a series of officially instigated outrages and indignities ... The conciliatory policy adopted by the British government from 1927 onwards only whetted the appetite of the Kuomintang for further concessions, the granting of which would have meant the abandonment of all those safeguards which alone have made it possible for Britons ... to reside and trade in this country ... When Japan hit back in 1931, the news was not unexpected or unwelcome in foreign circles generally ... They may not have approved of many of Japan's actions in Manchuria and Shanghai, but the fact remained that it was Japan alone who staved off the final surrender of foreign rights and safeguards in China.[6]

Meanwhile, a series of assassinations showed that fanatics among the Japanese officer corps were targeting government and business leaders. Junior officers in the IJN deemed the London Naval Treaty of 1930 an affront. In March 1932, a group of officers murdered the former Finance Minister, Inoue Junnosuke, and Takuma Dan, the director-general of Mitsui Holding Co. Two months later, on 15 May, eleven Navy officers shot dead Prime Minister Inukai Tsuyoshi. The officers were all court-martialled, but they received popular support including petitions written in blood and their sentences were extremely lenient.

Japanese strategy was confrontational. Puyi, the last emperor of the Qing dynasty, was persuaded to take over as head of state of Manchukuo, a Japanese puppet state in Manchuria not recognised by Britain, France or the United States. Meanwhile, Japanese forces pushed Chinese nationalist forces under Chiang Kai-shek out to Hebei province. Republican China called for the intervention of the League of Nations, so Tokyo withdrew its membership. In May 1933, China and Japan reached an agreement called the Tanggu Truce. Under its terms, Japanese forces occupied the Great Wall of

China and a demilitarised zone was drafted 100 kilometres south of the wall.

The naval commander-in-chief of the Far East station at this stage was Admiral Sir Frederic Dreyer, and he insisted that Japan was a threat to Britain in the Far East; war, he said, was 'inevitable'. In September 1933 he wrote angrily to Sinclair that Admiral Gerald Dickens, the Director of Naval Intelligence, had made incorrect assessments with serious implications for naval strategy:

> How in the name of hell can he expect the powers that be to put their shoulders to the wheel and give me the ships, men, harbour defence gear, etc., of which I am so lamentably short, if he, the D.N.I. [Director of Naval Intelligence], tells me that such a war is 'REMOTE'!![7]

Intercepts revealed that the Japanese maintained a secret source in London. On 6 March 1933, the Japanese naval attaché cabled the deputy chief of the IJN General Staff:

> We have received information from a reliable source to the effect that the British government will in two or three days cancel the prohibition of export of arms to Japan and China. In view of the source of this information it is particularly requested that you will arrange for it to be kept strictly secret.[8]

This cable was intercepted by the GC&CS and submitted by the SIS to the Foreign Office. The source was managed by the naval attaché only; they were not a confidential source or spy of the Japanese ambassador, otherwise they would have been identified in the ambassador's correspondence and assigned a codename. Instead, the source was likely to be a pro-Japanese official with access to the deliberations of the British government. Armed with the knowledge this source provided, Tokyo was confident that the gradually weakening British Empire would not confront Japan.

By late 1933, in the wake of the invasion of Manchuria and the battle for Shanghai, intercepts of Japanese diplomatic communications were demonstrating to the Foreign Office that Japan aimed to focus on diplomacy to boost relations with Britain, China and the United States. A cable from Foreign Minister Hirota to the Japanese ambassador in London on 25 October 1933 was intercepted and easily decoded:

> In the conference that has been going on since the 3rd instant between the five cabinet ministers viz premier and ministers for foreign affairs, finance, army and navy various important questions were discussed touching the mutual relations between diplomacy and national defence. A general agreement of opinion was reached and accordingly at a cabinet meeting on the 21st instant, after the premier had made his report, I followed with a verbal statement on the lines given in my separate telegram ... as regards international relations our policy should be accomplished by methods of diplomacy having in mind world peace. 2. as regards national defence we should be careful to make it proportionate to our national resources, and that we should not allow ourselves to be threatened by other powers not to incur their contempt.[9]

The No. 1952 Circular of the Ministry of Foreign Affairs, dated 25 October 1933, was also intercepted:

> The foundation of Manchukuo has created a great stir in the world, and it is imperative for Japan to establish friendly relations with the Great Powers without delay by diplomatic machinery in order to assure the peace in the Far East and to prevent international complications which may arise in the year 1935 and thereabouts, for which purpose the most pressing need is to foster the healthy development of Manchukuo. Moreover, among the changed diplomatic relationships due to the Manchurian incident the most important are those in respect of China, USSR and the United States which three powers may in the future, perhaps at an international conference, combine to take action against Japan.

With reference to Britain:

> Since the Manchurian incident not only has Japan been looked on with suspicion by foreign powers, but her economic relations have deteriorated owing to the advance of overseas

markets for Japanese goods. The most important country in this respect is Great Britain, but now that negotiations have been undertaken at Simla in regards to Japanese–Indian commercial interests their adjustment is in process of being contrived, so that by doing one's best to make the Simla conference a success in order to regulated economic relations with Great Britain, it looks as though friendly relations will be established between the two countries (Japan and Britain).[10]

London had to make a decision: either Japan had fulfilled its military goals and now wished for diplomacy, and thus should be viewed as a dangerous yet friendly power; or it merely aimed to legitimise its past interventions through diplomacy while it prepared for more, in which case a credible politico-military strategy of deterrence had to be drafted between the United States and Britain. In this context, pro-Japanese officials like Lindley, Piggott and Kennedy among others, including Churchill himself, argued for the pursuit of further diplomacy with Japan while ignoring their transgressions.

Meanwhile, intercepts had been interpreted as indicating that Britain need not feel threatened by the rise of Japan. The SIS in the Far East, and Japan in particular, was left underfunded because pro-Japanese voices at the Foreign Office insisted that such intercepts settled the debate. Nevertheless, in December 1933 Charles Orde, head of the Far Eastern Section of the Foreign Office, warned:

> … we should not … be influenced by fears of the harm that Japan could do to our interests in China to the extent of tamely yielding to her pretensions. If we show fear of Japan, the Chinese will be encouraged to attack us when they are not currying favour in order to enlist our support against her … we … cannot ignore the aggressive instincts of the Japanese, and the plans they cherish for an expansion in Asia which must react to our disadvantage if they realise that we are afraid of them. I therefore suggest that, besides meeting firmly the difficulties with which their industrial efficiency confronts us, we should, so far as we are able, but in no spirit of panic or immoderate haste, not hesitate to proceed with the

Singapore Base and the strengthening generally of our naval position in the Far East.[11]

By the end of the year in which Hitler had risen to power in Germany, Dreyer complained that the SIS in Japan had nothing meaningful to offer the Royal Navy. Harry Steptoe, the SIS spymaster in Shanghai who also had responsibility for Japan, wrote to London:

> Every effort [had been made] to find a person who will take over our Organization in [Japan] as a whole time job ... [But] to do the work successfully one has to be fluent in Japanese and the widespread xenophobia and suspicion in Japan made any initiative extremely risky; to attempt to build up an organization now, when every foreigner is so closely watched, and the spy scare so prevalent, is, if not an impossible task, an exceedingly delicate one.[12]

Despite the aggression in China and American frustration with Tokyo's foreign policy, Churchill remained pro-Japanese:

> I hope we should try in England to understand a little the position of Japan, an ancient state with the highest sense of national honour, and patriotism and with a teeming population and a remarkable energy. On the one side they see the dark menace of Soviet Russia. On the other the chaos of China.[13]

Furthermore, he condoned Japanese aggression in Korea and Manchuria:

> I have admiration and long-founded regard for the empire and people of Japan. I recognize the expansion needs of their teeming, vigorous and adventurous population. We have seen their work in Korea. It is stern, but good. We have seen their work in Manchuria. It is also good, but also stern.[14]

Lindley clearly had no trouble promoting his views on Japanese policy, nor did he struggle to block the efforts of the SIS. In 1934, the Treasury accepted that Japan was a threat to the British Empire in the Far East and argued that approaching Japan diplomatically would be financially beneficial to Britain. Britain, they claimed, should grant the Japanese sufficient concessions to appease them at the expense of China. The Foreign Office did not agree.

Despite this, the Foreign Office failed to take a strong stance against Japan; they did not draft a military-backed deterrence strategy even though Japanese imperialism in China was more than evident. Sir Robert Vansittart, the permanent undersecretary, argued that Russo-Japanese tensions compelled Tokyo not to turn against the British Empire. The Treasury at least believed Japan was a threat, even if their proposed solution was appeasement; the Foreign Office, meanwhile, seemingly believed there was no threat. Vansittart believed that, if approached, the Japanese would feel emboldened to act against the Soviet Union in the Far East; and as a consequence, the Soviet Union under Stalin would not support Britain against a renewed German threat in Europe.[15]

Because of intelligence from Manchuria, the War Office knew that the Japanese were actually in a disadvantageous position. In 1934, journalist Peter Fleming (brother of author Ian Fleming) toured the region and was directed to report on military matters by MI2c of the War Office; there was a strong interest in the numbers and dispositions of Japanese tanks and aircraft, and the conditions in Inner Mongolia. Another intelligence gatherer, Major Ferguson, reached Manchuria in July 1935 and reported that banditry was widespread; the Japanese controlled cities and rail lines only, and as many as 10,000 communist guerrillas were actively resisting them.[16]

In Whitehall, the prevailing belief was that Russia was the key threat to Britain and that Japan was less of a concern. The conclusion reached was that Japan was all bark and no bite – it had rearmed and boasted aggressive propaganda, but no attack on Siberia had materialised.[17] Evidently this position suited Piggott and Lindley. Stalin surprised London when he said that he did not back Mao against Chiang Kai-shek but sought a 'united' Chinese front against Japan. Whatever people's views about Japan's threat to Britain, a full-scale Sino-Japanese war was clearly imminent. Indeed, within a few years MI2c would be claiming that 'the initial clash may arise out of any trifling incident, and may occur almost anywhere in China'.[18]

Captain W. E. C. Tait, the Deputy Director of Naval Intelligence, warned of the 'policy of expansion in the Far East' and proposed a new regional inter-service intelligence office in Hong Kong. He was critical of the SIS in Japan, particularly the efforts of Steptoe to gather secret intelligence. In April 1934, Dreyer complained that intelligence reports coming from SIS lacked 'actual facts concerning fortifications' and 'warnings of definite preparations for hostilities in Japan or any of her possessions'. Dreyer wrote to Sinclair that in his opinion Steptoe 'talks too much'; he was 'indiscreet and boastful talk has left no doubt on people's minds generally as to what his real functions are'. 'Perhaps Steptoe is only a dummy and you have a real SIS working quite independent of him,' he remarked.[19]

Sinclair wrote to Dreyer in July 1934: 'I do not think that, even now, you or the G.O.C. (General Officer Commanding) realize the extreme difficulty of obtaining secret information about Japan or Formosa.' He assured the admiral that a new intelligence officer would be assigned to naval and military intelligence on Japan, although, as he complained in his turn, 'there appears to be no prospect whatsoever of obtaining any additional funds with which to finance this undertaking, which makes the task even more difficult than it otherwise would be'. In August 1934, a secret source covering Japanese affairs remarked that money was key in espionage so if the Admiralty 'require plans stolen ... serving [Japanese] officers bribed etc (which unquestionably is the most efficient method of obtaining what they require) they must provide far greater sums of money than are at present available'.[20]

By 1935, Sinclair admitted the position was 'unsatisfactory' in the Far East, 'especially in regard to Japan'. Even 'by diverting sums being spent, with valuable results, on other countries', the amount available for recent efforts in the region was 'wholly insufficient, and only suffices to maintain a skeleton organisation'. Sinclair stressed that, even when adequate funds were available, it took 'at least 2-3 years, under the most favourable circumstances, to establish a satisfactory S.S. [Secret Service] in any country'. Meanwhile, the SIS, 'living, as it does, a hand to mouth existence, with vast areas to cover', was able only 'to scratch the surface'. To 'obtain really inside information', he wrote, 'means spending big money'. He claimed that opportunities frequently occurred in which the might 'deal... with individuals in responsible positions', but 'the offer to them of the few hundreds a year, which represents the amount usually available, is naturally treated by them with contempt'. 'Whatever may be the outcome of the present crisis,' he concluded, 'it is plainly apparent that, in the future, Germany, Japan and Italy will have to be regarded as potential enemies from without, as well as Soviet Russia from within.'[21]

Charles Drage, a retired navy lieutenant who had served in China from 1923 to 1926, was appointed SIS station chief in Hong Kong with responsibility for Japan as well. Soon Drage and his chief associate started recruiting a 'mechanized type of agent', meaning Chinese seamen reaching Japan and Formosa. In early 1936, Drage informed Sinclair that secret agents of this type were reporting on four ports in Japan (Yokosuka, Kobe, Asaka and Hiroshima) and two in Formosa (Keelung and Taiku). Meanwhile, Captain John Vivian, the naval attaché in Tokyo, dismissed the Japanese navy as 'second rate' with officers of 'peculiarly slow brains'.[22]

By 1935, when Captain Kennedy joined the Japanese section of the GC&CS, he was allowed by SIS to remain in contact with the Japanese embassy and the evolving Japanese lobby in London. Ostensibly, Kennedy did not tell the Japanese that he was reading their messages but there is a strong possibility that their discussions might have led to the conclusion that he was curiously up to date on Japanese views. He had merely told them that he was working at the Foreign Office on assessments of the Far East.

Baron Tomii Shu of the Japanese embassy was closely following Kennedy's discussions with Japanese officials; any detail, any phrase mattered. On 18 January 1937, the baron visited the Far Eastern Department at the Foreign Office, whose head, Charles Orde, was always suspicious of Japanese policy and dismissed Piggott's assessments from Tokyo as 'Piggottry'.

Tomii inquired with Orde as to the department in which Kennedy worked. Afraid to give away that Kennedy was working on intelligence matters related to the Japanese language, Orde denied that Kennedy was working at the Foreign Office at all. This was a monumental mistake. When the baron returned to the embassy he mulled it over. For some time Kennedy must have been lying that he worked for the Foreign Office, but why a respected former officer and businessman would do tell such a lie was unclear – unless, that is, he was spying on them. In any case, the embassy continued to invite Kennedy to receptions but he noted in his diary that he felt that he was invited less frequently and there was a cold attitude towards him. On 28 November, at a reception, Kennedy chatted with Ambassador Shigemitsu Mamoru (who had replaced Ambassador Yoshida in October). Kennedy told the ambassador 'how the average Englishman regarded Japan's treatment of the Chinese interests'. The ambassador sounded 'equally outspoken with regard to Japan's attitude towards Great Britain', urging Britain to side with his nation and accept the new reality in China.[23]

The GC&CS had been reading the chief Japanese army and navy messages, having decoded their ciphers. Two years later, however, the IJA introduced a new cipher and in the subsequent years the Japanese made their systems more secure. It took until autumn 1939 for the GC&CS to return to a similar position, first decoding the IJN fleet code. Their diplomatic missions' communications, however, remained vulnerable to deciphering throughout the 1930s.[24]

On 26 February 1936, another coup attempt took place in Tokyo. Fanatical army officers murdered two former prime ministers and government officials, while Prime Minister Keisuke Okada escaped with his life. Eventually, three days later, the officers and their troops had to surrender to army forces supporting the government. This time, nineteen coup leaders were executed. This episode was the final event of the period of 'government by assassination'. In a 1936 article in *Collier's Magazine*, Churchill remarked:

I am one of the dwindling band of Members [of Parliament] who voted for the ratification of the original Anglo-Japanese Alliance. I watched with enthusiasm the loyal co-operation of Japan in the Great War. The impression left on my mind by many years of working with the Governments of the Mikado has been that the Japanese are sober, steady, grave and mature people; that they can be trusted to measure forces and factors with great care, and that they do not lose their heads, or plunge into mad, uncalculated adventures. But of late years we have been confronted with a somewhat different Japan. The elder statesmen and their sagacious power seem to have dispersed. For the last four or five years the political movement of Japan has seemed to effect itself through the murder of statesmen who were deemed too prudent or circumspect, or in other ways were objectionable to secret societies of Army officers. Great and honourable Japanese leaders have fallen in a swift succession to the sword or bullet of honourable assassins.[25]

In September 1936, Sinclair issued guidelines for Charles Drage to maintain a 'Coast Watching Organisation, in order to give advance information of [Japanese] troop movements or possible mobilization'. The chief wrote to Drage that 'the breakdowns (of radio communications) which are frequently occurring with this organisation, coupled with misleading reports such as you have furnished on this matter, give rise to the gravest anxiety here [in London]'.[26]

10

A SPY CLOSE TO THE
GENERAL

In 1935 and 1936, the SIS had a spy among the staff of General Terauchi; in fact, it was his personal adjutant in Taiwan (Formosa).[1] Recruited in Shanghai, he moved freely in the Taiwan Military Government as a staff officer. His key report was submitted in January 1937, and in it he informed British intelligence that Terauchi, during his tenure in Taiwan, lectured senior military officers about an invasion of Singapore and Hong Kong. The Japanese plan for an attack on Singapore was predicated on the idea that they would be near the port 'fourteen days before the arrival of the British fleet'. Plans for the attack on Hong Kong included a landing, probably at Swatow. In both operations Taiwan would be the jumping-off point, so three ports for embarkation were constructed on the south of the island.

The SIS and the Admiralty had already reported on Japanese war plans in relation to Hong Kong and Singapore, and the South Seas had been closely watched since 1931. From 1935, closer attention had been paid to the Singapore plans and it was in that year that the Japanese decided Taiwan should be the main base for any offensive against either target. In the planned 1931 offensive, three infantry divisions would participate. A few years later, the planned number of infantry divisions increased to five. In the 1936 summer manoeuvres in Taiwan, six divisions were assigned to the invasion of Hong Kong. The spy communicated to his SIS handler the plan for the six divisions to land at Swatow (their assigned main base) and at Hong Hai Bay (the advanced base). Japanese intelligence had noted the defensive line at Kowloon.

The Japanese staff officers calculated that they needed up to a month to deploy their invading force and arranged for bases in the Kagi, Teinan and Takao areas in Taiwan. According to the spy who brought with him the invasion plans, 'all arrangements for the concentration of war material and commissariat in these are completed'. The Japanese had drafted an air–land combined operation; the infantry would attack from the north supported by intensive air bombardment from the naval aviation and army air branch.

At Heito in Taiwan, the 8th Air Regiment was already deployed. The Japanese staff officers had drafted plans for the invasion of Singapore as a separate operation and as part of the general offensive in the South Seas. The Japanese were aware that British naval strategy placed a high value on Singapore; its capture would be devastating for future British naval operations in the Pacific. By now, the Japanese had revised their calculations and believed that twenty-five days would be needed for the Royal Navy fleet in the Mediterranean to reach Singapore. In contrast, the Japanese invading force needed only five days to steam from Taiwan. Moreover, 'plans to be executed as far as possible simultaneously with the combined attack for sabotage severing docks, electric light plants, essential services and civil and military aerodromes have been worked out'. The British spy in Taiwan claimed that intelligence collected for the invasion of Singapore was forwarded to Japanese intelligence commands and outposts in the Far East (including Shanghai) but 'not passed over to any one in Japan'. The air war plans focused on countering the RAF, defending the invading forces from British air assaults.

Espionage ensured that the Japanese General Staff would have a good view of the coastal defences with heavy artillery: 'The positions of all main batteries are known and it is believed that these can be reduced by naval bombardment alone.' However, the spy did not know anything about submarine plans and preparations.[2]

For the Admiralty staff officer in London, 'this report from secret source is most valuable and may be one of the various war plans which it is almost certain that the Japanese have made. It may on the other hand be the work of an individual staff officer who has worked on the problem and produced a "scheme".' Indeed, as we have seen, the first plans for an invasion of Hong Kong were drafted in 1931. One explanation for the increase in the invading force from three divisions to six was the 'greater resistance which can be anticipated from the improved quality of the Chinese army'. The Japanese needed three divisions to invade Hong Kong and another three to protect communication and supply lines 200 miles from Swatow. The landing at Hong Hai Bay, the Admiralty thought, was a surprise option since it was 'the least suited for landing an expedition and also the most difficult to defend from seaward'. The Admiralty had received a report claiming that for the invasion of Singapore the main force would concentrate in Japan and then be deployed in the Pelew (Palau) Islands under Japanese rule, which had capacities for repairing ships. The Director of Naval Intelligence confirmed the spy's reports with other secret sources with reference to the presence of the 8th Air Regiment in Taiwan.

Given that the plan required six divisions to attack Hong Kong and three to invade Singapore, the Admiralty concluded that either Hong Kong and Singapore would not be attacked simultaneously (at least not by forces based on Formosa) or that three divisions would be deployed against Hong Kong with another three coming from Japan. For the time being, less than one full infantry division was based in Taiwan.

The Japanese surely could not conceal such an invading force; six divisions meant 120,000 troops, and that meant 120 transports of at least 6,000 tons each. To handle this, Keelung in China could be a port of embarkation; the same applied to the Takao port in Formosa, which provided facilities for twenty transports up to 10,000 tons each. Anping port in China was also upgraded, and Mako in the Pescadores was identified as able to handle traffic for the invasion.

The Director of Naval Intelligence was deeply concerned. The plan of the attack on Singapore demanded immediate action focusing on early warning with reference to installations in Formosa and ship movements from there.[3] The spy had confirmed Japan's hostile intentions, active operational planning and its massing of capabilities for use against Hong Kong and Singapore.

Meanwhile, in Paris, the SIS station chief recruited a new agent offering information on Japanese intelligence in the puppet state of Manchukuo. The first report compiled by the agent was based 'on information that came to his knowledge whilst in Manchuria and he has amplified it (the intelligence) from conversations with Japanese and Manchukuo representatives in Paris, with whom he is on intimate terms'. The SIS representative was keen to instruct the agent to report on Japanese espionage in Britain to find out what they knew.[4]

Already in 1935, an SIS agent in the Far East had reported that the Japanese had set up an organisation in Harbin in northern China with the object of unifying all the right-wing Russian emigre groups in the Far East. Among the organisation's leading personnel were men named Rodzievski, Bakshaiev and Kislitzen, the latter two generals. The infamous General Kenji Doihara – dubbed 'the Lawrence of Manchuria' by the press – was also reportedly involved in the scheme.[5]

A new SIS spy asset in Paris claimed to have 'for some years inserted himself in the organization and activities of the Japanese S[ecret] S[ervice]'. He had recently been in Berlin and was 'on very friendly terms with a chief of the Japanese [secret] service in Germany, and often had occasion to discuss these matters with him'. Moreover, he conversed with Japanese and Chinese officials of Manchukuo serving as consular officials and consular police in France, along with employees of the South Manchurian Railway and other Japanese firms in China. In contrast with other sources, the informant insisted that General Doihara did not control Japanese espionage in the Soviet Union nor in southern China. He wrote that the Japanese secret service in the USSR was 'a highly developed organization ... employs principally White Russians, the leaders of whom, in this respect, are Ataman Semionov, Generals Backcheien [*sic*] and Kislitzin [*sic*]'.

Echoing the talk of a Harbin group, the source claimed that the Japanese employed a White Russian group named the 'Old Russian Fascist Party' led by Rodzievski. Rumour had it that the members of this group were 'specially trained to carry on espionage and sabotage' by Japanese instructors in two spy schools near Harbin; according to the new agent, about 140 secret operatives were under training 'constantly'. They were assigned to read Soviet press prohibited in Manchukuo, studied the Soviet constitution and taught 'to pass themselves off as good Soviet citizens'. At the same time, in Manchuria an 'immense number of servants and hotel employees' spied on Westerners. The headquarters of Japanese espionage were set up in Tientsin, while 'first-class' sub-division headquarters were situated in Peking, Mukden, Dairen, Kalgan and Hsikin, with 'second-class' subdivisions at Harbin, Pogranischaia and Ceicho (Sakhalin) and 'third-class' subdivisions operated in Dolonor, Hailar, Tsitsikar, Handochedsi and Sansin. The second- and third-class sub-divisions were put under the control of local Imperial Japanese Army commands and tasked with gathering intelligence on Russian troops deployed on the frontiers.[6]

The SIS representative in the Far East criticised this report: 'It would appear that some of the information supplied by the source is inaccurate and that most of the remainder is based on what amounts to common knowledge ... there is nothing in this report which suggests that it is based on fact'. Nevertheless, he admitted 'on the other hand it is probably correct in general implications'.[7] This criticism reveals bias towards a new, promising informer in Europe. The SIS representative commented:

[On servants being spies] comparatively speaking few Americans and British live in hotels in the Far East. It is certainly not so in Shanghai, Tientsin or Peking ... I cannot understand why the sub-divisions at important places like Manchuria, Hailar, Tsitsibar are second and third class divisions. They are obviously more important than Peking, Mukden and Hsinkiang ... All names mentioned above would be well known to anyone particularly White Russians interested in such matters in the Far East ...

[On central headquarters of espionage] there is no evidence available to us to show that this is the case. From close observation locally it appears to be much more likely that each authority, naval and military runs its own service ... The existence of the Old Russian Fascist Party is well known to me. I question very much the fact that its strength in Manchukuo would allow 140 pupils to be in constant training ... It is an established fact that following upon Japanese control in

Manchukuo a very large number of White Russians left that territory owing to the intolerable attitude of the Japanese towards them.[8]

It was mentioned that the number of British and French 'readily available to the Japanese for work on the Manchukuo–Russian frontier is extremely limited'; besides, no reports were filed for British individuals staying on and working in Pogranischaia, Ceicho, Hailar or Tsitsikar. For that matter, the SIS already knew from Polish intelligence that 'the Japanese were working in the closest contact with all White Russian organizations in Europe'.[9] The Poles did not reveal their closest liaison with Japanese intelligence, which in fact prevailed throughout the Second World War.

At this point, a brief explanation of the secret Japanese–Polish alliance is necessary to illuminate some finer points of Japanese espionage.

Since the Russo-Japanese War of 1904–05, Poland, viewing Russia's foreign policy with suspicion, began sharing intelligence with Japan. After the First World War, as well as sharing secret military intelligence this cooperation included training in ciphers and the study of Russian codes and cryptography. In the 1930s, Colonel Kowaleski, a Polish General Staff intelligence officer who was considered an authority on document analysis, lectured in Japan. Two or three Polish officers were meanwhile dispatched to Harbin to instruct the Kwantung Army intelligence staff, and in return the Japanese provided the Poles with Russian codes, intercepts and intelligence material from the Far East.[10]

After the invasion of Poland in September 1939 by Nazi Germany and Soviet Russia, the Polish government escaped to London. Once there, Colonel Stanislaw Gano, the head of the Polish intelligence service, asked Colonel Masao Ueda, the Japanese military attaché in Warsaw, to become a spymaster for Poland covering both Soviet Union and Germany. Ueda had served in Poland during 1938 and 1939 and had worked closely with Gano on intelligence concerning the Soviet Union.[11]

Gano was one of the Polish officers who wanted to extend the secret alliance with the Japanese. He had fought in the Russo-Polish War of 1919–1921, and from 1928 he served with military intelligence in the 2nd Bureau of the Polish General Staff. In 1933–35 he was military attaché in Helsinki, and afterward he returned to the 2nd Bureau. He had initially been arrested and interned in Romania after the invasion of Poland, but he soon escaped and eventually reached Britain.[12]

In 1940, Gano entered into secret correspondence with Ueda and both agreed for Polish intelligence officers to be sent to the Far East to work with their Japanese counterparts on intelligence gathering against the Soviet Union in Manchuria. In December 1941, Poland declared war on Japan after the Pearl Harbor attack. Colonel Revetow, the Polish military attaché in Tokyo, sent a request from the Polish government to the office of Major General Makoto Onodera, the Japanese military attaché in Stockholm, seeking to continue the secret intelligence-sharing arrangement. It was reported that 'within a short time General Sikorski, despite the fact that a state of war existed between Poland and Japan, answered that permission was given in accordance with the long tradition of collaboration between the two countries.' Revetow's assistant, Lieutenant Skora, continued working with the Japanese in cryptoanalysis.[13]

Major-General Onodera for his part worked with Rybikowski, a Polish intelligence officer who posed as a White Russian advisor to his office under the name Piotr Iwanow. '[He was] several times in direct contact with General Sikorski and the Polish General Staff in London.'[14] The Polish government in exile signed a treaty with the Soviet Union on 30 July 1941. Sikorski, who had authorised the secret collaboration with the Japanese, died in an air crash on 4 July 1943 in Gibraltar. In December 1942, General Ledochowski, a Polish officer who had secret contacts with the Japanese, died in the Vatican. Nevertheless, the Polish–Japanese intelligence sharing continued.

Onodera provided intelligence to the Polish government in exile on Soviet deployments in Europe and Asia (from Japanese, German, Hungarian and Finnish sources), the war potential of the Soviet Union (from Japanese and German sources), the Soviet Army order of battle (from German sources) and the war technology of Nazi Germany and the Soviet Union (from German sources).[15]

Since the 1930s, the Japanese had taken advantage of their consular offices as well as of the diplomatic missions of Manchukuo in Germany to expand their espionage networks while the Abwehr and the *Sicherheitsdienst* (SD) did not have sections devoted to counterintelligence against Japan, which they considered an ally. One of the assets in Berlin's Japanese embassy was Jerzy Kuncewicz (aka Jacubic), a naturalised Japanese who was a former intelligence officer of the Polish General Staff. Among his spy network was a Polish woman named Salomea Lapinska who posed as a cook at the Manchukuo legation in Berlin. She too was a naturalized Japanese citizen, and reported to First Secretary Hoshino and attachés Kasai and Yamada as well as to Nakagawa, the Manchurian consul at Hamburg. Hoshino was in fact the cover name of General Akikusa, described by the Office of Strategic Services as 'one of the best Japanese specialists on Soviet intelligence'. Akikusa coordinated the dispatch of reports from Onouchi, the Japanese military attaché in Riga and later in Helsinki.[16]

In 1939, a spy network encompassing Bialystok, Minsk and Smolensk was organised by Colonel Gano while Rybikowski arranged for information gathered by the agents to be delivered to Japanese couriers travelling back and forth between Tokyo, Moscow and Berlin. In Kaunas, the second largest city in Lithuania, consul Chiune Sugihara received their reports and sent them by Japanese courier to Riga, where Rybikowski gave them to Colonel Brzeskwinski, the Polish military attaché who was later assigned to Stockholm; he in turn forwarded them to London. From Koenigsberg, meanwhile, reports were sent by Japanese courier to Berlin, where they were taken by Jerzy Kuncewicz and dispatched to Onodera in Stockholm. Rybikowski and Brzeskwinski arranged for the reports to reach London. Their reports covered Soviet movements in Lithuania, the Soviet Army and Air Force and German troop concentrations.[17]

In 1940, Onodera and his Polish associates drafted a plan to renew intelligence reporting on Russia. They sent to Moscow a Polish intelligence officer with the cover name 'Thomas' who had been in hiding in Warsaw since 1939; he was about to approach

Yamaoka, the Japanese military attaché in Moscow, when the German invasion of the Soviet Union made his mission impossible and he was withdrawn.[18]

In February 1941, Onodera issued a special directive to his Polish network to focus on intelligence on German preparations for the invasion of Britain 'with particular emphasis on the operational date'. However, Onodera's secret German and Estonian sources revealed that Hitler was planning to invade the Soviet Union and not Britain. Even so, Tokyo believed strongly in the contrary reports of Oshima, military attaché in Berlin, who claimed that Germany was planning an invasion of Britain.[19]

The secret connections between the Poles and the Japanese had not gone unnoticed. The *Sicherheitspolizei* (SIPO) informed Goering in July 1941 that Sugihara had been kept under close surveillance since 1939, when he was serving as consul in Kaunas in Lithuania and then vice consul in Prague. He 'was to be considered a friend of England and of Poland'. Indeed 'since the time he was at Kowno (Kaunas), he has drawn attention to himself by his particular interest in German military affairs'. He was consul in Koenigsberg at the time of the report, but for the SIPO he was so 'active in his intelligence work that his stay at Koenigsberg threatens to break down the good relations which exist between Germany and Japan'. Sugihara had one Polish associate in spying, Jan-Stanislaw Perz, who held a Japanese passport, and he also knew Jerzy Kuncewicz.[20]

Eventually the SIPO identified the Piotr Iwanow who worked as an 'adviser' to Colonel Onodera as Rybikowski. In March 1941, Italian counter-intelligence informed Berlin that Kawahara, formerly secretary general of the Japanese embassy in Rome and at that time in Berlin, had meetings with Vladimir Ledochowski, a Jesuit Polish general. The Italians claimed that Ledochowski was receiving military intelligence reports from secret Polish sources through the Japanese diplomatic mission at Vilnius.

The Germans kept Jerzy Kuncewicz and Salomea Lapinska under close surveillance. On 6 July 1941, during a meeting in Berlin with a liaison agent of the Warsaw resistance, they were raided and arrested by the Gestapo. In the ensuing interrogation, Kuncewicz disclosed the existence of a Japanese espionage network under the military attaché Brigadier General Banzai, the chief of the Japanese intelligence service in Europe. His office was at No. 2 Wollendorf Square in the German capital. In all, he had about forty Japanese officers gathering intelligence in Germany. The SIPO reported:

> Every two or three months this office of General Banzai receives all the intelligence reports prepared by Japanese intelligence officers in the various capitals of Europe. The Japanese intelligence service is composed of the Service East and Service East. The Service East works against Russia; the Service West against Germany, England and France.[21]

The SIPO reported that Onodera was heading the 'Service East' sector, having taken over from Colonel Nishimura. The military attaché in Stockholm supervised the offices in Helsinki (under Colonel Onouchi) and Koenigsberg (under Consul Sugihara), the latter of which had three substations: one at Vilnius, directed by a former Polish student named Wojciechowski; one at Kaunas, headed by a Lithuanian named Koziolo; and one at Grodno in Belarus under a Pole called Rys. The Japanese had set up a 'mobile station' on the rail line between Bronowice and Bialystok (where a ghetto for the Jews was established). This spy line was established by a Polish captain named Kasprzik and for the time being it was run by a humble railway worker who was in reality Captain Tadeusz Olszewski. (The Bialystok Ghetto uprising would take place on 16 August 1943; though crushed by the occupation forces, it was the largest ghetto insurrection after the Warsaw uprising in April–May 1943.)

From captivity, Kuncewicz disclosed that Sugihara employed secret agents in Berlin and that there was a secret room in the Manchukuo embassy that acted as an office for Colonel Hoshino, attaché Yamana and a certain Azuni, all of whom spied on Germany. In addition, he said that Manchurian couriers from the consulate in Hamburg visited the Berlin embassy regularly to pass on intelligence. The Germans had intercepted a letter to Ledochowski dated 18 September 1940; it referred to the persecution of the Catholic priests in occupied Poland and Lithuania. A note from Kuncewicz was attached to the letter to Ledochowski, implicating the Japanese in the handling of secret correspondence. It read, 'The outside envelope should be addressed to Dr Furuuchi Secretary of the Japanese embassy in Berlin.'²² Kuncewicz told his captors that his network working for Onodera and Sugihara succeeded in obtaining information on German war preparations against Russia.²³

For the SIPO, 'even the Eastern network was engaged in a certain amount of activity against the Reich ... the fact that Kuncewicz succeeded in obtaining information on war preparations against Russia confirms this hypothesis'. The Germans were now working to decode messages destined for London that were found in the possession of the spy network.²⁴ Walter Schellenberg, a senior SD officer, directed the search for the Polish liaisons, being a protégé of Himmler. In his memoirs, he wrote that a reliable informer of the Abwehr counterintelligence section codenamed Y3 revealed that a liaison of the Polish resistance would go to Berlin and meet assets in a park. Surveillance of possible train passengers was narrowed to six suspects. Eventually two Poles, both about to visit a Japanese firm on business, were identified in the train and questioned – but not arrested.²⁵

Knowing that a secret meeting was going to take place in a park, Schellenberg contacted the Parks Department of Berlin and deployed secret operatives as gardeners and labourers who were to arrest the suspects if they tried to deliver something. Schellenberg narrated:

> 'K___' [Schellenberg did not give his full name in his memoirs – most probably it was Kuncewicz], the Pole identified as one of the secret couriers from Warsaw, appeared at 10 pm and met with a man. The agents watched him. 'K___' took a small packet and gave it a woman. Immediately the Gestapo agents arrested them. Meanwhile the other Pole 'Neb___' [as Schellenberg called him] was arrested also.²⁶

'"K___" looked as a Polish officer and had the solid calm of the Slav which nothing could shake,' Schellenberg remarked. He was 'a fanatical nationalist and my interrogators could get nowhere with him'. In the package he was about to hand Lapinska when they were arrested, a brush and a tube of toothpaste were found; both contained microfilm, one of which held a report of the political situation in Poland. The report was in English, French and Polish and analysed the psychological and practical mistakes of the occupying powers. Schellenberg judged it 'extremely well written and the contents excellently arranged'. In addition, 'the viewpoint was quite objective and not narrowly nationalistic'. Among other things, the report contained the tactics and methods of the resistance.[27]

Once the second microfilm was developed, it disclosed details of the German military deployments in Poland. The Supreme Command of the Wehrmacht 'were amazed at the accuracy of the figures, which were correct even to the most precise details'. Eventually 'K' revealed details of the secret arrangement with the Japanese and agreed with Schellenberg to spy for the Germans in the Soviet Union. According to Schellenberg, 'K' worked for the SD until 1945 when contact was broken. Evidently, he did not die in 1942 under Gestapo custody.[28]

Schellenberg discovered that Onodera was passing intelligence to both the British and Soviet intelligence. Dispatched by Schellenberg, a German agent posed as a representative of the Italian secret service until the end of 1944 and traded material with Onodera. Nevertheless, 'the material which we traded [with Onodera] in Stockholm was prepared by me personally, usually late at night. It was a very careful blend of false, even misleading, material and valid information, the latter mostly of a less important nature.' In return, the 'Italian' got intelligence material 'on Great Britain, for instance ... even got material that came directly from the British War Office. [According to the intelligence provided by Onodera to the 'Italian'] the Russians were already working with the secret service of the Chinese communists and used the Chinese skilfully, especially in diplomatic circles in London.'

Schellenberg suggested that the embassy of the Republic of China in London was penetrated by Soviet intelligence. He noted that Onodera 'showed great skill in making every part with whom he traded feel that they were the only ones with whom he shared his secrets. That we knew better was due to K____.' In the process Schellenberg discovered the role of 'Piotr' (Rybikowski), who also visited the Soviet embassy. According to Schellenberg, 'Piotr' was passing secrets to the Russians.[29]

In March 1946, the X-2 Branch of the US Strategic Services Unit (SSU) interrogated Colonel Joachim Rohleder, the head of

Abwehr IIIF, who confirmed the surveillance work of German counterintelligence against the Polish–Japanese network. They had first intercepted a letter from the Manchukuo embassy in Berlin to Rome to a Jesuit general.[30]

> A careful watch by my 'Hauskapelle', working under my orders, on the Manchurian embassy in Berlin resulted in a letter from the Embassy and destined to Italy, falling into German hands. The Embassy was suspected of carrying on intelligence work detrimental to Germany's prosecution of the war – a member of the Embassy had tried to recruit a German national as an agent.[31]

The typewritten letter was addressed to Ledochowski and had a handwritten signature. 'Practically illegible', it could have been Kuncewicz's. The letter was about the persecution of Catholic priests in Poland and Lithuania. Afterwards 'investigation carried out by my subordinates revealed that a Pole, Kuncewicz, though not on my official list, was in fact employed as assistant at the Manchurian Embassy, and had been supplied with a Manchurian passport'. The Abwehr informed the Gestapo, which had the Poles arrested.[32]

After the arrest of the Polish spies and their disclosure that they worked with the Japanese, the Nazi government protested officially to the Japanese ambassador at Berlin, Oshima, who blamed Onodera, who in turn demanded to be recalled or he would commit *hara-kiri*. Tokyo delayed its reply; the attack on Pearl Harbor and the entry of Japan into the war created new conditions which demanded that Onodera work harder on secret intelligence. He was not recalled and instead continued employing Rybikowski as a spy and liaison to the Polish government in London. The Germans meanwhile wanted him to oust the Pole, but Onodera did not change stance for three and a half years.

Already, 'Thomas' and one of his associates called Mischkiewitsch were working in intelligence gathering with the Manchukuo consulate in Warsaw and the Japanese embassy; they received orders from Akikusa.[33] Before the invasion of the Baltic countries, Rybikowski received also information from Finnish sources in Riga which did not dry up until August 1944.[34]

In early 1944, the Germans, with Swedish support, achieved the expulsion of Rybikowski. It was General Kelgren, the head of the attaché section of the Swedish General Staff, who paid a visit to Onodera's office telling him that his service had evidence that the 'White Russian' 'Iwanow' was a spy. Onodera was told he must fire him or the Swedish government would take direct and official action. He tried to persuade officers Petersen and Kaemp of the Swedish security service, but eventually relented. Rybikowski flew to Britain but kept up a correspondence with the Japanese spymaster until 1945.[35]

Both men had agreed for Onodera to pay Rybikowski in US dollars for information received from London. Rybikowski kept his side of the bargain and a Pole, Stephan Gadowski, was designated their liaison. Rybikowski's reports were handed to Brzeskwinski, the Polish military attaché in Stockholm, who gave them to Onodera. The Japanese received about twenty-five reports.[36] In the summer of 1944, the information received covered Allied movements in India and Burma. By the end of the year, the quality of the intelligence had declined. Onodera eventually figured that he being handed deception material, but he continued paying the Polish spy.[37]

After the German surrender in May 1945, Rybikowski sent letters to Onodera containing messages from Colonel Gano. 'One of Gano's messages announced the impending Soviet declaration of war against Japan and the other gave details of the movement of ten Russian divisions to the Far Eastern front.'[38] The Japanese were warned that Russia would turn against them in Manchuria.

Onodera continued correspondence with the Poles even after the Japanese defeat. In October 1945, Rybikowski came to Stockholm to see Onodera on behalf of Colonel Gano and offered him money and help. In January 1946, Onodera was in Naples waiting to be repatriated. A French colonel named Godefroy called for the Japanese officer and interviewed him. He showed Onodera a letter signed by Colonel Gano, who called the Japanese 'a faithful friend of Poland'.[39]

Onodera explained his methods to American interrogators in 1946. Their report read:

He got some of his best results by working with the General Staffs of small countries. They were usually better informed than anyone else with respect to their powerful neighbours; they had many possibilities for obtaining intelligence but did not possess the necessary finances. He found that if he was tactful, he could supply them with money and gradually create a situation whereby they were morally obliged to give him information because their debt was so large.[40]

The relationship with Poland was 'fruitful'. 'Onodera's own work was entirely dependent on the friendship and protection which he gave to Rybikowski.'[41]

Onodera had access to German intelligence reports in Stockholm covering the Soviet press, the British passport control office and the Swedish police. Having as a source Jacobsen, an Estonian intelligence officer, he secured 'good information' on German and Russian military about the planned invasion of Russia. From Colonel Richard Maasing, a Finnish intelligence officer, Onodera was informed of atomic bomb construction in the United States, German V-missiles and tank production in Russia. In addition, Onodera learned of US convoys to Britain, and US and British troop movements in the Far East. Onouchi, from his discussions with an Abwehr officer named Wagner (who was informed by Canaris, the head of the Abwehr), was informed of Allied deployments in India. Kraemer, another German intelligence officer, told Onouchi about US landings in Okinawa and the Philippines. The Japanese also received information about a US Air Force delegation to Russia. Colonel Petersen of the Swedish General Staff disclosed to Onodera details of Allied battle order on the European front; their discussions were on a monthly basis.[42]

Onodera got information on a US plan to attack the Aleutians one month in advance. 'Sufficiently in advance to be interesting,' he was given information about the planned US landings in Okinawa and the Philippines. A Finnish intelligence officer furnished Onodera with information on US diplomatic codes broken in 1941, but he revealed this to the Japanese in 1943. Rybikowski had provided Onodera with the Soviet war plans for the spring of 1942 for a strategic retreat to the Don–Stalingrad–Volga–Kuban line, plus the Soviet industry in the Urals and the military plan for the central front. Between February and June 1941, Onodera received information about the German preparations to attack Russia; Rybikowski was the main source. In 1943, Onodera believed that British intelligence leaked deceptive information to his network about the Russian entry into the war against Japan. The information came through Consul Vagy of the Hungarian legation; he was informed by a Jewish Hungarian refugee banker in Stockholm. It was reported just before the 1943 Japanese attachés' meeting in Rome, where it was discussed and reported to Tokyo. Onodera heard later that it had caused a controversy in the Imperial General Staff.[43]

Onodera's work is testament to the decades-old autonomy of Japanese spymasters, their resourcefulness in exploiting old antagonisms between Allies, their tradecraft and their tactics in recruiting committed spies.

Prior to the war, British espionage focused on Japanese yards and their shipbuilding programme. No matter how hard the Imperial Japanese Navy tried to keep secret the construction of a warship, in docks and yards officials, officers, sailors and workers talked openly. The secret sources of the SIS and naval intelligence were recruited spies, casual informers as well as travellers, businessmen asked to provide information once they returned from Japan. Just staying still and hearing others speaking in Japanese was the archetypical way of the spy. In a report dated 24 May 1937, it was stated, 'At the Kure yards an agent heard a conversation with Japanese naval ratings that two cruisers of 11,000 tons armed with 12-inch guns were being built...'[44]

On 10 May 1937, a British businessman returning from Japan informed British intelligence that battleships were being laid down at yards in Kure and Kawasaki in Kobe. He worked in the engineering sector and talked with Japanese engineers while in the country, and his reports were confirmed by other sources. By the end of July 1937, the British, American, German and French naval attachés in Tokyo together concluded that battleships were under construction at Kure and Yokosuka but there was 'no definitive evidence available'. There is a curious reference in the reports for 30 July 1937: 'Soviet intelligence believe that a battleship is building at Kure. Source of information unknown.'[45] In another report it is stated, 'Soviet intelligence says they have no evidence that battleship is being constructed at Yokosuka, but they apparently suspect it.'[46] This suggests consultations and intelligence sharing took place between Western naval attachés and their Soviet counterpart in Tokyo.

At the end of August 1937, the Italian naval attaché in Tokyo informed his British counterpart that he had learned from 'reliable' sources that ships 'will shortly be laid down at Kure and Kawasaki'. The warships would be of 46,000 tons each armed with up to 16-inch guns. The French naval attaché was dismissive, saying this tonnage was too high; the report was then amended to suggest the warships would reach 42,000 tons each.

In late September 1937, a businessman informed 'by a well-placed official in Kure yard' reported to British intelligence that 'new ships will be 37,000 tons with 18-inch guns'. In December 1937, a Japanese naval officer in Shanghai informed a secret source that battleships were under construction at Kure and Yokosuka; the battleships were of 35,000 tons with 16-inch guns. British intelligence by now believed the information regarding tonnage and guns was a Japanese attempt at counter-espionage.

In March 1937, a Chinese consular official in Canton told the British that a capital ship would 'definitely' be laid down at Yokosuka and another at Kure. In July 1938 a 'European businessman' was informed by a Japanese engineer in Shanghai that a battleship of over 30,000 tons was being constructed at Kure. Later that month, the British naval attaché in Tokyo cabled the Admiralty 'various wild rumours from USA' of warships of 46,000 tons under construction at Kure to be completed by August 1940. He filed a similar report about the Yokosuka yard, but the Admiralty discounted his reports. In summing up these reports, the Admiralty sounded frustrated:

Of the above eleven reports none is conclusive, no reliable agent has seen Kure building ship since the expiration of the treaty. DNI inclines to the belief that construction started about July 1937 though preparations were probably put in hand shortly after the decision regarding gun calibre was arrived at in March 1937. Yokosuka yards operating from April 1933 to November 1937 ships, built there [are] depot ship *Taigei*, cruiser *Suzuya*, oilers *Thurugizaio* and *Takasaki* and aircraft carrier *Hiryu*. Construction [is] rapid. Also build battleship *Mutsu*.[47]

A Chinese 'itinerant merchant' proved a reliable spy for British naval intelligence; it is not clear if he was managed by the SIS or by the British naval station in Shanghai. Most certainly there was no involvement of the British embassy in Tokyo with his activities. The Chinese reported that he saw at Yokosuka slips in January 1938 two large ships in construction, their hulls being red-leaded. In early April 1938, the British naval attaché saw a large vessel on No. 1 slip, 'apparently laid down about four months'. The next month a Chinese agent 'who mixed in academic engineering circles' told the British of two ships laid down in the latter part of 1937; one was certainly built at Yokosuka. Each ship was over 35,000 tons with 16-ichn guns and could reach 26 knots.[48]

With reference to the Kobe yards, spies reported for the first time in September 1938 that at Kawasaki slip No. 4 the battleships *Haruna* and *Ise* were under construction. It was also reported that battleships *Kirishima* and *Hyuga* were being built there. The Admiralty complained about information offered by the French: 'French intelligence service in the Far East is considered to be relatively inefficient, and as these reports are unconfirmed by other agents it is not considered that reliance should be paced on them. DNI does not believe that Japanese dry docks will be used for capital ship construction as long as other suitable building berths are available.'[49]

The Admiralty was frustrated:

No reliable reports have been received in NID [Naval Intelligence Division] concerning the tonnage of the capital ships believed to be now under construction in Japan. Estimates vary between 35,000 and 55,000 tons. The USA intelligence service has no reliable information. A secret source who may have known the original plans has mentioned two ships of 46,000 tons 'gross', and other of

36,000 tons projected. It seems unlikely that Japan would deliberately have furnished American and Britain with an excuse to 'escalate' by refusing to given an assurance that she was not building ships of over 35,00 tons unless she was in fact doing so.[50]

The DNI concluded that the Japanese had reached a 'definite decision' to arm their ships with 16-inch guns. Indeed 'there are indications that the Japanese have had difficulties with their triple [gun] mountings, and it is not known whether these have been overcome. In view of the fact that Japan nearly always sacrifices other qualities in order to mount a heavy armament it is believed that the new ships will mount more than the 9 [nine] 16-inch carried by the [Royal Navy's] *Nelson* class.'[51]

In August 1938, another report claimed that an 'Asiatic woman who mixed for a week in naval and dockyard circles in Yokosuka heard reference to cruiser building in the yard – 19,000 tons, [with] 12-inch guns'. Meanwhile the aforementioned Chinese spy-merchant, fluent in Japanese, managed to enter the yards. Between 6 and 24 January 1939 he submitted SIS eight reports. For the Admiralty, the information 'if true is of great importance as they [the reports] indicate a greater building capacity at Yokosuka, Sasebo and Maizuru [naval yards] than had previously been considered possible'.[52]

The spy-merchant reported that one capital ship was being built at Yokosuka – 34,000 tons, 676 metres in length, and with 16-inch guns – and another at Kawasaki. At Kure, one aircraft carrier of 25,000 tons named *Kairyu* was under construction. Another carrier named *Koryu* was under construction at Sasebo. The source for the spy-merchant was one of his friends who was described as an official in the town. In his 13 January 1939 report, the spy-merchant said that he had infiltrated Sasebo and had seen the warship himself and drafted sketches. He had also drafted sketches of a capital ship at Yokosuka, and these were deemed 'quite convincing' by the British assistant to the chief naval constructor in Hong Kong. The spy reported that it was now possible for the Yokosuka yard to build three cruisers simultaneously.

In London, the Director of Naval Intelligence considered 'that the existence of this vessel should be assumed – the evidence concerning the proposal to lay down a second "pocket cruiser" rests solely on the word of the merchant's friend the government official'.[53] At this point attention turned to a group of German engineers who had worked at the Maizuru yard. If the Chinese could trace them in Yokosuka, 'valuable corroboration will have been obtained'.[54]

11

A DOUBLE AGENT

In 1934, SIS chief Sinclair was nervous after reading intercepted cables between Captain Oka and the IJN General Staff in Tokyo. Oka was about to recruit a willing spy, a well-connected upper-class Englishman. The happy spymaster wrote:

A nephew of Sir Greene, a former permanent secretary of the Admiralty, has expressed an ardent wish that he would be delighted to take up intelligence duties on behalf of Japan against any country other than Britain, provided Britain is not an enemy at any time in the future. He lives in America, and would have introductions from Sir Greene and others in most other places. He has the entrée to any society. [He has] Excellent physique and could be employed on any work. During the war he was a military officer, and has had experience of employment in the coffee industry in South America. Here, is a member of the Queen's club. At present he is out of work and does not particularly like money-making employment. He has considerable property and is not embarrassed through unemployment, but desires work rather than money. It is considered that this person should be used as a spy and that he should he sent to America or some other suitable place and given suitable wok on an annual estimate of approximately 1,000 pounds and employed on intelligence ... he does not particularly desire salary work apart from necessary expenses for any work which he would be requested to undertake by our Navy ... I know that you will agree that it goes without saying that it is an extremely dangerous thing in war time to make Shinkawa [Rutland] alone the one important figure in our intelligence machine which uses an Englishman as its medium.[1]

The SIS, MI5 and the Admiralty were most interested in the case of William Herbert Greene, brother to noted author Graham Greene, who himself was later an SIS officer under Kim Philby. William Greene's telephone line was tapped and his correspondence opened. It emerged that he first called on Oka's office ostensibly 'to bring to his notice the efficiency of the captain of one of the Japanese steamers'. Immediately, Oka invited him for lunch; a couple of dinners followed with Oka paying the bill. Greene confessed that he was pro-Japanese and anti-American. Oka asked Greene if he could introduce him to prominent Americans, and so the offer to spy for Japan was made. Oka handed Greene £150 for expenses in £5 notes in order to commit him, and his recruitment took place in both meetings and in correspondence that was read by MI5. Oka, as we have seen, was not really security conscious; instead of meeting with Greene to exchange information, he wanted him to 'write what he wanted to tell him'.[2] He clearly did not suspect that their correspondence would be opened.

Greene, however, wished to play a double game. He showed up at the US embassy in London and called on Captain Anderson, the naval attaché, revealing to him that Oka was about to become his spymaster and that he would like to share intelligence on Japan with Anderson. The American officer angrily refused any further discussion while Greene asked in vain to be introduced to important figures.[3]

In March 1934, Greene appeared at the Admiralty claiming that his uncle, the former permanent undersecretary, had urged him to reveal that he was working for the Japanese. He was told 'his idea of spying on the Americans for the Japanese received no approval from the authorities and that he would get himself into very serious trouble'.[4] Colonel Washington warned him to stop playing with the Japanese and the Americans and return the money he had been paid. 'This advice was most unpalatable' to Greene who protested that he saw no reason, as he was not doing anything against this country.'⁵

In April, Anderson talked to the Director of Naval Intelligence in the Admiralty about the approach made by Greene, and Sinclair was promptly informed.⁶ Oka cabled the Director of Naval Intelligence in Tokyo:

> regarding the degree of reliance which can be placed on him [Greene], it is difficult to obtain conclusive proof in addition to the information I have obtained up to now, no matter what methods are tried, without about a year's trial and considering the result of this together with his capability. The social position and antecedents of his near relations are connected with the British middle to upper classes, considering this, his violent dislike for American and his great admiration for Japan, so far as I have been able to observe up to now I feel that there is adequate worth to make one take a chance with him to trust him and use him.⁷

Greene was assigned the codename Midorikawa. In October 1934, Oka paid Greene expenses to arrange a dinner with Colonel Forster of the Royal Marines, the assistant naval intelligence director, and his wife at Claridge's on the 24th. Greene was a master of discussion, drawing information from the high-ranking officer during the luxurious meal. He informed Oka, who wrote to Tokyo in a cable intercepted by the GC&CS:

> The Japanese proposals [on naval armaments] appear to have astonished the governments of Britain and America. They full appreciate the categorical nature of the Japanese demands in regard to expansion, and are doing all they can to check this. Not only does the sympathy of the British Navy towards Japan remain, but rather its flourishing development is giving rise to anxiety. However, in the long run, naval sympathy is powerless in advance of national policy. America intends to stick firmly to the previous ratios, and it seems certain that the conference will break up. It is believed that the Americans are afraid of Japan and that they would not fight Japan alone; Britain would join (according

to them) and this is sufficient indication that they are relying on the British Navy.[8]

It seemed to Oka that Greene was gleaning valuable intelligence.[9] He had also offered information from 'a high official at the Foreign Office':

Opinion in the cabinet is inclining towards Japan and is being alienated from America. A small number of very influential members of the cabinet maintain most emphatically these opinions. The fact that Britain is unable to maintain absolute supremacy in the Far East is already the question of the hour. Consequently, she should ally herself to Japan, and by way of compensation, obtain as profitable conditions as possible. On the other hand, the day has arrived when it is necessary to exert oneself in order to avoid quarrelling with America. [British officials understand] Japan has to dispose of a surplus population therefore there is no alternative but to open up the Dutch East Indies.[10]

Sinclair consulted with the Director of Naval Intelligence and together they quizzed the assistant director, who reassured them that he did not dine with Greene (though he was 'pestered' by him) and had not told Greene anything about naval armaments, which was the subject of an international conference happening in London. Sinclair concluded that Greene had pocketed the money from Oka, spent two days in Claridge's and then compiled a bogus report. The Director of Naval Intelligence wanted an official warning to be served on Greene, for him 'be told quite plainly that his idea of spying on the Americans for the Japanese received no approval from the authorities'.[11]

Oka, confusing the roles of spy and propagandist, also asked Greene to help him in the latter field despite Greene still being in his trial period. A letter survives in which he asks Greene how much he will need to pay for propaganda transmitted through the BBC:

Thanks to your advice I realize it fully now that the propaganda has started very recently. My dear friend don't be disappointed that I have been asking you to do only minor job, but on the contrary you got to understand that I have been waging a war against my government in order to get the enough fund to enable me to carry on this most interesting and effective business carried through ... When I was at our Naval College in Tokyo, in 1922 and 23, studying strategy and tactics as a student officer I used to admire Admiral Cradoc and his squadron ... we got to go systematically in order to persuade my people at home to understand the real value and the nature of the object we want to attain. In this connection I want you to give me the rough estimate to carry on the business. I want you to let me know when the BBC is going to broadcast together with the text.[12]

Upon being told the cost, Oka replied to Greene that he could not support an extensive campaign but enclosed £30 for Greene to arrange a pr-Japanese broadcast with the BBC and mentioned him that a commentator, retired Captain Bernard Actworth, sounded sympathetic towards Japan.[13] The British Director of Naval Intelligence arranged for the BBC to be warned in case Greene attempted 'to plant someone on them' for pro-Japanese propaganda.[14] On 17 January 1935, Oka sent his superiors the information offered by Greene:

Since the latter half of the naval conference and especially since America became so very nervous under the mistaken impression that an agreement existed between Britain and Japan, their propaganda campaign vis-à-vis Britain has become much more open ... I received the following intelligence from a reliable source (Midorikawa) [Greene]:

1. The British Admiralty do not like the positive American anti-Japanese propaganda in England, but they find it convenient,
2. It is confirmed that the recent Japanese actions have made the British position in the Far East difficult, and it is not difficult to see that in regard to these conversations the actions of the British Navy are naturally based on the principle of achieving something.[15]

Greene provided gossip, speculation and fabrications. What he gave Oka led the IJN General Staff to believe that Britain and America were weak and felt threatened by the rise of Japan. Tokyo naval and military leaders grew confident that Imperial Japan could not be deterred by the decaying British Empire in its aspiration for hegemony in the Far East.

In January 1935, Sinclair urged the Director of Naval Intelligence to issue 'a final warning' to Greene, and this occurred on the 21st. Anyhow, the chief of the SIS did not 'consider it advisable to take any action against him at present'.[16] Greene was manipulating publicly available information; he had no access to classified documents or secret information pertaining to the Official Secrets Act.

By March 1935, Oka decided to dismiss Greene: 'The approved period for using Midorikawa expires this month, and as in the present situation there is no special work I can give him, and also as it is difficult to see that he could be specially effective, I am considering severing relations for the time being.'[17] In the same cable, Oka mentioned that he employed a retired lieutenant colonel, Malone, as a propaganda agent distributing pro-Japanese pamphlets in the House of Lords and Commons.[18] Oka wrote that he had 'completed an agreement' with Malone. Some political information and gossip probably derived from this man:

> ... talk is concentrating on a bay on the east coast of Africa (a place, the name of which begins with S.) from the point of view of the value of Singapore in war operations against Japan and particularly for the purpose of the protection of Australia. Regarding the forthcoming general election ... It will probably take place about August and at the latest at the beginning of October. There is no doubt that there will be a change to the Labour Party. This will not cause a violent change in the attitude towards America, nor will it result in anything in the nature of Anglo-American cooperation against Japan.[19]

Undeterred, Greene now went to the ever-suspicious Soviet military attaché and offered his services for espionage. On 14 October 1935, MI5 director-general Vernon Kell received a letter from the Foreign Office: 'I enclose a letter from the Soviet embassy regarding an approach that has been made to them by a certain W. H. Greene offering his services as an intelligence agent.'[20] Greene promptly left for Spain, where civil war was brewing.

Two years later, on 3 November 1937, Greene appeared at the Admiralty. He told a naval intelligence officer, who surprisingly agreed to see him, that his creditors were going to declare him bankrupt and so he was offering to spy on the Japanese embassy for British naval intelligence. He revealed his recent sojourn in Spain, which was at war, and boasted he was 'well qualified for a "job" as he has recently made three trips to [rural] Spain and Madrid and had met several "Admiralty men" who were "fools"'. Greene lied that Colonel Washington of the Royal Marines had earlier wanted him to stop working for the Japanese and had therefore caused him to lose income. He did not divulge that he had ignored Washington and that it was Oka who had stopped employing him.

On 14 December, Greene again went to the Admiralty; this time, he received an audience with the Director of Naval Intelligence.[21] Greene surprised him by telling him that he was back in the employ of the Japanese, having received £800. He wanted the Director of Naval Intelligence to back him and arrange a pro-Japanese BBC broadcast on maritime matters. Greene offered himself as a double agent since 'if this (the BBC broadcast) could be done it would keep him in favour with Oka and that he (Greene) in return would be able to get some information which would be of value ... Oka is not paying him for nothing and sooner or later he will ask him to do something important; he would then in a position to do something for us (the Admiralty).'[22]

The Director of Naval Intelligence refused to help Greene and warned him to stop working for the Japanese. He angered Greene by telling him that Oka used him only for propaganda and nothing of importance like espionage, prompting Greene to try to demonstrate his closeness with Oka by claiming the Japanese naval attaché organised his espionage operations at a Japanese restaurant off Tottenham Court road but 'he could not remember the address'. He also claimed that Oka paid him to have two great days at Claridge's.[23]

Greene tried to impress the director by telling him that Oka was strongly interested in the upcoming general elections and that the

Japanese did not believe in a Labour victory. He continued asking for help with the BBC broadcast, and promised that he would write a report on Oka's espionage activities. He further disclosed that he had approached the American naval attaché, at which point he was yet again warned to stop playing espionage games, prompting him to furiously protest that 'he was not doing anything against this country, why should he not continue his connection with the Japanese naval attaché until the latter definitely asked him to engage in specific espionage work'. He was again warned 'he was embarking on a course of action which might land him in very grave and serious difficulties'.[24]

After this meeting, Greene hit back. He went to the Communist newspaper *Daily Worker* and revealed that he worked for the Japanese. The 22 December 1937 edition ran with the headline 'I was in the Pay of Japan':

A secret agent tells his story to the *Daily Worker*. The *Daily Worker* yesterday talked Mr Herbert Greene, lately on the pay-roll of the Japanese naval intelligence service operating secretly in London. His statements are timely. He is the nephew of Sir William Greene, for six years one of the highest officials of the British Admiralty. The Japanese paid his expenses at the rate of £800 per year.[25]

The next day, the *Daily Worker* published another article in which Greene claimed dramatically that he was 'warned' by the Japanese that they would take 'drastic action' against him. The Japanese embassy did not comment.[26] The *Daily Worker* were interested in drawing a connection between anti-British espionage and the upper class, hence their emphasis on Greene's relations.

British and Japanese intelligence tried to avoid Greene, who was a walking embarrassment for any spymaster trying to plot delicate operations in interwar London. Nevertheless, in spring 1938 he was circulating his legend at barber shops. An MI5 officer reported:

While I was in the barber's shop at the Grosvenor hotel today, a man, who appeared to be somewhat the worse for drink, came in and started a conversation with the barber on the situation in

Japan. I could not catch much of what he said but he appeared to be rather well informed. After he had left, I asked the barber (whom I have known for a number of years) casually who he was, and whether he was a regular client. The barber replied that the man in question often came to the hotel for meals, and had told a member of staff that he had been approached by the Japanese who had taken him on as an espionage agent at a salary of 20 per month. The barber went to say, however, that all was well, because the man was also used by the War Office as a double cross agent, mis-information being supplied through him to the Japanese.[27]

In the summer of 1938, Greene persuaded Robert Hale Ltd to publish his 286-page book *Secret Agent in Spain*, in which he claimed that he was recruited into 'secret intelligence' at an office in London. Reviewers took him at his word; his adventures seemed plausible. A reviewer remarked:

This must be one of the few books – if not the only one – to have been written by an active member of an Intelligence Service during the progress of the war in which he was playing a part. One January morning a telephone call invited the author [Greene] to visit a certain office in the City. There, the proposition was put up to him that he should undertake Secret Service work in Spain. He accepted- and thus started upon the most exciting year in his life. Bombing, shelling ad sabotage were the least of the dangers that confronted him, for after a while it became apparent that he was suspected of espionage. Thenceforth, every kind of attempt, ranging from poisoning to burning, was made upon his life...The book gives a true insight into the dangers and nerve-racking strain suffered by those who work, often alone and unaided, in a foreign country, where every steps fraught with peril. The author is brother of Graham Greene, the well-known novelist, and a nephew of Sr W. Graham Greene, KCB, late Permanent Secretary to the Admiralty.[28]

No evidence had been found that Greene worked for the SIS in Spain. Had he done so, publishing his book would have resulted in a criminal prosecution under the Official Secrets Act; had his publishers believed him, they would have been afraid of this. Greene's writing looked authentic because he was accustomed to meeting with spymasters such as Oka and the officers in the Admiralty. His fictitious plots in Spain could be based on hearsay from the conflict areas he visited. In truth, Greene was employed as an ambulance driver in Spain but was dismissed for his ineptitude.[29]

After the invasion of Poland on 1 September 1939, Greene, aged forty-one, tried to get a commission. On 14 September 1939, MI5 reported that Greene 'was unsuitable for any position which may give him access to confidential documents, apparatus or information'. The military was warned: 'Greene is a thoroughly unreliable type of person, is addicted to drink and should not be allowed to hold a position in H.M. Forces.'[30]

Greene joined as a soldier and in October 1941 was discharged from the Pioneer Corps. Together with his wife he took up work in a hostel for evacuee children at Reigate. For those tasked with keeping him under occasional surveillance, he seemed satisfied in his new job, keeping himself away from plots and intrigues.[31]

For the SIS, MI5 and the Admiralty, Greene was an unscrupulous upper-class character who had the nerve to try to play one side against the other. He did not have access to secret intelligence nor classified documents. Whatever he heard in social conversations he turned into digestible intelligence for Oka, who, without confirming anything with other sources, cabled Tokyo. He was in his own way dangerous, because his forwarding of gossip and pro-Japanese sentiment gave confidence to decision makers in Tokyo, who were increasingly convinced that Britain was weak and thus felt emboldened to pursue expansion in the Far East.

12

MANIPULATION

M ajor General Piggott, who was military attaché at the British embassy in Tokyo from 1936 to 1939, was named a 'public danger' and *'âme damnée'* by the Foreign Office.[1] Indeed, it was reported that 'General Piggott's sympathies are well known to be 100% Japanese. In [Foreign Secretary] Halifax's view there is no doubt that he has considerably contributed to the easing of tension in Anglo-Japanese relations, even though some of his critics feel that his views are too much one way'.[2]

Piggott was obsessed with his personal mission to improve Anglo-Japanese relations, and this was well known to the Japanese who cultivated him, providing him with special access to their generals and headquarters, ensuring he communicated their positions to the War Office and the Foreign Office. In the meantime, military intelligence in London was furious with his failure to provide anything of value. For years, he blocked attempts to organise espionage in Japan. A close reading of his autobiography shows him boasting of the meetings he had with high-ranking Japanese officers and demonstrates how he was manipulated by the Japanese military into believing their lies and representing policies inimical to British interests. Piggott's reports in the 1920s and 1930s had the effect of effectively *delaying* the Foreign Office and the War Office realising that the war with Japan was coming at a time when Japan claimed land and power in China, where Hong Kong, Shanghai and neighbouring Singapore were key colonies and dominions.

Upon being informed that Piggott had been chosen for a second tour as military attaché, Sir Robert Clive, then British ambassador, warned:

> My own impression confirmed by others who know General Piggott is that in regard to Anglo-Japanese relations his feelings outrun his sense of realities and that his judgement is warped. ... It might be embarrassing therefore to have on my staff an officer on whose judgement I could not rely and with whom I might differ on broad questions of policy.[3]

Nevertheless, upon the appointment of Sir Robert Craigie as the new ambassador to Tokyo, Piggott gained influence on policy. Both men knew each other from the consultations of the 1921 Washington conference, and Craigie's aim was the improvement of Anglo-Japanese relations. Soon Piggott started producing distorted assessments:

> At present [1938] the only safe guide to the future development of the pro- and anti-British factions in the Army, is the undoubted fact, I repeat fact, that the heads of the army (Generals Sugiyama, Tada, Umezu, Homma ... Hata, Ikeda etc.) wish to restore and strengthen friendship with Great Britain.[4]

This was inaccurate. Japanese imperialism could not coexist with British interests in the Far East and China. Besides, there was a young generation of independent-minded generals – Tojo, Itagaki, Oshima, Ishiwara and Muto – ready to confront Britain and the United States.[5]

Extending privileges to Piggott ensured the Japanese positions would be defended in cables and memorandums to the Foreign Office as well as influencing the ambassador's stance. He boasted:

> In return for services rendered in the preliminaries to the Tientsin conference, 'M [General Kennichi Oshima] kept me generally informed of what was going on about proposed alliance. Great pressure was being exerted on the [Japanese] Government by Germany and her Japanese admirers, but

resistance to the plan developed in many quarters- the Court, the navy, financial circles, and in some sections of the army. Nevertheless, the Prime Minister, in 'M' words "is slowly being pressed towards the gate he does not wish to enter" had the Tientsin issue still been alive the forces in his support would have been correspondingly weakened.

For Piggott, after Japan's withdrawal from the League of Nations

... there was a noticeable relaxation of tension. The voices of the fanatics and alarmists were hushed, and throughout 1934 and 1935 Anglo-Japanese relations improved considerably. There were various reasons for this, the principal one being a feeling of relief on both sides that there had been no actual collision over a mater in which the British public could not or would not take a profound interest. To the question 'Does this Manchurian affair really concern us?' The man in the street answered 'No'.[6]

He was allowed to visit the headquarters of military intelligence:

In addition to the headquarters of the garrison, there was also a so-called Special Bureau. The latter had various military and other activities, chiefly intelligence and liaison, but it dabbled in most things. The officer in charge of the Bureau (General Miura), and the garrison Commander (General Sonobe) showed themselves frank and friendly, no doubt taking their cue from the good relations existing between the consular representatives of the two countries. It was annoying, however, to encounter complete secrecy as to the numbers and composition of the garrison, which at a guess might have been a division; I was enchanted to find that the bluff and genial Sonobe shares my feelings of irritation. He said that the authorities in Tokyo were 'obsessed with this ridiculous secrecy- we are not allowed to mention a unit's number, and every unit is designated by the name of its commander. How can I possibly remember the names of all the subordinate commanders in my division? My staff's time is wasted keeping track of the continual changes. *Domo, komatta* (I am fed up)'.

This was a good example of the relaxation of reserve that is often to be found in Japanese outside their own country; General Sonobe's remarks could hardly have been made in Japan without serious repercussions on his career.[7]

Piggott visited Hsinking, the new capital of the Japanese puppet state Manchukuo. There he met with the commander-in-chief and ambassador, General Ueda, 'a tall and striking figure, in a position not very dissimilar to that once held in Egypt by Lord Kitchener'. His chief of staff, General Itagaki, 'a silent man much preoccupied with his responsibilities, military and political, invited me to dinner'. He added:

> One of the colonels, Akira Muto, sat near me – a fortunate contact which bore valuable fruit three years later. There was one officer destined to become world famous whom I should have liked to meet, but unfortunately he was away from Army Headquarters: Lieutenant General Hideki Tojo, Head of the Military Police. His deputy Major-General Fujie, was as communicative as General Sonobe at Mukden. For my benefit he expounded the ramifications and categories of the police organization in considerable detail, somewhat to the surprise of a junior officers whom he summoned to refresh his memory about some figures; this officer, thinking that we had been talking French, rather naively asked his superior in Japanese whether it was 'in order to divulge these matters to a foreigner'. General Fujie curtly told him that it was all right – 'a special case'; he laughed when the young man had left the room and said he was very zealous but narrow-minded. We resumed acquaintance in Tokyo where we were of some service to each other, as will be seen.[8]

In the city, Piggott dined with officers and Japanese businessmen at the Bankers' Club:

> It was difficult to learn much about trade and commerce in two days, but a letter of introduction provided in Tokyo by the President of the Manchurian Electric Development Company (General T. Yoshida) made me free of their Hsinking offices.[9]

With reference to the atrocities and war crimes committed in the sacking of Nanking, for Piggott only 'certain units' of the Japanese army were undisciplined. He yet again defended Japanese actions:

A curious feature of the Japanese attitude was that they objected more to British unfriendliness to Japan and moral support of China, which were both abstract manifestations of our views, than they did to the concrete facts that the Germans not only supplied arms to their enemy, but also were presented by a Military Mission, under General Falkenhausen, which continued to train and advise the Chinese armies for many months after the outbreak of hostilities. This was not merely a form of differing Japanese mentality, but was strict realism; the Japanese did not object to the Germans earning some money by selling arms to the Chinese, as they (the Japanese) expected to capture them (the arms) quite soon. British resentment against Japan, apart from general disapproval of her invasion of China, which the Japanese announcement of 'no indemnities, no annexation' did little to allay, was based mainly on the injury to British trade caused by the restrictions imposed under the plea of military necessity.[10]

Meanwhile, the British military attaché in China, Lieutenant Colonel C. R. Spear, reached northern China embedded in a Chinese army unit. Eventually he, as Piggott narrated,

was found in plain clothes behind the Japanese lines without any permit from their military authorities, on his way from Shanghai to Peking. The view of the Japanese commander, which, it must be admitted, was shared by all foreign military attachés in Tokyo, was that Colonel Spear had no business to be where he was in such circumstances; whether by bad luck or bad management, he was in an equivocal position which the Japanese were bound to investigate.[11]

Piggott was instructed to fly to China, find commander-in-chief General Sugiyama – 'an old friend of mine' as Piggott boasted – and secure the release of Spear.

It would have been fatal to call upon General Sugiyama first; here was a case in which some branches of his staff had been involved from the beginning, and they would have resented a direct approach to the commander in chief ... My plan now was to use a lever never before employed and to ask a favour in return for my efforts, so long continued, to understand and explain the Japanese point of view; in other words, to make a personal appeal *ad misericordiam*. I had never done it before, and disliked doing it now, but it was important to secure Spear's released by any means, even at the risk of a rebuff ... some of the officers had taken part in the Tientsin discussions the previous month, including Major-General Muto, and seemed genuinely pleased to see me. My visit was apparently not resented after all, and several officers even said they admired my having flown 'all the way from Tokyo specially for the sake of a brother-officer'. The most encouraging moment of the day was when I was given a clear indication that General Sugiyama himself would probably discuss the whole matter with me in the course of a day or two.[12]

In his official residence (and not at headquarters), Sugiyama met with Piggott for 'two hours talk over a whisky and soda'. Piggott noted, 'In accordance with Japanese custom, the principal object of our meeting was reached by circuitous routes.' Sugiyama played part by putting emphasis on 'his heavy load of responsibilities' for the 'safety' of his army and keeping law and order in China:

He [Sugiyama] pointed to a large dossier, observing it had been 'prepared by my legal branch, all about Colonel Spear's journey, much of it sworn evidence by Chinese witnesses; it is a serious matter'. He said he had not made up his mind whether to send the case for trial by curt martial or not. He seemed sympathetic, thanked me for making so long a journey, and was sorry to hear of my forthcoming departure; had I any points to bring up?[13]

Piggott argued:

There was no anti-Japanese motive in Colonel Spear's expedition. As regards his alleged anti-Japanese statements to Chinese troops ... he [Spear] could hardly have made pro-Japanese statements with the Chinese Army! I then told the Commander in Chief that Spear had won the Military Cross for gallantry when the Chinese armies attacked the British consulate at Nanking in 1927, a fact which impressed him considerably. He promised to take into account all I had said.

A few days later, on 8 September 1939, Piggott was informed by telephone message from Major Miyamoto at Army Headquarters that General Sugiyama 'after full consideration of all the facts, supplemented by what I had told him, had consulted again with his staff and had finally decided not to send Colonel Spear to court-martial; he added that he would be released that afternoon'.[14] Colonel Spear 'looked well ... the nervous strain must have been considerable'.[15]

By granting Piggott special access and personal privileges, the Japanese could rest assured that the attaché would always cable London to 'explain the Japanese point of view'. Piggott was passionate about private diplomacy:

The task of maintaining close touch with my own contemporaries in the Japanese Army (including the Minister of War himself), and at the same time cultivating the very important 'middle strata', is extremely difficult. Courtesy and old friendship with the former demand constant meetings; and tact is necessary in order to avoid the appearance of neglecting the younger generation. By 'doubling' most of my entertainments, and at considerable physical, mental and financial exertion, I have so far been able to maintain contacts in both 'strata'.[16]

At the War Office, however, frustration with the paucity of military intelligence was escalating:

When Piggott took up his post as military attaché, Tokyo, he was convinced that his primary task was the promotion of better relations between the Japanese and British armies and, therefore, between the respective governments of those countries. From the MI2 point of view this is a wrong appreciation of an MA's (Military Attaché's) duties but General Piggott's conviction is so strong on this subject that I doubt if it can be shaken ... From the narrower aspect of military intelligence, his work is not so satisfactory, especially from the point of view of the compilation of the handbook. His self-imposed task of improving relations, and the number of contacts he has to maintain for that purpose absorb a great proportion of his time and energy, to the detriment of the collection of purely military intelligence. His reports are of interest as containing pen pictures of distinguished Japanese officers, the general Anglo-Japanese atmosphere in Japan and the attitude of the Japanese Army towards England, but they contain comparatively little of direct military intelligence value. They fall noticeably short of those of his predecessor, Colonel James ... one reason for this, I believe, is that he purposely avoids tapping one of Colonel's best sources of information in the person of the Soviet MA, because he feels it may prejudice his position with his friends in the Japanese Army ... it is doubtful if any representations from the War Office will persuade him to subordinate it to the collection of detailed military information.[17]

The reference to the Soviet military attaché indicates some sort of naval intelligence sharing on Japan in the past.

In a bid to rectify the situation, the War Office and the Foreign Office approved the appointment of an assistant military attaché, George Wards, to focus on military intelligence. This failed dismally, however, because Piggott, while happy to have an assistant as he had requested, wrote back that he did not consider intelligence gathering appropriate:

With the advent of war conditions, and the consequent intensification of secrecy, normal sources of information have become still more restricted; while contacts with Japanese officers are less easy to maintain owing to the anti-British feeling engendered in the fighting services by the hysterical and one-sided attitude of the English press. None of my colleagues, with all of whom my relations have been close and cordial, have had quite the same difficulties on a similar score. The presence of 'intelligence centres' in the Far East, with their machinery for duplication and distribution, and many sources of information not open to the military attaché, has raised the question as to what information the military attaché can supply to these centres, bearing in mind the fact that the military authorities in India, Canada, Australia, and New Zealand, are also desirous of receiving his reports on a military nature. There are two practical sides of this question, namely, the physical capacity of the Military Attaché's office for re-duplicating reports, and the dividing line between political and military information. Major [George] Wards [the assistant military attaché] visited our headquarters in Singapore and Hong Kong on route to Japan, and gathered that the information required was mainly identifications, movements of troops and tactical methods. In war time the two former classes of information are naturally most jealously guarded, and any illicit attempts on my part to obtain them would merely increase the embarrassments of my present position.[18]

Piggott distorted the threat assessments: 'I must state, moreover, categorically that Japan has no present intentions inimical either to Singapore or Hong Kong. Information, such as tactical methods, new equipment, etc. has no special urgency, and appears in due course in the War Office Intelligence summaries.'[19]

As we explored in previous chapters, the Japanese had long since drafted plans for an invasion of Hong Kong and Singapore. Piggott told Craigie that he communicated directly with the chief of the Imperial General Staff in London – bypassing military intelligence – on 'matters of importance'. He was warned by the War Office that 'such procedure is entirely unauthorized and potentially embarrassing'.[20]

Piggott acted as if he was a committed and important agent with an explicit task to avert threat assessments and intelligence gathering while insisting that social contacts had an influence on Japanese foreign policy and strategy. Instead, his 'dinner diplomacy' was causing more trouble than expected: on 24 March 1939, Piggott held a dinner for one Colonel Kagesa. Cowley, the British Consul in Tokyo, attended also. Kagesa made reference to a statement by R. A. Butler, the Foreign Office undersecretary, in the House of Commons that Britain was considering 'other kinds of assistance to China'. Piggott remarked that Butler 'was obliged to say this in order to placate the Opposition and public order'. The Foreign Office was furious, and Craigie was warned:

> We do not wish to make heavy weather of the incident and ask the War Office to reprimand him [Piggott], but I think you should call his attention to the grave impropriety of what he said and point out to him that, if these unofficial conversations are to do any good, neither side ought to give utterance to misleading, still less to false, statements.'[21]

Craigie hit back, pointing to his own secret sources:

> I may tell you in confidence that one argument which the Japanese Prime Minister used in order to prevail over the reluctance of the Japanese Army to hold the Tientsin conversations in Tokyo was precisely that General Piggott and I were sufficiently well known in Army circles to enable the military representatives to feel that they would not be dealing with total strangers impervious to reasonable argument. It has therefore been a little disappointing to me that in the first notice which the Far Eastern Department have taken of these informal meetings, involving the exercise of much tact and careful preliminary arrangement, to say nothing of expense, you should have singled out an expression of opinion which might perhaps have been phrased somewhat differently for such severe strictures. I am left here with the feeling that such efforts as we are able to make here to prevent the state of our relations with Japan from going from bad to worse are viewed with suspicion and misgiving by the Far Eastern Department and that only when we are engaged in our normal duty of protesting and recriminating can you really sleep comfortably in your beds.[22]

Prime Minister Neville Chamberlain trusted Craigie more than his counterparts in London. He even wrote to his sister Hilda on 15 July 1939:

> Thanks to the ineptitude of our Foreign Office we have been manoeuvred into a false position where we are single-handed and yet are being attacked over a policy as essential for America, France and Germany as ourselves ... The only thing that gives me any confidence is Craigie's attitude. He always seems to preserve his calm and never seems to get rattled ... But the anti-Japanese bias of the FO (Foreign Office) in the past has never given him a chance. If he gets us through this mess I shall insist on his having an honour to mark our gratitude.[23]

Edmund Hall-Patch, the financial adviser to the Tokyo and Shanghai British embassies, felt differently:

> [Piggott] is ... looming too large as an interpreter of Japanese motives to the Ambassador, and as an exponent of our point of view to many Japanese who think his influence is greater than it really is ... I do not place great faith in him in either capacity. Not that he is actuated by base motives: far from it, but he genuinely believes that the Japanese are people of much the same stamp as ourselves ... In other times, in other circumstances his 'get together boys' and his heartiness with the Japanese might be valuable. But not now.[24]

The independent-minded Japanese officers, the middle and high ranks, saw that Piggott could be manipulated because he was obsessed with all things Japanese and held an important position in the British embassy. Unwittingly, however, Piggott manipulated the Japanese by giving the impression that he had greater influence in the embassy than he truly had.

'Piggottry' had been used in the Foreign Office to describe the work of the military attaché, and this chapter shows what 'Piggottry' was all about – and how difficult it was to criticise the man. Chamberlain supported Craigie and, by extension, Piggott, and Foreign Secretary Halifax backed the ambassador's work in consultations at the Foreign Office. Military intelligence gathering therefore remained in a dismal state for a number of years, bolstering the incorrect belief that there was no immediate or medium-term threat to Hong Kong and Singapore.

Piggott's attitude and bias remained evident in his post-war memoirs, which avoid blaming the Japanese for the atrocities they committed. In the final analysis, his work was so beneficial to the Japanese spymasters that it would have had the same outcome had he been employed by them to block intelligence gathering and derail the formulation of a credible deterrent against Japanese aggression towards British interests and colonies in the Far East.

13

ARMIES OF SPIES

The naval base under construction in Singapore was a key target for Japanese spies who managed to buy intelligence from a British subject in 1932. This was a bad year for the British, as an RAF airman sold secret intelligence on an air base as well. The following year, the Japanese approached a British civilian motivated by money and employed him to steal drawings of the naval base. In Singapore and Malaya, the rise of the Japanese threat compelled the police to establish special 'Japanese' sections for counterintelligence investigations.

In 1934, Lieutenant Commander Kaseda Tetsubiko of the IJN reached Singapore under the alias Kashima Teizo. Accompanied by an associate, he approached an RAF warrant officer and attempted to persuade him to sell a codebook. Special Branch put the two operatives under surveillance and soon arrested them. London was informed, but at the Foreign Office no one wanted a hint of crisis with Japan at this time and the spies were merely deported. Another Japanese agent, an associate of Kaseda, was arrested when he tried to buy plans on the RAF base in Seletar but he poisoned himself before he could be questioned.

Elsewhere, Special Branch found documents in the home of one Kokubo Hiromichi. The documents showed that he was in communication with four Royal Artillery servicemen on Blakang Mati, an island with heavy guns deployed, and was trying to persuade them to provide him with intelligence. Arrested and interrogated, Kokubo was deported in March 1935.

Another spy, with the codename Goma Shohei, was the younger brother of transport minister Nakajima Tsunekichi, and he reached Singapore in 1936 with a stated purpose of working for the East Asiatic Economic Investigation Bureau. Surveillance led to his arrest, and interrogation revealed that he called on Chinese and Tamil workers to help him carry out espionage on British troops and naval stations. The choice was yet again to deport him, this time alongside four other Japanese, in February 1938. Tokyo complained about their treatment in custody.

After these tensions, a diplomatic crisis erupted when Assistant Superintendent J. S. H. Brett of the Singapore Special Branch boarded the Japanese ship *Hakone Maru* to search the baggage of Akiyama Motioichu, who held a diplomatic passport. Another protest from Tokyo compelled London to consider avoiding confrontation with Japanese agents to avert further crises.[1]

By October 1940, the main conclusion of British intelligence in the Far East read:

A continual flow of reports from trained, reliable and semi-trained agents coupled with the efforts of literally thousands of enthusiastic amateur spies must make the task of efficient collation an insuperable one. Although we have no evidence of the results at the Tokyo end, it is considered probably that are not of a high standard.[2]

British spymasters noted the basic problem of the Japanese spymasters, mainly supporting forces in China, Manchuria and south-east Asia, after the fall of France and Holland: collation and analysis were not deemed priorities in the Imperial General Staff. Major General Ishiwara Kanji, an outspoken and undisciplined officer, cut his teeth in Manchuria where he employed dozens of operatives, from professional spies to rogue Japanese, Chinese and Russians. He reorganised the General Staff in 1937, and blamed staff officers for not producing tactical intelligence that would lead to action. Focusing his attacks on the Intelligence Bureau's China Section, Ishiwara called officers/analysts 'completely worthless, [not doing] real work, just sit[ting] on your butts and theorizing'.[3]

Japanese intelligence showed interest in training operatives: the War Ministry established the Training Unit for Rear Duty Agents

(*Kōhō Kinmu Yōin Yōseijo*) near the Yasukuni Shrine in Tokyo in March 1938, and the following year it was formally transferred to the Nakano school of espionage under the General Staff Office as the Army Communications Research Institute (*Rikugunshō Tsūshin Kenkyūjo*). The Nakano school and its branch in Shizuoka had trained more than 2,500 secret operatives by the end of the war.[4] British intelligence commented sarcastically:

> It may be a fortuitous circumstance which makes the Japanese such a good barber and such an ardent photographer; it is certainly more than remarkable that there are so many Japanese barbers and photographers to be found in so many somewhat remote places on the continent of Asia, in the East Indies and South Sea Islands. This is even more remarkable when it is considered that the Japanese, as a people, are not great colonisers (*sic*) – they have a great affection for their own island with its geishas and cherry-blossoms; while Manchuria is too cold for them, the East Indies are too hot. The same is true of the innumerable small merchants and fishing companies. All of them are in fact part of the vast web of commercial espionage which Japan has spread, and is still spreading, over the areas she plans to dominate. While carrying on their normal occupations these little men are constantly and methodically filling their notebooks with every conceivable item of information, much of this information no doubt of little or no value. Some of them may be trained agents planted to connect intelligence of a particular nature. Others will just collect it for the fun of it; if one day they are called upon to say their piece they will be prepared and will surely be well rewarded – even without a reward, the resultant gain of face is well worth the trouble involved.[5]

On paper, the Japanese had thousands of spies; in reality, most of these individuals relayed only information that was openly available.

The Far East Combined Bureau, an outpost of the British GC&CS, was set up in Hong Kong in March 1935 to monitor Japanese, Chinese and Russian (Soviet) intelligence and radio traffic. By 1940, its findings had led British spymasters to observe the 'apparent inconsistency' of Japanese methods:

> It is known, for example, that they spend quite fantastic sums of money on the collection of quite a ridiculously unimportant details; again they vainly continue to try to win over the Chinese in Burma and Malaya with pro-Wang-Ching-Wei [the head of the Chinese government of collaborators] propaganda, when it is patently obvious to any intelligent observer that their whole campaign is a waste of time and money; they cannot understand that the Chinese are an intelligent, stubborn and conservative people. They spend so much effort for such poor results. This vast organisation for the collection of intelligence cannot produce results which are in any way justified by the expenditure of labour and money.[6]

The Japanese seemed to take an interest in the Middle East as well, with similar results:

> As far as direct political advantage to Japan is concerned the outstanding feature of this multifarious activity is the apparent meagreness of the results obtained. Their commerce is undoubtedly increasing in the area under review, but the overhead represented by the expenses of their clandestine activities must reduce profits to a vanishing point, and, according to their own admission, as seen from censored correspondence, their political intrigues are hardly more successful, owing to the strict control and supervision of the British authorities, and it must be added the clumsiness and ineptitude may of their personnel display.[7]

For years, British military and naval intelligence, as well as the SIS, were studying the architecture of Japanese intelligence. The 'special service' was responsible to open 'the way for the army, first by the collection of intelligence and then by the instigation of revolution'. These spymasters and their operatives employed tactics like subversive propaganda and suborning of colonial government officials. By the time of the Japanese invasion, a puppet regime was almost in place ready to take up the reins. Informers kept the

Japanese General Staff and the divisional headquarters apprised of 'the political sympathies, degree of loyalty and movements of various foreign governments' officials.

At the same time, every effort was being made in the distribution of propaganda in the foreign press. For instance, there existed the China Affairs Board, a military intelligence service focusing on China. This service employed a network, assumed to be widespread, of commercial enterprises with branches in Thailand, Indochina and the East Indies. The companies reported on intelligence matters to the local Japanese consulate general, and the consuls provided spies with instructions and financing. In fact, consuls 'are under direct orders from Tokyo to carry on spying or engage spies on behalf of any government departments'. In India, the Japanese consuls 'are engaged in the organization of the "cultural approach" in schools and communities'. Many Japanese consuls were graduates of spy schools, being former navy officers. Meanwhile, the South Manchurian Railway officials, many of whom 'appear in places far remote from Manchuria, is another concern which is intimately connected to the army and with military intelligence in particular'.[8]

IJN intelligence maintained special service stations and operated within the China Affairs Board, with spymasters focusing on naval intelligence declining to 'engage to any great extent in political, economic and propaganda activities; certainly not on anything like the same scale as the military intelligence service'. The naval attachés in foreign capitals developed networks of informers like their predecessors. The most important naval intelligence stations were in Shanghai, Tsingtao and Canton. No doubt there was antagonism and jealousy with the army intelligence; indeed, a British intelligence report claimed that the head of station in Tientsin reported directly to Tokyo on Japanese army operations.

The Hainan branch of Nomura Co. operated as a 'post box' for naval intelligence at this time. The shipping line Nippon Yusen Kaisha, meanwhile, provided cover for secret agents as did the local Japanese banks. In addition to the government and military/naval intelligence, secret societies such as the Black Dragon Society were influential. British intelligence concluded, 'It now appears that some and possibly all the intelligence departments of these various secret societies have come under the influence or direction of the

Japanese government in the shape of the ministries of Foreign Affairs, Overseas Affairs and Commerce and Industry.' However, this was wrong in that it discounted the ideological independence of society members – former officers among them – as well as the independent mindset of Japanese generals and spymasters, which had been demonstrated in recent assassinations.

British intelligence in fact had 'irrefutable evidence' that the so-called East Asiatic Economic Investigations Bureau was an offshoot of the Black Dragon society and was the intelligence organisation of a subsidiary company, Oriental Development Company of the South Manchurian Railway; later control of the East Asiatic Economic Investigations Bureau passed to the Japanese Ministry of Foreign Affairs. The director of this bureau, Dr Shumei Okawa, 'a notable historian and revolutionary who has been responsible for various political assassinations in his times', funded a school for espionage in Tokyo in 1938. The Ministry of Foreign Affairs and the War Ministry controlled this school, cooperating also with the Ministry of the Marine and the South Manchurian Railway.[9]

Furthermore, it was established that the Nippon Trade Agency was 'an important part of the Japanese espionage system'. The Nippon branches in Calcutta, Karachi, Singapore, Bangkok, Sydney, Alexandria and Baghdad, along with those soon to open in Tunis, Djibouti and Madras, were key hubs of espionage. 'Unimpeachable sources of information' confirmed that secret agents were posted as apprentices in the Japanese government-controlled South Seas Development Association, operating offices in Malaya, the East Indies and the Pacific.[10] In Malaya 'it is incorrect, even if it were possible, to dissociate commercial or any other Japanese activity from espionage ... the truth is that it is everywhere'.[11]

According to a Japanese General Staff officer interrogated post-war by the Americans, the *Kempeitai* were responsible for innumerable atrocities in the Japanese-occupied territories in China and south-east Asia. They were supported the *Tokkō* secret police, who 'mingled with the troops, and to some extent with the local inhabitants and to keep their ears alert for "careless talk" and examples of low morale'.[12] The *Kempeitai* 'were easily distinguishable from regular troops as they were allowed to let their hair grow long, so as to enable them to successfully impersonate civilians. When on this duty they carried pistols under their clothing.'[13]

In spring 1939, Italian secret agents in Shanghai gained access to a Royal Navy building and obtained a copy of a secret report dated 5 May 1939. It was written by the commander-in-chief of the fleet in China, Sir Percy Noble, and addressed to the First Sea Lord, and in it noble was clear that Britain would be unable to defend both the Middle East and the Far East simultaneously; London had to make a strategic choice, and the conclusion was that Singapore and Malaya could be defended only with American help. The Italians provided the German ambassador in Rome with a copy of the Noble report; based on what came after, the Germans probably passed it to the Japanese.[14]

14

MURDER

On 27 July 1940, as the Battle of Britain escalated and fear of invasion soared, Lieutenant General Tojo Hideki, Minister of War and soon-to-be Prime Minister of Japan, declared that the Imperial Japanese Army would 'not hesitate to take drastic measures against Japanese who assisted Foreign Secret agents and those who were pro-British'.[1]

Frantic reporting followed. The *Kempeitai*, arrested British subjects on charges of espionage, and among those arrested was the fifty-five-year-old journalist Melville James Cox, a Reuters correspondent in Tokyo who had spent almost thirty-five years in the Far East. One morning at breakfast, two Japanese officers and an interpreter went to his house and asked him to come with them. He was allowed to send a total of five letters to his wife.

Back in 1936, Cox had posted information on the upgrading of warship *Nagato* in a letter signed 'Jimmy' posted from the Teikoku Hotel in Tokyo. The *Kempeitai* had intercepted the letter; 'Jimmy' was not identified, but analysis showed that he had to be a European or American frequenting the hotel. 'Jimmy' was interested in shipbuilding, a specialised subject pertaining to national security. Surveillance over a long period showed that Cox – whose first name was James (thus 'Jimmy') – was visiting the Teikoku Hotel. Comparisons between the letter and Cox's own handwriting showed similarities.[2]

Soon after his arrest, Cox fell to his death from the police building in Kudan. The official statement claimed that a guard had grabbed him in an attempt to stop him from jumping, but his body was found roughly 20 feet from the wall of the building. Besides, the window was small; just 3 square feet, the sill being a little over 2½ feet from the floor.[3]

Other British subjects arrested at this time were retired Captain James RN (the representative of the Federation of British Industries in Tokyo); L. T. Woolley (working with the Rising Sun Petroleum Company, Yokohama); R. Holder (working with Messrs Brunner, Mond & Co. in Kobe, and President of the Kobe branch of the British Association of Japan); E. W. James (the manager of Cameron & Co. in Kobe, and President of the Kobe and Osaka Foreign Chamber of Commerce, and Honorary Consul for Sweden); F. M. Jonas, also working for Messrs Nickel & Lyons, Kobe; J. P. T. Drummond (working with Frazar & Co. in Osaka); H. M. McNaughton, a British merchant and Honorary Consul for Greece; J. F. James (working with Messrs Nickel & Lyons in Kobe); S. A. Ringer, British merchant and vice-consul at Shimonoseki; F. E. E. Ringer, a British merchant and vice-consul at Nagasaki; de Trafford a school teacher working in Nagasaki; and E. G. Price, a British merchant in Kobe.

Foreign Secretary Viscount Halifax, Churchill's erstwhile rival, stated in the House of Lords:

> On July 29 the Ministries of War and Justice in Tokyo made a. joint announcement to the effect that: In view of the ever-increasing activities of foreign organs of espionage and conspiracy in this country of late, the military police, under the direction of prosecutors, arrested, as a first step on July 27, those constituting part of a British espionage network covering the entire country. It is hardly necessary for me to state that there is no foundation whatsoever for this allegation by the Japanese Government. A further joint announcement by the Japanese Ministries of War and Justice stated that Mr. Melville James Cox, Reuters correspondent at Tokyo, was arrested on a charge of espionage and threw himself from a third-storey room of the Tokyo military police headquarters on July 29 and died at 3.46 p.m.[4]

The British government retaliated; suspected spymasters in London, India and Singapore were arrested and put into custody. One of them was Shinozaki Mamoru, the press officer of the Japanese Consulate General in Singapore. Shinozaki was reporting to Colonel Tanikawa Kazuo and Captain Kunitake Teruhito of the Imperial General Staff. Most significantly, the Japanese controlled two spies, Gunner Frank Gardener of the Royal Artillery and Corporal Compton of the RAF; they had provided him with information on British deployments in Malaya.

Japanese arrests continued. Vanya Ringer, a British resident in Nagasaki, was arrested, like Cox accused of espionage and threatened with the same fate. Eventually, she was repatriated together with Cox's wife. According to a secret source of British ambassador Robert Craigie, General Tojo had ordered the arrest of the Britons aiming to intimidate London.[5] Craigie himself had of course been working for stable Anglo-Japanese relations and continuously argued for easing of restrictions against Japan, as in this letter from July 1940:

It is most repugnant for me to have to urge compliance with this Japanese request [for closing the Burma road to the supply of Chinese forces], but I do so in the hope and belief that when we have defeated Germany we and the United States will be able to teach Japan a lesson which she will never forget.[6]

Piggott, meanwhile, wrote that the ambassador 'continued his friendly intercourse with the soldiers, and few Ambassadors of any country can have had so many acquaintances in the Imperial Army as he'.[7]

Throughout 1939 Craigie had maintained confidential sources, including Japanese officials like Ikeda Seihin, former finance minister Yoshida Shigeru and generals Koiso Kuniaki and Araki Sadao. They told him that the Ministry of Foreign Affairs had arguments with General Kenichi Oshima on the strategy to be followed and that there were the 'expansionist' army top brass and the moderate civilian leadership to be borne in mind. As a result, Craigie had insisted on improving relations with Tokyo and disregarding American policy towards Japan. Another unnamed confidential source assured him that Tokyo was willing to improve relations with London and Washington.[8]

On 17 July 1940, Craigie and Foreign Minister Arita signed the Burma Road Agreement, which banned the transport of war materials, including petrol, to China until 18 October. Protests from China and the United States showed the tightrope that British policy was walking. Craigie did not hesitate to protest:

> ... the Americans are forever inciting us to assume an attitude of utmost firmness towards Japan, only to tell us, when the inevitable crisis comes, that they are of course not in a position to use force. I have been aware of this tendency from the start but the Far Eastern Department of the Foreign Office have been less wary - or perhaps less well-acquainted with American methods - than I have been.[9]

Churchill, the imperialist strategist turning into a pragmatist tactician, admitted to his antagonistic Foreign Secretary Lord Halifax on 17 July 1940:

> I have never liked the idea of our trying to make a peace between Japan and China. I am sure that all this talk of a 'just and equitable peace' is moonshine and known to be so. I think it is a great pity to use it. It might act as some palliation for the action which has been forced upon us by the plight in which we lie. I have yielded to it but it is certainly not in our interests that China and Japan should end their quarrel, and I am delighted that Chiang Kai-shek should rest his objections to our conduct so largely upon our references to peace.[10]

The Foreign Office and the War Office needed time over the next three months to build up the defences in the Far East; a Japanese advance in Southeast Asia was deemed most probable. Imperial forces were moving to Thailand and Indochina.[11] Meanwhile, in Tokyo the British ambassador described life under close surveillance: 'All official telephones are tapped.'[12] No doubt for years the military attaché's office at the British embassy in Tokyo could not be assumed safe from espionage. Major-General Piggott himself hailed, rather naively, 'the faithful old Japanese clerk in the military attaché's office, Genro Hikida [who] retired in September

[1938] after eighteen years' continuous work, receiving a gratuity from the Army Council'.[13]

Despite Craigie's moderation, on Saturday 13 December 1941 the *Kempeitai* raided the embassy to arrest Herbert Vere Redman, the head of the information department, on charges of anti-Japanese propaganda. The ambassador tried to block their entry but was pushed violently aside. Redman was interrogated for months and eventually released. Redman's arrest compelled Foreign Secretary Anthony Eden to order the arrest of Kaoru Matsumoto, a member of the Japanese embassy staff in London.[14]

15

FALSE ALARM

It was a top-secret triumph for MI5 – they had bugged the telephone lines inside the Japanese embassy in London. Telephone conversations between military and naval attachés and staff could now be monitored; the very words of the interlocutors could be studied, and reliable conclusions could be reached, as well as leads for further investigations.

Early on 5 February 1941, alarm bells rang. A foreign journalist with colloquial Japanese proficiency was translating the telephone conversations for MI5, and he realised that the embassy was on a war footing. The first phone conversations of consular staff and attachés revealed the Japanese ambassador had received urgent instructions from Tokyo. From now on, the embassy staff would have to observe 'formality' in their relations with British officials, and British journalists would have limited access to them. 'Friendships' with British subjects were to be 'curtailed' and most importantly the staff had to be ready to leave London at 'short notice'.

Already, from military intelligence and diplomatic sources, the Foreign Office was well aware that after a special conference on 19 January the Japanese leadership had resolved to 'intimidate' Thailand and Vichy Indochina into a peace deal. The intention was that Japanese forces could then be deployed there for use in immediate operations against the Dutch Indies.

Throughout January 1941, Foreign Minister Matsuoka Yosuke had boasted that the alliance with Berlin and Rome was the 'central pillar of Japan's foreign policy'. He put emphasis on the fact that the Greater East Asia Co-Prosperity Sphere included the colonial possessions of the European powers in the Far East.[1] In secret consultations Matsuoka disagreed with the army leadership's desire for a rapid advance in south-east Asia; as an imperialist diplomat, he looked for a show of force with exercises. He did not want the United States and Britain to be provoked into war.

On 20 January, the Foreign Affairs Ministry in Tokyo cabled the Japanese Consul-General in Singapore:

> ... future intelligence and propaganda policy will be mainly directed southwards in order to secure supplies of war commodities. Promotion of agitation, political plots, propaganda and intelligence (particularly naval and military) must be expedited and intensified so that new order in greater East Asia may be expedited.[2]

This was intercepted and promptly decrypted by British intelligence and forwarded to the Foreign Office (on 23 January), together with other intercepted communications between the Japanese minister in Bangkok and Tokyo. There was a clear intention of the Japanese military to acquire bases in Thailand.

Dutch military intelligence forwarded their British counterparts intercepted Japanese communications demonstrating preparations for war and espionage activities in the colony.[3] A key source of military intelligence on the Japanese deployments was the radio direction-finding equipment of the FECB at Singapore. On 1 February, intercepted telephone conversations were added to the list of secret intelligence sources, and the governor of East Java informed the British consul in Surabaya that an intercepted telephone conversation between two prominent Japanese at Surabaya and Lawang 'referred to news just received that Japanese attack would take place February 10th'. The Japanese were 'immediately arrested'; they denied everything. The governor reassured the consul that in case of war he could round up all Japanese in the colony.[4] The specific date and the reliability of tapping phones as a secret source made officials in London rather nervous.

Throughout the crisis, MI5 monitored the phone conversations of counsellors and attachés only; not of the ambassador himself. They were generally interested in a few subjects of discussion: actual instructions received from Tokyo, grave predictions of the next set of instructions, rumours of a Japanese diplomatic mission in Europe, and assessments of the evolving Anglo-Japanese relations and Japanese strategy in the Far East.

The Far East Combined Bureau (FECB) listed the 'essential preliminaries' for a Japanese offensive in the South Seas: troops and transport concentrations, 'unusual' naval movements and the concentration of shore-based aircraft. They listed as 'non-essential preliminaries' the Anglo-Japanese diplomatic exchanges, the declarations of restriction of entry into sea or ground areas where troops or transport were concentrated, the evacuation of Japanese nationals and the reduction in commercial and financial activity, as well as the interruption of communications, sabotage, 'side show or feints' (incidents in other countries) and propaganda. The 'non-essential' preliminaries did not make it possible to discern a date for the commencement of hostilities, but 'a number of them taken together should give useful information, though possibly of a negative character'.[5]

As far as the FECB were concerned, the true sources of information warning of a Japanese attack would be: sightings by British and Allied men-of-war and merchant ships; sightings by British reporting officers; Chinese military intelligence; US Naval and military intelligence; Dutch intelligence; wireless transmissions and direction-finding intelligence; 'Y' (intercepts); and the SIS. It was possible for Japanese warships to be sighted early in the seas close to Hong Kong, Singapore and the Dutch East Indies; merchant ships could report on Japanese warships, but it would take precious time, even if the reporting proved reliable. For the time being, American gunboats on the Yangtze 'proved uncommunicative' in reporting to the Royal Navy the movements of the Imperial Japanese fleet.

The FECB believed that 'Chinese military intelligence, if worked up to rather more than its present state of liaison with us, should provide early information regarding troop movements in the Canton area. Information from other areas e.g. Formosa and Hainan is uncertain and usually much delayed.' Formosa was reported by spies as being a key base for Japanese forces. As for other sources, 'US intelligence up to the present had given little but alarmist and baseless rumours' and the Anglo-Dutch intelligence cooperation was 'fairly close [but] the material received so far does not represent an appreciable addition to our own'. Dutch air reconnaissance could locate the Japanese forces in their offensive operations 'but this may only give us the shortest notice'. With reference to intercepts of wireless transmissions, 'there is a strong probability that major Fleet movements from Japan would be detected before the units reached Formosa'. The FECB was pessimistic as to the contribution of the SIS: 'It is extremely doubtful that SIS, through either its own agents or its foreign contacts, will give any reliable warning of attack.'[6]

The FECB was emphatic that enemy troop concentrations would be noted in Formosa and Hainan while the Japanese would avoid deploying troops in Canton to 'avoid publicity'. Pessimism was expressed yet again: 'Reliable information of a concentration in Hainan or Formosa is most unlikely to be obtained in time to be of use.' With reference to the concentration of transport ships, 'the most likely' locations were the Pescadores and Yulinghan (on South Hainan). Japanese ships could steam in from the Pescadores, Yulinghan, the Dutch East Indies, Borneo, Thailand or even Malaya 'without any certainty of their being detected until in sight of land'. Intercepts of Japanese ship communications and direction-finding intelligence would reveal 'unusual naval movements' like the reinforcement of the fleet from squadrons coming from Japan. As for the concentration of shore-based aircraft, the normal Japanese procedure was to deploy squadrons from Japan, China or elsewhere in airfields for attack. Nevertheless, it was 'most improbable that the aircraft would be unloaded and assembled further south than Hainan or Takao (in Formosa). These bases are too far from the probable Japanese objectives to be used for the attack.'[7]

On 5 February, the Joint Intelligence Subcommittee assessed all available secret and open intelligence to decide the extent to which 'essential' preliminary and 'non-essential' preliminary preparations

were put in place. The committee concluded that Japan initially planned to move against the Dutch East Indies 'in the near future'. The first draft of conclusions predicted that British colonies and possessions would face a Japanese invasion within a few months. The threat would combine with a German offensive in Europe – probably against the Balkans – or the invasion of Britain.

By the end of the same day, however, the conclusions had changed. The Chiefs of Staff Committee examined the draft of the Joint Intelligence Subcommittee and reasoned that 'the gravity of the situation in the Far East, to which the Joint Intelligence Subcommittee have drawn our attention in their report, is now reinforced by a most secret intelligence report'.[8]

This, of course, was MI5's intelligence from the tapping the phone lines inside the Japanese embassy that very day.[9] A concerned Anthony Eden cabled Halifax, newly installed as ambassador in Washington:

Evidence is accumulating that the Japanese may already have decided to push on southward, even if this means war. Press reports indicate that Japan is using her position as mediators between Thailand and Indo-China to gain (besides a preferential economic position) naval base at Camranh Bay, air bases in Southern Indo-China, and control of Indo-China customs. There is also reason to suppose that some military agreement with Thailand directed against our territories and the Netherlands East Indies is under consideration. Following are a few 'straws in the wind': Sir R. Craigie reports general feeling amongst Japanese that crisis in the Far East will come within the next few weeks; cancellation of sailings of Japanese ships to the United States and reports of commandeering of ships by the Japanese government. Reports so far received from our naval authorities in Singapore do not confirm that general measures of this kind have been taken; continuance of Japanese supplies of munitions to Thailand; intercepted telephone conversation between two Japanese at Surabaya and Lawang to the effect that Japanese attack would take place 10th February governor of East Java attaches no undue importance to conversation, but thinks it cannot be disregarded; statement by Japanese naval officers to students of Malay language that time was very short indeed (from Tokyo); [cargo ship] *Asaka Maru* taking naval mission to Berlin. Time-table of this ship seems to indicate action not contemplated until mid-March; reports from French source in Indo-China of [Japanese military] concentrations in Formosa and Hainan. While some of these indications may be conclusive in themselves, they suggest that further move is impending, and I shall be glad if you will communicate them in confidence to State Department. United States naval attaché in London has been given most of this information. Sir Craigie ... has drawn attention once more to the danger of the Japanese squeezing out Singapore through Indo-China and Thailand...[10]

On 6 February, having read the MI5 report, informed Halifax:

We now have sure indication that members of Japanese embassy here were warned on February 4th to reduce to the minimum contacts with British friends here, and to hold themselves ready to leave London at short notice. Meeting was held at the embassy yesterday to discuss supplementary instructions which evidently relate to some scheme for co-operation with Germany advocated by Army Party in Japan...inform State Department in strict confidence.[11]

The same day, the tapped phone conversations of increasingly excited Japanese diplomats revealed rather vaguely that 'news of some impending Japanese action is expected in London shortly. This news to come from Tokyo as a result of reports from Berlin and Washington.' The report listing the intelligence included analysis from other sources, creating the impression that the monitored conversations covered all the areas narrated. The summary read:

It seems certain the Japanese government has made up its mind as to future policy. The implication is that this policy is actively pro-German and anti-British. An agreement with Russia is important to Japan in her proposed venture, and some progress has been made in this sense. Mentioned by

Matsuoka and not denied by Tass news agency. It is unlikely USA will take any active part in the war or will interfere against Japan. Japan acted as a mediator in the Thailand-Indo-China despite from motives of self-interest... There is some doubt as to how much the USA have heard of impending Japanese action. There is some annoyance felt over recent official Japanese instructions that friendships and relations with British subjects are to be severed.[12]

At 9 p.m. that evening, Eden sent another urgent message to Halifax:

From same source [tapped phone lines] we now learn that Japanese embassy are expecting the notification from Tokyo 'at any time', though there is some indication that this depends on news to be expected from Berlin and Washington before February 18th, and that the Japanese government have made up their mind on a course arranged with Berlin which caused misgivings to some members of the embassy. There are hints that agreement is being reached with Russia and with Chinese communists. Action contemplated will be carefully planned so as not to affect interests of United States, who are not expected to move. Movement of United States fleet is at present regarded as routine manoeuvres. It is stated that Japanese mediation in Thailand-Indo-China dispute is only part of a large scheme. Members of embassy are actually speaking of 'war with Great Britain, if indeed it is on us'. I have given substance of these telegrams to Mr [Harry] Hopkins [the influential advisor] who thinks that you should try to see President [Roosevelt] and Mr [Cordell] Hull [the US Secretary of State] together on the subject. If United States government could order any naval movement that would clearly not be of ordinary routine nature, that might show Japanese government that United States government were watching closely trend of events. [13]

Eden and the War Office were well aware that Malaya did not host sufficient British forces to confront Japanese aggression, so Eden did not want to introduce economic sanctions lest they 'provoke' Tokyo. His options were limited. London had to employ propaganda and diplomacy to deter Tokyo from invading British colonies as well as setting up bases in Thailand and Indochina. Propaganda included pieces in the press warning of impending war as well as leaking the rumour that Britain was about to dispatch a Royal Navy fleet to Singapore with a mission to fight the Japanese, which reached the ever-vigilant Japanese embassy in London. The evolving British diplomatic strategy also included putting pressure on Washington to accept that the Japanese menace must be countered by decisive Allied diplomatic action.[14] Eden was influenced by the gloomy assessment of Permanent Undersecretary Sir Alexander Cadogan, who confided in his diary on 6 February: 'Some more very bad-looking Jap[anese] telephone conversations, from which it appears that they have decided to attack us.'[15]

The same day, Hopkins was informed of the crisis by the Foreign Office; his reply was that Washington would 'react immediately' to any further Japanese aggression in south-east Asia.[16]

The tapped phone conversations continued producing intelligence that was summarised together with other information. On 7 February, the summary read:

> Military members of a [Japanese] 'mission' are to go from Berlin to Moscow. One member of the mission is to go to Lisbon, staying at Vichy on the way for a talk with Japanese and General Huntziger [commander of Vichy land forces and Minister of War]. After delivering his report at Lisbon he will go to Madrid and thence back to Berlin. The instructions received from Tokyo to break off friendships with British subjects must be carried out carefully so as not to arouse suspicion. Journalists and official friends must be avoided. An important cable is expected from Tokyo soon after 14th February.[17]

Meanwhile, the Joint Intelligence Subcommittee concluded that a propaganda campaign with press articles and releases could 'deter Japan, showing the world that war was imminent'. The Chiefs of Staff Committee proposed putting strong pressure on the Americans to side with Britain openly.[18]

The same day, Eden summoned the Japanese ambassador, Shigemitsu Mamoru, to the Foreign Office. He protested about the 'deterioration' of bilateral relations, referring to the speeches of Foreign Minister Matsuoka and the advance in south-east Asia with the attempted Japanese 'mediation' of the Thai–French dispute. Surprisingly, he also mentioned rumours of war circulating in Tokyo that had been reported by Craigie. Shigemitsu was not expecting this and seemed surprised. Nevertheless, he stated that it was a British overreaction; no war was coming. He replied:

It is geographically quite natural that Japan should hold the leading position in East Asia, and this cannot be helped. It is no different from the special interests which Britain and the United States of America feel in the neighboring geographical countries … In stating the crisis in Anglo-Japanese relations, you do not try to understand the other party's standpoint but rather find fault with the Japan's policy [sic] and lay the blame on Japan.[19]

On 8 February, the tapped phone conversations revealed more:

Considerable importance is being attached by the Japanese embassy staff to current reference to Japan in British press. Particular points being watched for are suggestions that British government is showing extra interest or anxiety. References to the 'mission' from Berlin. Japanese know that Japan is attracting the attention of official British circles in London at present. An important naval investigation has been made. The results are to be cabled to Tokyo from Lisbon.[20]

Understandably, this provoked confusion and further gloomy assessments at MI5 and the Foreign Office.

The next day, Eden rushed to issue instructions to Ambassador Craigie in Tokyo:

In the event of war, your staff and staffs of consulates under your superintendence will be of great value to our war effort. I am somewhat concerned lest Japanese military authorities who are doubtless aware of this fact may influence Japanese government to prevent departure, in particular of consuls, and possibly to intern them for the duration of the war. While it is true that we could hold a number of Japanese consuls throughout the empire as hostages, the loss to Japan on balance would not be so great as the loss to us. Your Ministry of Information staff will also be of great value, and if, as appears not unlikely, their activities are curbed by Japanese interference to the extent that they are unable to function effectively, it is for consideration whether it would not be better for them, or at any rate for key members such as [Herbert Vere] Redman [the head of the information department of the embassy], to leave unobtrusively for Singapore while there is still time. As regards consuls, it is necessary to weigh the advantage of maintaining a full staff at maximum efficiency until the last moment against the disadvantage of losing men who, in view of the very small number of persons available with a real knowledge of Japan and the Japanese, would be of the utmost value if war breaks out. Any general exodus at this stage cannot be contemplated as it would attract attention and cause undue alarm. Nevertheless, I should like you to bear in mind the possibility of getting our key men away. You may think it well for this purpose to grant leave in suitable cases and make any moves which you may consider desirable. I need hardly impress upon you the necessity for keeping this matter strictly secret.[21]

Redman was a key member of the embassy but was not covered by diplomatic immunity; in the coming months, he would be arrested and harshly treated but survived.

While the situation was unfolding, tensions had been increasing between Ambassador Shigemitsu and members of the British government. Shigemitsu had met with Foreign Office undersecretary R. A. Butler, with the result that Permanent Undersecretary Cadogan fumed: 'Like all Japanese, he thinks he can put over the most blatant nonsense...'[22]

Cadogan and others, including Eden, were predisposed against Shigemitsu, viewing him as utterly dishonest. With the benefit of hindsight, however, it is clear that the ambassador had been trying to stabilise Anglo-Japanese relations since he began his tenure. Historian Antony Best remarked that Shigemitsu 'was neither the

Anglophile liberal portrayed by his admirers nor the militarist diplomat painted by his detractors. He was first and foremost a nationalist, and as Ambassador to the Court of Saint James from 1938 to 1941 he did his best to improve relations with Britain on terms beneficial to Japan.'[23]

The smooth-mannered ambassador believed that Imperial Japan could carve out influence and territories in the Far East, from Manchuria to Indochina, by easing out the declining British Empire. He was a man in the mould of Yamagata Aritomo, attempting to employ nineteenth-century imperial strategy and diplomacy in the late 1930s.

On 12 February, the tapped phone lines revealed Japanese fears of 'leakage of information'. The same day, the Director of Naval Intelligence reported:

> There is no unusual disposition of the Japanese mercantile Marine ... if Japan has decided to take hostile action on, say, 1st March, it is unlikely that any indication of such action could be expected from shipping movements more than a fortnight before, i.e. on about 15th February. [24]

Meanwhile, on the same day, Ohashi Chuichi, the Vice Minister for Foreign Affairs, had a conference with Ambassador Craigie in Tokyo. The Japanese official, who was deeply frustrated with the British press campaign, denied that Japan was planning to go to war against Britain.[25]

The daily summary continued its darkening tone on 13 February:

> There is a strong feeling that war is inevitable. The British military situation in the Far East is considered weak. Appearance of articles in the British press on Japan are taken as a sign of uneasiness in this country. Japan will give the USA no case for declaring war against her. Instructions have been issued to certain Japanese consulates in England to destroy all papers etc. which might be of use to British government in the event of war.[26]

On 14 February, Craigie wrote Eden from Tokyo: 'No evidence available in Tokyo suggests however that Japanese are preparing for an immediate attack on British territory either in·conjunction with German offensive elsewhere or independent of it.'[27] The same day, Butler also wrote to Eden: 'Now that the press has had its first fling on the Far East, we are trying to control it, particularly over the weekend. We do not want it to go too far.'[28] A follower of Halifax, Butler disliked Eden and had gained Churchill's ire by urging appeasement with Hitler.

The summary for 15 February suggested a changing landscape:

> T. [presumably military attaché General Tatsumi Eiichi] says that Counsellor Kam had been full of elation at the prospect of going to war with Britain but was now angered at the thought that Japan would now climb down. T. thought that though such a course would be a humiliation it was nevertheless wise at this time not to enter into the war. T. went on to say that the present time was not so much in Japan's favour as last October or September, but that when Britain was engaged in a desperate tussle with Germany would be Japan's time. Kam opined that when the British were heavily engaged elsewhere and had allowed their vigilance to relax in the Far East, Japan could easily strike. Sooner or later, Japan must fight Britain. T. considered the crisis had not altogether simmered down and could not understand how Britain had become aware of what was likely to happen. Kam said there must have been a leakage of information and was amazed at the speed with which HMG (His Majesty's Government) had acted and the rapidity of the British press campaign. He was sure it was the attitude of the US that had caused events to be held up ... T. ... could not understand how Britain had become aware of what was likely to happen ... but said the Amb. [Shigemitsu] seemed relieved and was like a man who had a load lifted from him.[29]

On 15 February, intercepts of diplomatic communications resulting from US intelligence officials providing a Purple cipher machine to the GC&CS at Bletchley Park indicated that Foreign Minister Matsuoka was planning a visit to Europe. Churchill himself read this intercept and concluded that war could not be imminent if Matsuoka was visiting.[30] Craigie had a meeting with Matsuoka that day, and the Foreign Minister reaffirmed that Japan had no intentions to wage war on Britain. The Japanese foreign secretary 'was surprised to learn of the undue concern of the secretary of state, based no doubt on information from British embassy, Tokyo and other sources; there was no way of ascertaining what kind of information the British government had been receiving, but the minister for foreign affairs would like to state that, so far as he could see, there were no grounds for alarming views on the situation in East Asia'.[31]

On 16 February, Churchill wrote to Cadogan:

These [tapped] conversations and the delayed telegram have the air of being true, and make one feel the earlier conversations were real. If so, there is a decided easement, and the danger for the moment seems to have passed. The delayed telegram strongly favours this as naturally if they were not going to act, they would try to make amends to the Germans and Italians by sending their man on a diplomatic demonstration. Altogether I must feel very considerably assured. I have always been doubtful whether they would face it.[32]

Matsuoka hinted at British espionage producing unreliable intelligence. Moreover, he 'could not be but anxious about the movements of the British and United States Governments in their attempt to expedite and enlarge warlike preparations in order to meet any supposed contingencies on the Pacific and South Seas'.[33] The same day, the phone tapping revealed that the Japanese military attaché had met with his Soviet counterpart in London. Monitoring the conversations revealed a great deal:

[The attaché] is excited at news that there are 10 Japanese Divisions concentrated round Hong Kong but considers the report exaggerated. Kam (a Japanese embassy counsellor) is certain USA will keep out of war and that any joint declarations by USA, Great Britain, Holland and Australia will be bluff. Kam states recent Japanese change of attitude is undeniably for a purpose. Kam believes Eden has quietly gone abroad. Discussions on possibility of Great Britain negotiations for peace follows considered unlikely possibility of Japanese attack on Canada is considered, but it is thought this would bring in the USA. Certain code words are passed Yan (another counsellor) to Kam.[34]

On 17 February, a news bulletin from the Kuomintang's press agency read, 'Six Japanese divisions are now stationed on Hainan Island in French Indochina and Spratly Islands and Four Divisions are in Formosa.' Hong Kong was in danger.[35]

On 20 February, the monitoring of the phone lines inside the Japanese embassy divulged more:

> Kam considers that we know too much. Alternatively [he thinks] the British press campaign is a bluff. Japanese ambassador has taken particular note of final paragraph of the leading article in the [*Daily*] *Telegraph*, as being rather significant. Reference is also made to an article in the *Yorkshire Post*.[36]

The last paragraph of the *Telegraph* article, 'Dragon's Teeth', published the same day, read:

> ... it is only to be wished that Japan would show the way by restoring the peace she has been disturbing for the past five years ... It is she who started the war in China, and it is she who can restore peace to-morrow by the simple act of liquidating that aggression. The 'sphere of common prosperity' she so urgently desires can be had for the asking, but as her five years experience might have taught her, the only practicable means of attaining it is by peace, not conquest. She has found that the dragon's teeth, once sown, produce crops of all manner of unexpected trouble. Only she can uproot them, but if she could bring herself to such a step the obstacles to a mutually advantageous understanding with Britain and the United States would swiftly vanish.

The *Yorkshire Post* article, meanwhile, concerned the 8th Australian Infantry Division, which had departed Sydney on 4 February aboard liner-turned-troopship *Queen Mary*. On 18 February, the division had reached Singapore. (Nevertheless, for the *Daily*

Telegraph 'Malaya is the last place in the world most of them expected to see'.). The *Post* article that troubled Kam read:

> The Royal Navy has competed a fine piece of transportation work in bringing over the Pacific a giant convoy of Australian troops to Malaya. It is probably the largest military force that has crossed the Pacific Ocean, and although there is no opposing fleet in those waters, it is known that German raiders are afloat on the Australian route ... Admiral Layton, Commander in Chief of the China Station, states the arrival of the Force is another demonstration of command of the sea, and of the ability of the Navy to escort troops to any part of the British Empire ... It would seem that the great convoy crossed before the Japanese were aware of the movement. Tokyo says that, if any considerable force had arrived, a statement will be made ... American interest in the Australians' arrival is the keener because of President Roosevelt's announcement that naval areas in the Pacific have been zones off and all stations linked up in co-operation with the British ... The force which has arrived in Malaya is of a special kind, made up of volunteers from all the States. The equipment is of Australian manufacture, including the field guns. This makes the despatch of the force historic as a self-contained army, staffed and provided with no outside aid, and is a reminder of what Australia will do as the war goes on...[37]

Also on 20 February, Craigie cabled the Foreign Office:

> ... the situation is today easier than it was a week ago, and that the combined firm stand by the United States, Australia, the Netherlands and ourselves has had a most salutary effect in calling bluff of the Japanese military is the opinion unanimously held by all colleagues with whom I am in contact.[38]

On 24 February, the monitoring of phone conversations produced confusing intelligence: 'An arrangement is made by which an Englishman [no name given] is to be picked up at a secret

rendezvous for a conversation with the Japanese ambassador.'³⁹
The next day, phone conversations revealed:

Kam says that Japanese ambassador has decided to make his preparations without waiting for details from Lisbon – otherwise there may not be time. Kam feels that Matsuoka has taken up an uncompromising attitude and has made Japan's position quite clear, particularly in view of his statement that Japan must control Oceania. Kam adds that doubts as to whether this term includes Australia, Philippines and NEI (Netherlands East Indies) will soon be resolved ... admiration is expressed [by Japanese in embassy] for Churchill who is considered a far greater man than Hitler.⁴⁰

An intercepted cable from the Foreign Ministry in Tokyo to the Japanese Consul-General in Sydney, Australia demonstrated the response of the Japanese:

All talk of impending crisis in Far East is nothing more than British propaganda aimed at winning over American public opinion, checking Japan's southward advance and hindering improvements of her relations with Thailand and Indo-China.⁴¹

There followed a lull in leaked communications, prompting some speculation.

In mid-May 1941, Major H. I. Chapman of the MI2c at the War Office made a bid to assess the value of secret intelligence in the crisis as he was 'becoming more and more sceptical of the authenticity of this information'. He concluded:

(a) A number of the conversations do not ring true. This point I have made before.
(b) between 5 Feb and 25 Feb we had a spate of what appeared to be very significant information. Since then – i.e. over a period of nearly three months – we have had only one report. These dates are interesting. 5 Feb was after the Far Eastern Committee had decided from information from 'open' sources that our relations with Japan were

likely to become critical, and the period 5-25th Feb corresponds fairly accurately with that covered by our own 'anti-Japanese' propaganda campaign in the press. It seems highly unlikely that these conversations would begin and end so abruptly with such a curious incidence of dates. It would be more natural for them to begin gradually, rise to a crescendo, then die away – again gradually.

(c) B.J.'s [intercepts] and original material of the same kind have been searched in vain for any confirmation…

(d) Two days after Items 2 + 3 [the information for instructions of embassy officials to distance from British officials] were received I was invited to lunch by the Japanese. I have since often seen them and have noticed no coolness.

(e) The reference to General Huntziger in Item 13 [the visit of a Japanese diplomat from Berlin before reaching Lisbon] is not understood.

(f) The 10 divisions [to be deployed near Hong Kong] referred to in Item 32 is such an obvious mistake that a Japanese officer would have contradicted it.

(g) I understand MI5 followed up Item 43 [the secret rendezvous of an unknown 'Englishman' with the Japanese ambassador, overheard on 24 February] without success.

(h) I am told that the 'reception' of information from this source is very bad, and that even English is not at all clear. In the present case the language difficulties would be considerable.

(i) I am told that one officer [of MI5] employed on duties in connexion (*sic*) with this type of information recently voluntarily resigned as he felt certain no proper results could be obtained.

On the other hand it must be agreed that certain items are undoubtedly true and accurate. The conclusion which I am forced make is that there is a definite possibility that some of the reports we have had are much more highly coloured than they should be, and, in some cases, have given entirely false impressions. So far our general conclusions on Japanese intentions have not materially been influenced by these reports, as they were made on evidence available to us from 'open' sources, before receipt of these reports. It is possible however that should we get more startling reports in the near future, our conclusions may be influenced. This would be dangerous.[42]

The operator/translator heard the conversations of officials and staff as they narrated the instructions, and he translated their words. The Japanese sounded excited as they talked about war; thus they themselves 'coloured' their remarks. The embassy staff's war rumours and talk mirrored the war rumours reported to Eden by Craigie. Most significantly, the intercepted phone conversations of Japanese officials in in Java talking about war confirmed London's fear.

The foreign secretary, the permanent secretary and the chiefs of staff assigned primary importance to the intercepted conversations, which supported intelligence from military and diplomatic sources suggesting Japan was about to go to war against Britain in the Far East. Nevertheless, the intelligence received from the phone tapping did not meet the criteria of 'essential preliminaries' and 'non-essential preliminaries' prior to a Japanese attack as listed in December 1940 and employed in assessment by the Joint Intelligence Subcommittee.

The crisis of February 1941 showed that the conversations of embassy officials and staff were not gospel. Indeed, the panic of the Japanese in the embassy caused panic at MI5 and eventually at the Foreign Office, culminating in Eden summoning Ambassador Shigemitsu.

The phone tapping reports were of great value because they seemed to confirm earlier reports of Japanese aggression. It must be noted also that if Eden was given the document entitled 'Japanese Intentions' that is included in file WO 208/855 he would have been quite misled, for in the listed 'items of intelligence' the information gleaned from phone tapping was grouped together with other intelligence, creating the impression that everything listed came from phone tapping.

The lesson learned from this crisis, which was more than a mere 'war scare', was that propaganda alone could provide a deterrent. It could have gone better; both Craigie and the Foreign Office were unaware of the indecisiveness evident in discussions between the top Japanese imperial navy and figures, and this was the result of espionage in Tokyo having been blocked for years by the likes of Piggott. Craigie depended on his own confidential contacts, who were officials.

But who was the mysterious Englishman due to meet with the ambassador? Guy Liddell, director of counter-espionage at MI5, offers some insight in his diary entry for 11 December 1941:

> I returned at midday. While I was away Special Material indicated that an Englishman had correspondence which was of a compromising nature and had to be destroyed. He was in conversation with Nakimura [the military attaché]. It was felt that the Englishman could only be Lord Sempill and his apartment and office were subsequently raided. Only a few Air Ministry and Admiralty reports of no particularly interest were recovered. He has, of course, committed a technical breach of the regulations but we are fairly confident that he had not retained the documents for any ulterior purpose. There was a scare later in that the ambassador's house in Grosvenor Square contained a transmitter. Post Office wireless vans were quite confident. It transpired eventually that the transmissions were from a house occupied by the Poles in an adjoining street. The Foreign Office was quite prepared to let us go in if we found anything to search all the other embassy premises. They were fortified in this idea by the news that our chancery in Tokyo had been searched for wireless equipment. The Foreign Office is now considering whether we should in any case search all Japanese embassy premises, on grounds of reciprocity.[43]

It is not improbable that during the February crisis the ambassador asked for a secret meeting with Sempill, a member of the British political elite who could communicate to him the government's intentions. However, Sempill could not evade MI5 surveillance.

16

HIS LORDSHIP

In the circles of the elite there existed a maze of lies and truth, a combination of the leaking of classified intelligence to known adversaries and casual gossip overheard. Information about British foreign policy and strategy regarding Japan was kept under lock and key in classified Foreign Office memoranda, but the gist of information – that Britain was not willing to confront Japan – was aired at dozens of dinner parties and balls and found its way back to the Japanese.

William Francis Forbes-Sempill, 19th Lord Sempill, was born on 24 September 1893. Scion of a Scottish noble family, he attended Eton and worked as an apprentice at the Rolls-Royce factory in 1910. At the outbreak of the First World War, he joined the Royal Flying Corps as a second lieutenant under probation, graduating from fighter pilot to experimental pilot the following year. In August 1915 he was appointed to instruction duties, but at the end of that year he resigned his commission and took service with the Royal Naval Air Service, soon becoming a squadron leader. In April 1918, the Royal Air Force was established and Sempill was appointed deputy director of its personnel department; that year, during a high-risk flight, he skilfully navigated his plane and was awarded the Air Force Cross for his troubles. He then served under the Air Ministry before being seconded to the Ministry of Munitions. In 1919 he retired from active service, becoming a test pilot and a well-connected public figure, and it was at this point that he was sent on the aforementioned civilian mission to Japan to train officers and encourage the Japanese to purchase British aircraft.

In the 1920s and 1930s, in the full knowledge that Japan was antagonistic to Britain in the Far East, Lord Sempill took payment from Japan in exchange for technological intelligence. He breached the Official Secrets Act. Nevertheless, he was no spy in the 'mole-in-the-elite' pattern. Rather, he was pessimistic about the future of the British Empire in the east and felt it was a good time to make money in commercial activities and consultancies with the Japanese companies that were rising to replace the empire. In a self-fulfilling prophecy, his gossip about politics and official policy helped convince the Japanese that Britain was weak in the Far East.

All the while, the SIS and MI5 proved meticulous in shadowing Sempill as he leaked technical intelligence on British aircraft. On 1 February 1924, MI5 intercepted a letter from Sempill addressed to Captain Toyoda Teijiro, the Japanese naval attaché in London. He wrote that in an earlier letter he had given him 'particulars regarding large bombs'. He warned the Japanese of 'the moves that are being made against you'.[1] Evidently, he was trying to gain the trust of Toyoda, who was disappointed by the recent lapse of the Anglo-Japanese Treaty. Sempill had returned from his mission in Japan and for some time styled himself as 'acting captain of the Imperial Japanese Navy' despite knowing that the Admiralty was suspicious of Japanese naval programs.

According to MI5, Sempill was 'on terms of closest friendship' with Toyoda, who 'is engaged in military espionage':

> ... the correspondence between Sempill and Toyoda leaves no room for doubt that Sempill is allowing himself to be used by Toyoda for the purpose of securing confidential information which Toyoda could not otherwise secure. It is also clear that Sempill is aware of the impropriety of what he is doing and that precautious are being taken by the two that the facts shall not come to light.[2]

Toyoda, greedy for information that might further his career in Tokyo, was not a security-sensitive spymaster. Sempill had to instruct him to 'be very careful how you use any information you get and don't couple the name of any individuals with it. I will tell you more when we meet again but I know just exactly how the wind blows, and the need for being super cautious.'³

On 15 May 1924, Toyoda wrote to Sempill thanking him for offering him drawings and specifications, stating he would 'mention Sempill's views with regards to the advantages which might be derived from the Blackburn School type Flying Boat as a training machine' for the IJN. The Air Ministry was informed by MI5 about this, but they replied that it was 'of no particular interest'. In July, Toyoda requested details of a sound-detection device that the British were keeping secret; he also asked for information about improvements to parachutes, the Handley-Page aircraft and other flying machines, and at the end of the month he received from Sempill details on landing and flying the Plover aeroplane with a Jaguar engine and information about fighters that could land on decks. In October, Sempill informed Toyoda of an aeroplane engine classified as 'secret' by the Air Ministry, and in the same month he told Toyoda that Air Vice Marshal Arthur Vyell Vyvyan was about to retire and suggested 'he would be invaluable to the I.J.N.' Nevertheless, he urged Toyoda not to contact Vyvyan for the time being.

The SIS was aware that Sempill was codenamed 'Kamumu' in outward cables,⁴ In other cables he was referred as 'Colonel Sempiru'.

As 1925 dawned Sempill, codenamed 'Kamumu' or 'Colonel Sempiru' in Japanese cables,⁵ continued to provide Toyoda with information. Just before the year began he warned his contact that 'trouble will be avoided if Toyoda knows in advance the moves [of anti-Japanese circles in the government and business] that are being made'. Toyoda in turn offered Sempill a report of naval aviation in Japan in January, while Sempill wrote to Toyoda of a Mackie generator ordered by the Air Ministry in April. The Mackie generator was deemed 'secret' but soon there was 'nothing secret about it ... the [Air Ministry was] anxious that it be taken up commercially'.⁶ Toyoda was interested in a wireless signalling device and a testing apparatus and asked Sempill for particulars in May and June before writing to thank Sempill for the information he had provided. Toyoda was then introduced to a retired commander of the Royal Navy, Boothby, who was an expert on airships. Sempill for his part asked Toyoda in July whether a particular aeroplane engine was employed in Japan because 'Rolls-Royce have asked me to advise them and I naturally to advise them to your greatest advantage'. In November, Toyoda asked Sempill for details of the Royal Navy aeroplanes under development, assuring him, 'I am confident that so far as lies in your power you will do your best to help me.'[7]

Employing his charisma, Sempill, in cooperation with executives of the Westland Company, arranged for Japanese 'patent agents' to take a look at the classified 'secret "Dreadnought" machine'.[8]

Toyoda was issuing tasks to Sempill, who was eager to maintain his relationship with the Japanese. Toyoda tasked Sempill with answering a questionnaire on deck-landing technology, remarking, 'I am setting you a somewhat arduous and lengthy task ... there are certain machines of which you will be bound to withhold details in accordance with the request of the Air Ministry.'[9]

Sir Victor Wellesley at the Foreign Office tried to persuade Kell, then director general of MI5, to prosecute Sempill.[10] Kell was cautious; he could not take Sempill to court owing to a 'lack of any definite piece of secret information'.[11] Nevertheless, MI5 would continue watching Sempill and the modest payments he received from Toyoda for his consultancy services. Toyoda listed as 'aviation investigation expenditure' payments to Sempill: £200 for 1924; £100 for 1925; £75 for 1926; £75 for 1927. Intercepted correspondence offered MI5 a full understanding of the contract between the business-first Sempill and the Japanese.[12]

Aware of the suspicions following him, Sempill hit back by seeking an inquiry in which he could clear his name. He wrote to Piggott, then serving with military intelligence at the War Office: 'Had I been acting in the manner suggested by official action [i.e., MI5 monitoring], I would never have allowed information to be transmitted by post.'[13] Kell directed his officers to inform Piggott about the 'true facts', and Piggott agreed, replying to Sempill.[14] The cleared and amended letter from Piggott read:

> I think that you will admit that you were guilty of certain indiscretions, and you can scarcely be surprised that H.M. Government took a serious view of the affair ... your wisest course for the future is not to attempt to re-open the matter,

in any way, but to take case to proceed with the utmost discretion in similar circumstances, should they arise again ... In due course it will, I feel sure, be appreciated in the proper quarters that you are genuinely anxious to act as a loyal British subject in any dealings in which you may be engaged.[15]

Indirectly, Piggott revealed to Sempill that MI5's case against him was weak. Moreover, he gave no indication that Japan was a hostile nation regarding its positions in the Far East. Evidently Piggott had his own motives; his personal mission to promote good relations with Japan meant a scandal involving Japanese espionage could never reach the public on his watch. Around this time he supported Kell's election as chairman of the Japan Society in London, but he stood down after a year.[16]

After the affair died down, Sempill spent the 1930s enjoying the life of an aristocrat and business consultant for the Japanese, who gradually lost interest in British aviation technology. During this time, no intercepts of Japanese cables showed Sempill sharing secret intelligence with Tokyo.

In October 1939, Sempill joined the Department of Air Materiel as an acting commander in the Royal Naval Volunteer Reserve. He later claimed that he offered his services and the Fifth Sea Lord of the Admiralty replied, 'Come at once.' Sempill stated that he was 'instructed to organise a section of which I was always the sole member, dealing with aircraft accidents and maintenance and general technical intelligence'.[17]

Sempill had access to classified 'secret' documents on the procurement, development, testing and acquisition of carrier fighters, and he moved freely in the Admiralty, talking with senior staff. However, by now the Japanese had developed their own naval aviation industry and they were less interested in technical intelligence. By April 1941, Sempill possessed sufficient standing to speak in the House of Lords about American aircraft.[18]

Nevertheless, Sempill maintained his business office and so continued communications with the Japanese naval attaché for the purposes of his business. He worked under a consultancy agreement with the Mitsubishi office in London, and MI5 intercepted letters from Mitsubishi headquarters in Tokyo addressed to their London representative. In the letters there was a clear reference to the 'use both direct and indirect made of Lord Sempill by our Military and Naval Attachés in London'. A payment of £300 was authorized for 1940. MI5 informed naval intelligence of this, and Commander Sheffield of naval intelligence asked Sempill to submit a report on his connection with the Japanese embassy and Mitsubishi. The ageing Kell – who would retire in April 1941 – informed Director of Naval Intelligence Rear-Admiral John Godfrey and Lord Swinton, recently appointed to a new Security Executive, that Sempill might constitute a security threat.[19]

Sempill was asked to resubmit reports on his activities. By autumn an agreement was reached with Sempill:

> ... it is not their [Admiralty's] Lordships' desire to prevent [Sempill] from discussing political and economic questions in political and official circles, but it must ask him to give a written undertaking that ... he will in matters connected with the Services ... have no contact of any kind either with the Japanese or with anyone else who is likely to make use of such information for the benefit of the Japanese ... he may be directed to produce written evidence that he has terminated his connection with the Mitsubishi Company and that no honorarium or fee will be paid to him for services to the Company since the beginning of the war [*sic*].[20]

Swinton agreed with MI5 that Sempill was a security risk for the Admiralty, but to no avail. Godfrey and the Admiralty did not turn against Sempill, but instead 'decided to accept his explanations and continue his employment'. A furious Swinton then wrote to Churchill.[21]

MI5 was shadowing Sempill as the tapping crisis of February 1941 unfolded and an intercept revealed that Japanese assistant military attaché Colonel Nakano Yoshio was seeking intelligence on British ships in the China Sea and was in touch with an unidentified 'European'. At the same time, Japanese ambassador Shigemitsu Mamoru contacted the Foreign Ministry in Tokyo with details about the vessel *Asaka Maru*. This message was intercepted, and senior officers at MI5 concluded that there had to be a secret source inside the Admiralty.

Asaka Maru, 'a special service ship', had steamed from Yokohama to Portugal with a mission to transfer war materiel to Japan. Eden had briefed the war cabinet on 10 February that he feared an escalation of hostilities if the Royal Navy made an attempt at 'contraband control'. Eden pushed for President Roosevelt to be informed about the vessel's mission, and when told Roosevelt was cautious. The same view was taken by the First Sea Lord of the Admiralty, Sir Dudley Pound. Initially Churchill was positive about an SOE sabotage operation. Churchill, reviewed Shigemitsu's intercepted cable:

> ... the ostensible status of the Special service ship in relation to its departure for Bilbao is that she is to load cargo. Measures to deal with the situation that has thus arisen are under careful consideration. When my 'contact' was asked his opinion by the leading Naval Authorities, it was fortunate that I had your instructions as a guide to enable him to reply. Subsequently a report was received from the embassy in Tokyo (ambassador via British naval attaché) and the Government is considering its procedure. It appears that under the control of the Prime Minister Churchill, taking a general view of the relations between the two countries, there will be no interference with the ship's cargo at any rate, and that a carefully worded protest will be made in regard to the recurrence of such circumstances. My 'Contact' has tried to prevent this for some time Great Britain has allowed Brazilian merchant vessels facilities under certain conditions for cargoes of German goods. The German broadcast boasted that the British blockades was meaningless on this account and this is the reason why the British promptly stiffened up their procedure in cases like this. The foregoing was for the private information of the 'Contact' who was told by the British side that they did not wish me to know all the ins and outs of this question. I have arranged as follows with the naval attaché ... Special service ships to be quick and cautious in their movements and to get away from European waters with the least possible delay; the most reticence to be observed in all quarters and, as regards the cargo, to have on the surface nothing whatever to do with it.[22]

The Prime Minister concluded: 'There are some indications that the Japanese anticipated that we should not do more than make a strong protest [of the sailing of *Asaka Maru*].'[23]

London had already experienced a crisis with Japan beginning on 6 January 1940 when the *Asaka Maru* departed from San Francisco. On 21 January she was intercepted by HMS *Liverpool* in international waters off Nozaki, Japan, and fifty Germans were arrested on board. The Japanese government issued a strong protest at that time, citing article 47 of the 1909 London Declaration on neutrality.

For the current crisis, MI5 requested that the Naval Intelligence Division at the Admiralty try to identify the 'contact' of the Japanese ambassador. For MI5, the secret source had 'to be employed at the Admiralty and to have a particular knowledge of Japan or of the Far East in general'.[24] For the SIS and MI5, the source was Sempill,[25] and Godfrey began worrying that Sempill might be the source of the leak. The *Asaka Maru* returned to Yokohama in April, and the Royal Navy did not attempt to intercept her – besides, Eden did not want to hand the Japanese a *casus belli*.

During the same period, Sempill was vocal in his agreement with Piggott and other Japanophiles that there should be a four-power pact involving Japan, Britain, the United States and China. Piggott and Sempill's fellow travellers were A. F. H. Edwardes, an advisor to the Japanese embassy; George Sale, a director of the Sale-Tilney import-export firm; and a retired commander named McGrath who was also director of Cannon Boveri Co.:

This pro-Japanese lobby approached former Japanese ambassador Francis Lindley and Ernest Bevin, then Minister of Labour and National Service, after which Sempill was ecstatic:

We have got absolutely to whip out then and there before we leave that room a paper which can carry on a four power pact idea which I have submitted to Bevin, which he is keen on and agrees to, and say definitely what is to be done and how it is to be done.[26]

On 6 August 1941, Sempill urged the pro-Japanese Lord Maurice Hankey to influence Churchill 'over the head of the Foreign Office'.[27]

MI5 informed Churchill:

... in the course of this intrigue Sempill made a speech in the House of Lords from a memorandum prepared by Edwardes. The Japanese Ambassador Shigemitsu was very enthusiastic about this idea, but according to Edwardes it fell through owing to the obstructionism of Sir Alexander Cadogan.[28]

Cadogan had received reports of intercepted phone calls between Sempill and Edwardes courtesy of MI5, and his view was clear: 'A most amusing talk between Edwardes and that green amateur Sempill, who has evidently been completely hoodwinked by the Japs ... It's amusing, watching the sorry futility of these ridiculous, busybody dupes! Edwardes ought to be jugged & Sempill certified.'[29]

Now under the direction of David Petrie, a veteran of counterintelligence operations against the Japanese, MI5 continued watching Sempill. His business had an overdraft of £13,000, and for Liddell this was yet more proof of a motive for Sempill. On the other hand, Churchill's intelligence advisor Major Desmond Morton concluded the existence of such a high overdraft was evidence that Sempill 'has not received payments for services from improper quarters'.[30]

Shigemitsu left London in July 1941, at which point *charge d'affaires* Kamimura Shinichi took the helm at the Japanese embassy. Intercepted telegrams he sent to Tokyo led to the belief that he had intelligence 'privately from Government circles' informing him about discussions due to be held between the US president's envoy, Averell Harriman, and Lord Beaverbrook on war supplies to Russia, which had just been invaded by Nazi Germany, and on Eden's diplomatic schedule. Kamimura had cited a source 'from government circles' who confided to him that an Allied conference excluded China 'in order not to excite Japan unnecessarily',[31] hinting at British weakness.

Churchill read the intercepted telegram and wrote to Eden, commenting, '[T]his man [Kamimura] seems well informed. Can we not get some information on his contacts?'[32]

In September, Eden brought up a list of seven suspected contacts. Sempill ('who is suspected of receiving a subvention from Japanese funds') was listed,[33] and other suspects included Professor Gerothwohl, who was 'probably the Japanese Embassy's best source', and Sir Edward Grigg, the joint parliamentary under-secretary for war and a friend of Hankey.[34] This was alarming. Seven officials talking about strategy and diplomacy towards Japan was too many, even if they were only offering personal views without reference to classified documents. Churchill was furious:

> I regard the attached document as most serious. At any moment we may be at war with Japan, and here are all these Englishmen, many of them respectable, two of whom I know personally, moving around collecting information and sending it to the Japanese Embassy. I cannot believe that the Master of Sempill [*sic*] and Commander McGrath have any idea of what their position would be on the morrow of a Japanese declaration of war. Immediate internment would be the least of their troubles … none of them must have access to any Government Department. It is impossible for Lord Sempill to continue to be employed at the Admiralty, I do not know in what capacity.[35]

Ever close to the action, Liddell recorded in his diary for 23 September 1941:

> Lord Swinton came at 6 pm to discuss the Prime Minister's anxieties about various British subjects who were making contact with the Japanese so we went over the whole ground with him. He will reply to the Prime Minister, who had become very excited about the whole matter … Lord Sempill should, in accordance with our advice given years ago, be removed from the Admiralty … [Lord] Swinton would speak to McGrath, that George Sale knew very little but was inclined to put business before the country, and that Piggott was a pathological Japophile (*sic*), but honest.[36]

Months earlier, he had already pointed in this direction:

> The Japanese assistant military attaché A. Nakamo is obviously doing intelligence work. Special Material shows that he is trying to get information about the movements of

our ships to the China Seas (*sic*) and that for this purpose he has been in touch with some European. We are having him kept under close observation and also putting Lord Sempill under observation. The Japanese are very difficult to watch as to a European they all look alike and there is the additional difficulty of the [Blitz] blackout and four exits from the military attaché's office.[37]

The following month, the matter was still on Churchill's mind: 'It seems to me intolerable that Lord Sempill should be employed at the Admiralty in these circumstances.'[38] Yet on 16 October he was backpedalling: 'I had not contemplated Lord Sempill being required to resign his commission but only to be employed elsewhere than at the Admiralty. The matter should be treated as one of employment and not as one of status.'[39] Evidently the Prime Minister feared a political embarrassment.

MI5 continued to monitor Sempill's phone and in October he was seen in public with Japanese military attaché General Tatsumi. The Admiralty feared that a 'peremptory dismissal' of Sempill would provoke 'undesirable repercussions in Tokyo';[40] others felt that Sempill could be usefully employed as a confidential channel of communication with the Japanese.

On 4 December 1941, Churchill was handed a brief message from SIS chief Stewart Menzies:

I have just received information that the Japanese Embassy at Washington has received somewhat similar instructions to these sent to London [embassy of Japan] regarding the destruction of cyphers as well as the cyphers machine.[41]

Even so, British intelligence had not foreseen what was to come.

On 7 December 1941, in a huge turning point for the Second World War, Japanese naval fighters attacked Pearl Harbor.

The following day, as Japan attacked Singapore, Hong Kong and Malaya, Britain declared war on the Empire of Japan. Churchill wrote to the Japanese ambassador in London:

In view of these wanton acts of unprovoked aggression committed in flagrant violation of International Law and particularly of Article I of the Third Hague Convention relative to the opening of hostilities, to which both Japan and the United Kingdom are parties, His Majesty's Ambassador at Tokyo has been instructed to inform the Imperial Japanese Government in the name of His Majesty's Government in the United Kingdom that a state of war exists between our two countries.

I have the honour to be, with high consideration,

Sir,
Your obedient servant,
Winston S. Churchill

The Prime Minister remarked later with sarcasm, 'Some people did not like this ceremonial style [of my letter]. But after all, when you have to kill a man, it costs nothing to be polite.'[42]

On 10 December, HMS *Prince of Wales*, armed with ten 14-inch guns, and HMS *Repulse*, with six 15-inch guns, were attacked off Malaya by Imperial Japanese Navy bombers. In the first wave, a total of nine torpedoes were launched against HMS *Prince of Wales* and one found the target; in the second wave, three torpedoes hit the warship. HMS *Repulse* was hit by a total of four torpedoes. Aerial bombs were also used. Eventually, both warships sank. Vice Admiral Sir Tom Spencer Vaughan Phillips, commanding the *Prince of Wales*, went down with his ship.

The following morning, Churchill was informed of the catastrophe. He was devastated:

In all the war, I never received a more direct shock ... As I turned over and twisted in bed the full horror of the news sank in upon me. There were no British or American ships in the Indian Ocean or the Pacific except the American survivors of Pearl Harbor ... Japan was supreme, and we everywhere were weak and naked.[43]

While HMS *Prince of Wales* was sinking in the Pacific, Inspector Grant from the Metropolitan Police Special Branch entered the Austria Club in London, where Sempill was having an evening dinner with Sir George Frankenstein, and asked Sempill to follow him. He informed his lordship about searches that were to be conducted at his home and his business address. This had come about because MI5 had intercepted a phone call between Kamimura and Sempill regarding the destruction of certain documents. Indeed, the police found secret documents but of 'no particular interest ... for any ulterior purpose', as Liddell remarked. Sempill was interviewed by Special Branch and MI5 at Scotland Yard. A warrant for internment under Defence Regulation 18 (B) was submitted to Home Secretary Herbert Morrison, but he did not sign it.[44] After all, it would be a grave political scandal for a member of the House of Lords to be detained on these terms in a time of war.

More than anything else, Sempill was a political embarrassment for Churchill. He did not have access to secret intelligence such as documents on British strategy or policy towards Japan. Had he been a spy, Shigemitsu would not have named him 'a contact'. Had he provided secret intelligence throughout the 1930s, the Japanese embassy would have cabled Tokyo about that intelligence and the GC&CS would have intercepted the communications. Gossip about diplomacy and logical deductions did not amount to espionage but nonetheless produced actionable and reliable intelligence reinforcing the unshakable conclusion of the Japanese leadership that the British Empire in the Far East was weak and could not, or would not, check the expansion of the Japanese Empire in south-east Asia.

Sempill and his wife Lady Cecilia proved to be thorns in the side of British diplomacy and intelligence throughout the war and after. In 1943, while Sempill was visiting Canada, the British High Commissioner cabled London to complain that Sempill was causing 'embarrassment ... by reason of indiscreet political speeches'. He wanted the Dominions Office to recall him at once.[45] Sempill announced that he would go to New York to visit his friend William Stephenson, at that time SIS spymaster in the city and working with American intelligence, prompting panic at the prospect of the indiscreet Sempill talking to everyone about Stephenson. A frantic cable read, 'Stephenson should be warned so that he might be on his guard in his dealings with Sempill.'[46]

Lady Cecilia, meanwhile, was boasting that her husband was employed 'in a very secret job by the Ministry of Supply'.[47] This was not true – nobody trusted Sempill. Cecilia herself proved indiscreet, and could even have damaged the prospects of the invasion of France. In early February 1944, a Royal Navy officer lunched with his sister; she was friends with Lady Cecilia, who joined them and began speaking about military matters. The officer reported that she was 'one the most indiscreet and talkative people he has ever met'. She also repeated German propaganda:

> Lady Cecilia said that there were 20,000 Sikhs in France fighting for the Germans and wearing the emblem of Free India. There were also a large number of Free Poles, Free Czechs, Greeks, etc. She said openly to an almost complete stranger that she had information about the exact date of the invasion. She implied that she had inside information and gave the end of February or the following moon as the date in question ... She talked freely about the Germans' secret weapon and said that the Press had much information about this ... the Germans had extensive concrete works along the French coast for flying off radio controlled 'Queen Bees' to raid London ... She ridiculed the Americans [troops] in this country and said that she knew from an authoritative source that the spearheads of all attacks on the Continent would be British.[48]

Meanwhile, the FBI was following Sempill in the United States, where he drew the attentions of General Clayton Bissell. The US embassy in London was asked to gather information on Sempill, and it seems the British government was keen to avoid embarrassment. Roger Hollis, the future MI5 director general, feared that 'Sempill with his very wide contacts is not unlikely to hear what we say about him'.[49]

Eventually, after a conference with MI5 Director-General David Petrie, it was decided that General P. A. Peabody, the US military attaché in London, should be informed that 'we had had no reason to believe that he [Sempill] was engaged in any espionage or subversive activities, but that he had been, for obvious reasons, friendly with the Japanese in the past; that politically, he was a person of no great importance'.[50] Further details of the Sempills' claims over the course of war were not released to the Americans.

Once the war was over, Sempill was involved in the publication of a Paris-based weekly, the *South European Observer*. The SIS representative in the city, along with MI5, discovered that it had a pro-Soviet line. Indeed, it was reported that Sempill told his associates and editors 'that the apparent pro-Russian bias displayed in the initial numbers of the *South European Observer* was to be the necessity for enabling the paper to be introduced into the Russian zone [of Europe]'.[51]

Sempill's attitudes confused the public, the elite and the intelligence services, who all saw political motives in his work. In fact, the final conclusion of MI5 was that Sempill was only interested in making money, and 'in order to do so it was conceivable that he might try to use the Soviets in some way'.[52]

CONCLUSION

Intercepts of Japanese communications provided the SIS, MI5 and the Admiralty with a clear view of the operational and strategic intentions of Japanese spymasters, and a close reading revealed the Japanese understanding of espionage and operational doctrine.

For the Japanese, conducting espionage was an assignment under a legal contract funded by public spending. Information was to be supplied and money given in return; nothing more. The secret agent would not be offered status in Japan or a better way of living. The secret agent would not be recruited based on ideology, nor would the spymaster expect their asset to abide by Tokyo's imperialistic ideology.

The secret agent would have to agree to a trial period as a kind of apprentice spy: 'He agreed to commence work for a test period of about 6 months, as a first trial for himself and give us an opportunity of trying out his abilities.'[1]

Since espionage was financed through public spending, the Japanese spymasters would personally negotiate with the secret agent to get the best price. This generated meetings and correspondence, which created opportunities for the asset to be compromised, indicating a competitive business mentality rather than secrecy-oriented tradecraft. The spymasters did not fear their correspondence or meetings being read by British intelligence; on one occasion there was a warning that 'lengthy telegrams may arouse the suspicion of the British and result in a leakage of secrecy',[2] but this did not change the common practices of Japanese spymasters.

Japan's chief adversary was not Britain but the United States, and it was considered vital to have secret agents under contract deployed there: 'On our part it is considered absolutely essential that he [the prospective spy] should reside in America ... it was *sine qua non* that his headquarters should be in America- during the recruitment negotiations.'[3] A spymaster/naval attaché was directed from Tokyo to push on the negotiations for the above spy: 'Prevail on him to manage on the above mentioned advance, get him to submit...'[4] The Director of Naval Intelligence put emphasis on a 'fidelity agreement for five years, [for the spy] to reside in America, with the proviso that, if circumstance required, the period can be extended'. Expenses would be paid per year 'for the sake of secrecy, and other considerations'. The secret agent was informed that 'during the term of the agreement', should he 'die, or should his livelihood and that of his wife suffer some serious damage due to reason connected with his intelligence mission, the sum of 100,000 yen will be handed over to him or his wife or after consideration of the degree of loss, a sum less than 100,000 yen'.[5]

The Japanese paid handsomely for intelligence. An air staff intelligence officer expressed his surprise at 'how much' the Japanese 'are prepared to spend on seeking information about the USA and Greene was only one of many'.[6]

The Japanese Director of Naval Intelligence concluded 'in wartime it is necessary to attach great important to San Francisco on account of [US fleet] mobilization and other considerations...' He added that 'regarding wartime intelligence, our policy is to search at once among Germans or Frenchmen for a reserve system, so as to avoid relying on an Englishman alone, therefore, the general plan here is to make use of [name not declassified] in case of necessity in future'.[7]

Pearl Harbor was the key place for espionage:

By way of preparation he [the spy] should by placing an agent in H (Honolulu), Los Angeles and London. Report on any resolve for war against Japan and the opportunity they would wish to commencing hostilities. [He would report] Information from which we would appreciate war operations against Japan and the state of affairs concerning their [American] training in war strategy. The attitude towards the 1936 disarmament agreement. Relations with the principal powers Britain, China, Russia, France, Germany.[8]

The Japanese spymasters did not employ middlemen; they themselves arranged and attended meetings with secret sources, confident that Asiatic features would not draw attention in London or other European and American cities.

Tokyo had a 'policy to collect preliminary intelligence for war time principally by using people other than Englishmen'.[9] The Japanese espionage machine had not developed a sophisticated system getting money to its agents, so the spymaster would always run the risk of being caught with unexplained money; in the case of the Japanese naval attaché in London, the Director of Naval Intelligence ruled that 'apart from the transfer of money, it is intended that future negotiations will not be through the naval attaché London'.[10]

The naval attaché in London wrote to Tokyo: 'The difficulties of transferring the money [in this case to Frederick Rutland in the United States] are greater than we imagined, and though we have exhausted discussion of all the plans we were able to think of, we had no other bright idea and decided to buy bearer bonds to transfer them in Paris and dispose of them there. We could invite him to Vancouver, Canada or to Paris.'[11]

Despite being a chief spymaster, the naval attaché felt it was safe for him to meet with a foreign secret agent:

> As a formula for future meetings (I am at present investigating and will make a detailed report when this is completed), I think it would be best for the Director of Naval Intelligence or his deputy to meet the man and if possible the naval attaché, London etc. once a year. The best place for this would be Los Angeles with Vancouver as the next best place, and Hawaii or Shanghai as a last resort.[12]

As for darker work than mere spying, no evidence appeared in the intercepts of a 'special service' section to arrange for assassinations in Britain, its colonies or other European countries. The Japanese spymaster does not resort to violence by threatening or murdering rogue agents. Deception was not something developed in Japanese tradecraft; 'false flag recruitment', whereby an agent is fooled into believing he is working for a different country, appears non-existent in archival material examined.

The same applies for seduction, whereby prospective blackmail victims are enticed with the promise of sexual favours; there is no evidence of this in the relevant directives cabled from Tokyo. In contrast, the narratives of intrigue and seduction are noted in Shanghai and Hong Kong.[13] In the examples covered in this work, the Japanese naval attaché in London and the head of naval intelligence in Tokyo did not possess suitable contacts, knowledge or skills to recruit the right individuals to perform a 'honey trap' operation in the British capital. They preferred to simply gather intelligence from people identified as being of high social status.

During his travels in China in the 1930s, Peter Fleming fell in with a Japanese company hunting Chinese bandits. In his account of this time he remarked:

> ... it was in short virtually certain that we had been brushing all the time against an unseen web of [Chinese] spies; and *news travels fast in the East* (author's emphasis), in fact as well as in sensational fiction.[14]

Indeed, in rural China, Shanghai and London, the Japanese spymaster was absorbed in the hunt for information of any kind. He sent Tokyo thousands of dispatches and distorted the view of the Japanese naval and military leadership, wrongly emboldening them to believe that they could follow an expansive strategy without Britain and the United States confronting them. This became an orthodoxy in Japanese strategic thinking, and it led to defeat.

The Anglo-Japanese secret war commenced in the 1900s as a result of Japanese complacency after their victory over Russia. In 1909, British military intelligence officers started realising that militarist Japan could be a threat to the British Empire in the Far East, and in that year the SIS and MI5 were established. Colonel J. A. R. Haldane in military intelligence warned, 'In fact it has been truly said that the Japanese army is preceded by geisha and spies, so if ever we hear of numbers of them landing in India or any of our colonies, we may be prepared for trouble...'[15]

British intelligence in India, the Far East and London recruited spies to monitor Japanese intentions. The employment of Indians to spy in Japan is a fine example of the British recruitment and management of secret sources, along with the tradecraft employed; the British Secretary of State was duly informed by the ambassador about the achievements of the spies, meaning awareness of clandestine spycraft went all the way up the chain to leading politicians.

On the other hand, British officers trained in Japan and imbued with a fondness for the country brought back to Britain a naïve and distorted view of Japanese strategy and military and naval power. They were unwitting allies of Japanese intelligence, both gathering intelligence and passing it on to obtain favour and influencing British policy along pro-Japanese lines.

Gradually, a paucity of funds for the SIS, the pro-Japanese attitude of figures at the War Office and Foreign Office, and an overreliance on deciphering Japanese diplomatic cables led to a lack of interest in recruiting spies inside the Japanese political and military elite. The British ambassadors, with the exception of Greene, defended their personal information-gathering schemes with their confidential contacts (generally officials of government departments or political parties).

Spies in the Japanese army and navy would have helped London to understand that the autonomous officer corps (with its many rough spymasters serving in China) was preparing for war despite the political crises and assassinations of politicians in the 1920s and 1930s. As we have seen, it was a spy in Taiwan who disclosed the plans for the invasion of Hong Kong and Singapore.

Secret coups were also achieved by spies working for British intelligence in Japanese naval yards. Indeed, despite xenophobia, paranoia and counter-espionage, it was still possible to glean intelligence in Japan. Politicians, officials, officers, businessmen, office employees and workers – all proud of their country's imperial policy in the Far East – would talk at length on 'interesting' issues to anybody who would listen.

The early successes of Japanese forces in the Second World War, and the element of surprise employed, do not mean that the Japanese intelligence machine was well developed and modernized; as we have seen, it was unsubtle, a blunt instrument.

However, 'intellectual integrity', the quality so valued by SIS spymaster George Kenneth Young, was sorely lacking among British foreign and defence policy elites, who always discounted the possibility of Japan elbowing out British strategic, military and commercial interests in the Far East. Indeed, British business interests in China (sidelined by Japanese businessmen and the military) did not play a pivotal role in British long-term policy over Japan; instead, from the 1900s onwards Britain simply reacted in a modest fashion to each crisis with Japan, and this led to Japanese overconfidence. Complacency was always in evidence among the British political elite.

At meetings of the British cabinet, the prospect of Japan expanding its empire was considered so unlikely that there was no coherent military and political strategy to deter it. Politicians like Churchill expected the United States to take the lead in the Pacific; weakened by the First World War, the British sought only to follow. British imperial strategists were correct in their belief that that an alliance with the United States would ensure Japan's defeat, but they were sorely mistaken in thinking that the United States would be willing to ensure the continuation of the British Empire in the Far East.

ENDNOTES

Preface

1. 'Quit now, critics urge Johnson as Tory leadership race begins' *The Times*, 8 July 2022
2. Frank, Richard, *Downfall: The End of the Imperial Japanese Empire* (New York: Penguin, 1999), pp. 316-318
3. Quoted in Blake, George, *No Other Choice: An Autobiography* (New York: Simon & Shuster, 1990), p. 168
4. Dickinson, Frederick R. *War and National Reinvention: Japan in the Great War, 1914-1919* (Cambridge MA: Harvard University Asia Center, 1999), p. 241
5. Allison, Graham, *Destined for War: Can America and China Escape Thucydides's Trap?* (New York: Houghton Mifflin Harcourt, 2017); Freedman, Lawrence, 'Book review: Destined for War: Can America and China Escape Thucydides' Trap?' *PRISM*. National Defense University, 14 September 2017
6. See Langer, William, *The Diplomacy of Imperialism, 1890-1902* (New York: Knopf, 1956)
7. Quoted in Hackett, Roger F. *Yamagata Aritomo in the Rise of Modern Japan, 1838-1922* (Cambridge MA: Harvard University Press, 1971), p. 159
8. Quoted in ibid., p. 270

1 An Alliance with an Antagonist

1. See Hackett, Roger F, *Yamagata Aritomo in the Rise of Modern Japan, 1838-1922* (Cambridge MA: Harvard University Press, 1971), pp. 6-23

2. Quoted in ibid., p. 30

3. Quoted in ibid., p. 66

4. Felton, *Japan's Gestapo*, p. 11

5. Hirose Yoshihiro, 'Yamagata Aritomo's Seiban Iken' Opinion on the Taiwan Expedition) p. 56, available at: https://www.surugadai. ac.jp/sogo/media/bulletin/Bunjo10-02/Bunjo10-02hirose.pdf

6. Quoited in Hasckett, *Yamagata Aritomo in the Rise of Modern Japan*. p. 146

7. Quoted in Samuels, Richard J. *Special Duty: A History of the Japanese Intelligence Community* (Ithaca: Cornell University Press, 2019), p. 32

8. Berton, *Russo-Japanese Relations*, p. 14

9. Quoted in O'Brien, Philips Payson ed. *The Anglo-Japanese Alliance, 1902-1922* (London: Routledge Curzon, 2004), p. 49

10. Quoted in Takeshi Sugawara, *A Matter of Imperial Defence: Arthur Balfour and the Anglo-Japanese Alliance, 1894-1923* (PhD Thesis, University of East Anglia, 2014), p. 203

11. Quoted in Chapman, John, 'British Naval Estimation of Japan and Russia, 1894-1905' in *On the Periphery of the Russo-Japanese War*, (Discussion Paper No. IS/04/475; The Suntory Centre, London School of Economics and Political Science, April 2004), p. 44

12. Ibid.

13. Satow to Dickins, 27 Jan 1905 quoted Heere, Cornelis, *Japan and the British World, 1904-14* (PhD Thesis London Schools of Economics and Political Science, 2016), p. 25

14. Quoted in Sugawara, *A Matter of Imperial Defence*, p. 197

15. 'Trade Prospects in Manchuria', *North China Herald*, 8 June 1906 quoted in Heere, *Japan and the British World, 1904-14*, p. 82

16. Quoted in ibid., pp. 81-83

17. Quoted in ibid., p. 92

18. Berton, Peter, *Russo-Japanese Relations, 1905–1917: From enemies to allies* (New York: Routledge, 2012), p. 4

19. Quoted in Heere, *Japan and the British World*, p. 93

20. Ibid.

21. Quoted in Masuda Hajimu, 'Rumors of War: Immigration Disputes and the Social Construction of American-Japanese Relations, 1905-1913' *Diplomatic History*, Vol.33, No. 1 (January 2009), pp. 1-37

22. Ibid., p. 10

23. Ibid., p. 19
24. Rivera, Carlos R. *Big Stick and Short Sword: The American and Japanese Navies as Hypothetical Enemies* (PhD Thesis, Ohio State University, 1995), p. 308
25. Dickinson, Frederick, R. War *and National Reinvention: Japan in the Great War, 1914-1919* (Massachusetts: Harvard University Asia Centre, 1999), pp. 27-28
26. Quoted in Steeds, David, 'The Anglo-Japanese Alliance and American Hegemony' in *Studies in the Anglo-Japanese Alliance, 1902-1923* (Discussion Paper No. IS/03/443; The Suntory Centre, London School of Economic and Political Science, January 2003), p. 32
27. Grey to MacDonald, 1909, FO 800/68 TNA
28. Lea, Homer, *The Valor of Ignorance* (New York: Harper, 1909), p. 55
29. Ibid., p. 159
30. Ibid., pp. 162, 173, 232
31. Ibid., p. 192.
32. Berton, Peter, 'A New Russo-Japanese Alliance? Diplomacy in the Far East during World War I' *Acta Slavica Iaponica*, Vol.11 (1993), pp. 57-78.
33. Stefanie Affeldt & Wulf D. Hund 'Conflicts in racism: Broome and White Australia' *Race & Class*, Vol. 61(2) pp. 43–61
34. Quoted in Heere, *Japan and the British World*, p. 123
35. Quoted in ibid., p. 131
36. Quoted in ibid., p. 156
37. Quoted in Ong Chit Chung, *Operation Matador, World War II: Britain's attempt to foil the Japanese invasion of Malaya and Singapore* (Singapore: Marshal Cavendish, 2011), p. 3.
38. Quoted in Sugawara, *A Matter of Imperial Defence*, p. 205
39. Quoted in Dickinson, *War and National Reinvention*, pp. 142-43
40. 'Japan's Fiscal and Financial Policy,' *The Economist*, 30 July 1910 quoted in Heere, *Japan and the British World*, p. 158
41. Quoted in Frederick R. Dickinson 'Japan debates the Anglo-Japanese Alliance: The second revision of 1911' in O'Brien ed. *The Anglo-Japanese Alliance*, p. 111
42. Ibid.
43. Quoted in Dickinson, *War and National Reinvention*, p. 45

44. Quoted in Maurer, John H. 'Winston has gone mad': Churchill, the British Admiralty, and the Rise of Japanese Naval Power, *Journal of Strategic Studies*, Vol.35 No.6 (2012), p. 785

45. British embassy (Washington) to Foreign Office, 17 January 1914; British embassy (Tokyo) to Foreign Office, 20 April 1914, all in FO 371/2011 TNA

46. Robert R. James (ed.), *Winston S. Churchill: His Complete Speeches, 1897–1963*, London: Chelsea House, 1974, vol. V, pp. 2262–6

47. Quoted in Dickinson, *War and National Reinvention*, p. 45

2 'The Empire Is the Master'

1. Quoted in ibid.

2. Ibid., p. 46

3. Churchill to Grey, 12 August 1914 quoted in Saxon, Timothy D. 'Anglo-Japanese Naval Cooperation, 1914-1918' *Naval War College Review*, Vol.53 No 1 (Winter 2000), p. 66

4. Ibid., p. 68

5. Parkinson, John, 'Wakamiya Maru off Tsingtao: September 1914' available at: http://www.gwpda.org/naval/wtsing.htm

6. Quoted in Dickinson, *War and National Reinvention*, p. 45

7. Lowe, Peter 'Great Britain and Japan's entrance into the Great War, 1914–1915' in O' Brien, Philips Payson ed. *The Anglo-Japanese Alliance, 1902-1922* (London: Routledge Curzon, 2004), p. 164

8. Quoted in Dickinson, *War and National Reinvention*, p. 54.

9. Berton, *Russo-Japanese Relations*, p. 36

10. Lowe, Peter 'Great Britain and Japan's entrance into the Great War, 1914–1915' in O' Brien, Philips Payson ed. *The Anglo-Japanese Alliance, 1902-1922* (London: Routledge Curzon, 2004), p. 168

11. Quoted in ibid.

12. Quoted in ibid.

13. Quoted in ibid.

14. Quoted in Dickinson, *War and National Reinvention*, p. 107

15. Lowe, 'Great Britain and Japan's entrance into the Great War, 1914–1915' in O' Brien ed. *The Anglo-Japanese Alliance, 1902-1922*, pp. 170-71

16. Quoted in Best, Antony, 'Britain, Japan, and the Crisis over China, 1915–16' in Oliviero Frattolillo & Best, Antony eds. *Japan and the Great War* (Basingstoke: Palgrave Macmillan, 2015), p. 56

17. Nicolson minute, 30 March 1915 quoted in ibid.
18. Ibid., pp. 59-60.
19. Greene to Grey, 4 January 1916, FO 800/68 TNA
20. Quoted in Dickinson, *War and National Reinvention*, p. 144
21. Berton, *Russo-Japanese Relations*, p. 46
22. Greene to Grey, 5 December 1914, FO 800/68 TNA
23. Quoted in Ferris, John, 'Armaments and allies: The Anglo-Japanese strategic relationship, 1911–1921' in O'Brien ed. *The Anglo-Japanese Alliance*, p. 250
24. Greene to Grey, 5 December 1914, FO 800/68 TNA
25. Bose to Balfour, 2 February 1917, FO 800/210 TNA
26. Quoted in Saxon,'Anglo-Japanese Naval Cooperation, 1914-1918', p. 75
27. Quoted in Nish, Ian, 'Early Retirement: Britain's retreat from Asia, 1905–23' in Best, Antony ed. *Britain's Retreat from Empire in East Asia, 1905–80* (New York: Routledge, 2017), p. 15
28. Quoted in Saxon, 'Anglo-Japanese Naval Cooperation, 1914-1918', p. 79
29. Ibid.
30. Quoted in Dickinson, *War and National Reinvention*, p. 180; see also Linkhoeva, Tatiana, 'The Russian Revolution and the Emergence of Japanese Anticommunism', *Revolutionary Russia*, Vol. 31, No.2 (2018) pp. 261-278
31. Best, Antony, 'Major-General F.S.G. Piggott and Anglo-Japanese Relations, 1917-63' Maj.Gen F.S.G. Piggott (1883–1966) in Cortazzi, Hugh, ed. *Britain and Japan: Biographical Portraits*, Vol. VIII (2013), pp. 102-116
32. Piggott to Hankey 29 October 1956 quoted in ibid.
33. Ibid.
34. Piggott, Francis, *Broken Thread: An Autobiography* (Aldershot: Gale & Polden, 1950), p. 50
35. Lyons (N Dept) minute 19 Feb. 1918. TNA FO371/3289 30285/383/38 quoted in Best, Antony 'Britain, intelligence and the Japanese intervention in Siberia' in Best ed. *Britain's Retreat from Empire in East Asia*, p. 59
36. Quoted in ibid.
37. Quoted in ibid.
38. Note by Cumming, 1 January 1918, FO 371/3298 TNA

39. Pardoe, J. M. R. *Captain Malcolm Kennedy and Japan 1917-1945* (PhD Thesis, University of Sheffield, 1989), unpaginated, available at <https://www.sheffield.ac.uk/polopoly_fs/1.694153!/file/KennedyBiography.pdf>

40. Quoted in Dickinson, *War and National Reinvention*, p. 189

41. Quoted in ibid., p. 200

42. All quoted in Best 'Britain, intelligence and the Japanese intervention in Siberia', p. 62

43. See Fleming, Peter, *The Fate of Admiral Kolchak* (London: Rupert Hart Davis 1963; Birlinn Edition, 2001)

44. Best 'Britain, intelligence and the Japanese intervention in Siberia, p. 64; memorandum by Lord Curzon 'Siberia', 20 December 1919, CAB 24/95 TNA

45. Best 'Britain, intelligence and the Japanese intervention in Siberia', p. 68

46. Japanese ambassador (Paris) to ambassador (London) 23 May 1921 HW 12/22

47. Japanese ambassador (London) to Japanese minister (Brussels) 4 June 1921 HW 12/23

48. Behringer, Paul Welch, 'Forewarned Is Forearmed': Intelligence, Japan's Siberian Intervention, and the Washington Conference', *The International History Review*, Vol. 38 Issue 3 (2016), pp. 1-16

49. Quoted in Dickinson, *War and National Reinvention*, p. 234

50. Quoted in ibid., p. 235

51. Pardoe, J. M. R. *Captain Malcolm Kennedy and Japan 1917-1945* (PhD Thesis, University of Sheffield, 1989), p. 26, available at <https://www.sheffield.ac.uk/polopoly_fs/1.694153!/file/KennedyBiography.pdf>

52. Quoted in Nish 'Early Retirement' in Best ed. Britain's Retreat from Empire in East Asia, p. 17

53. Vinson J. Chal, 'The Drafting of the Four-Power Treaty of the Washington Conference', *Journal of Modern History*, Vol. 25, No. 1 (March 1953), pp. 40–4

54. Katsuya Tsukamoto, *Japan's "Carrier Revolution" in the Interwar Period* (PhD Thesis, The Fletcher School of Law and Diplomacy, February 2016), pp. 48-50

55. Bix, Herbert P. *Hirohito and the Making of Modern Japan* (New York: Harper Collins, 2000), pp. 103-120; Piggott, F.S.G. *Broken Thread: An Autobiography* (London: 1950), pp. 117-134

3 The Spymasters of the Emperor

1. Section X (c) Phase I- the period before relief of Singapore. Course of Action open to Japan, June 1938, ADM 116/4393
2. Section X; The period before the relief of Singapore, Passage of the Fleet, February 1939, ADM 116/4393
3. Ian Fleming, *Britain and Japan: Biographical Portraits*, Vol. VI (Leiden: Brill, 2007), p. 255
4. Fleming, Ian, *You Only Live Twice* (1964) available at https://gutenberg.ca/ebooks/flemingi-youonlylivetwice/flemingi-youonlylivetwice-oo-h.html
5. Masunaga, Shingo, 'The Interwar Japanese Intelligence Activities in the Baltic States, 1918-1940' *Acta Historica Tallinnensia*, Vol 24 (2018), p. 90 n.62
6. Ibid.
7. Orbach, *Curse on this Country*, p. 154
8. Japanese naval attaché (London) to Director of Naval intelligence, March 1, 1934, KV 2/338 TNA
9. Felton, *Japan's Gestapo*, p. 11
10. Ibid., p. 34
11. Yansuji Nagai, 'Diplomat's 1895 letter confesses to assassination of Korean queen' *The Asahi Shimbun*, 12 November 2021 available at: <https://www.asahi.com/ajw/articles/14482741> accessed 24 January 2022
12. Orbach, *Curse on this Country*, pp. 101-104
13. Gregory J. Nedved, 'Decryption in Progress: The Sino-Japanese War of 1894-1895' *Cryptologic Quarterly*, Vol.36 No.3 (2017) pp. 5-15
14. Ibid., p. 16.
15. Gregory J. Nedved, 'Decryption in Progress: The Sino-Japanese War of 1894-1895' *Cryptologic Quarterly*, Vol.36 No.3 (2017) pp. 5-18; Gregory J. Nedved (2018) The Sino-Japanese War of 1894–1895: Partially decrypted', *Cryptologia*, Vol. 42, No.2 (2018), pp. 95-105.
16. Paine S. C. M. *The Sino-Japanese War of 1894-1895: Perceptions, Power, and Primacy* (Cambridge: Cambridge University Press, 2003), pp. 263
17. Ibid., p. 263.
18. Ibid., pp. 284-288.

19. Orbach, Danny, '*The Military-Adventurous Complex: Officers, adventurers, and Japanese expansion in East Asia, 1884–1937*' *Modern Asian Studies*, Vol.53, No.2 (2019) p. 347
20. Ibid.
21. Quoted in ibid., p. 348
22. Ibid.
23. John Chapman, 'British Naval Estimation of Japan and Russia, 1894-1905' in *On the Periphery of the Russo-Japanese War*, Part 1 Discussion Paper No. IS/04/475 April 2004, The Suntory Centre, London School of Economics and Political Science, p. 28
24. Quoted in Hall, Simon, *Blinded by the Rising Sun: Japanese Military Intelligence from the First Sino-Japanese War to the end of World War II* (PhD Thesis University of Adelaide, 2016), p. 62
25. Samuels, *Special Duty*, p. 272 n.10
26. Ibid., p. 37
27. Quoted in Olavi K. Fält and Antti Kujala eds. (translation by Inaba Chiharu) 'Colonel Akashi's Report on His Secret Cooperation with the Russian Revolutionary Parties during the Russo-Japanese War' *Studia Historica* Vol.31 (1988), p. 52
28. Ibid.
29. Quoted in ibid., p. 46
30. Zuckerman, Fredric S. *The Tsarist Secret Police Abroad: Policing Europe in a Modernising World* (Basingstoke: Palgrave/Macmillan, 2003), pp. 159-161
31. Quoted in ibid., p. 48
32. Ibid.
33. Chapman, *British Naval Estimation of Japan and Russia, 1894-1905*, pp. 37, 44
34. Chiharu Inaba, Military co-operation under the first Anglo-Japanese Alliance, 1902–1905 in O'Brien ed. *The Anglo-Japanese Alliance, 1902-1922*, pp. 70-71
35. Ibid.
36. Ibid., pp. 72-73
37. Ibid., pp. 75-77
38. Cook Andrew, Ace of Spies: The True Story of Sidney Reilly (Stroud: The History Press, 2004), pp. 51-55

39. Sergeev, Evgeny, *Russian Military Intelligence in the War with Japan, 1904-05: Secret Operations on Land and at Sea* (London: Routledge, 2007), pp. 56-57

40. Guidelines, September 1909, ADM 116/1231C TNA

41. Ferris, 'Armaments and allies' in O'Brien ed. *The Anglo-Japanese Alliance, 1902-1922*, pp. 259-260

42. Colonel J.A.L. Haldane, 'Japanese and Russian Intelligence Systems', March 1909, WO106/6150 TNA

43. Kondo Motaki, 'Japan's Contribution to Naval Architecture', *Transactions of the Institute of Naval Architects*, London, 1925, vol. LXVII, p. 39 quoted in Ferris, 'Armaments and allies', in O'Brien ed. *The Anglo-Japanese Alliance, 1902-1922*, p. 258

44. Ferris, ibid., p. 268

45. Quoted in Sergeev, *Russian Military Intelligence in the War with Japan*, pp. 23-24

46. Hall, *Blinded by the Rising Sun*, pp. 81-82

47. Ibid., p. 45; Japanese and Russian Intelligence Systems, 1909, WO 106/6150 TNA

48. 'Japanese and Russian Intelligence Systems', WO 106/6150 TNA

49. Ibid.

50. Ibid.

51. Ibid.

52. Quoted in Kyoichi Tachikawa, 'Japanese Pre-War Military Attaché System', *NIDS Journal of Defense and Security*, Vol.16, Dec. 2015, p. 165

53. Japanese Prisoner of war Interrogation, Research Report no 134/ Allied Translator and Inter Section/Supreme Commander for the Allied Powers, 1 June 1946

54. Quoted in Dickson, *War and National Reinvention*, p. 131

55. Ibid., p. 133

56. Memorandum by MI2c, 14 July 1917, WO 106/869

57. Quoted in Pardoe, *Captain Malcolm Kennedy & Japan*, p. 36

58. Minute by J.R. MacKinnon, 19 November 1921, BT 60/3/2 TNA

4 *On His Majesty's Secret Service*

1. Popplewell, *Intelligence and Imperial Defence*, p. 281

2. Greene to Grey, 9 May 1914, FO 371/2013

3. Ibid.

4. Ibid.

5. Greene to Grey 2 June 1914. Ibid. FO 371/2013 TNA

6. Popplewell, *Intelligence and Imperial Defence*, p. 184

7. Aide memoire by military attaché, 15 April 1914 FO 371/2013 TNA

8. British embassy Tokyo to Governor of Hong Kong, 2 May 1914, FO 371/2013 TNA

9. Greene to Langley, 5 October 1917 FO 369/1003 TNA.

10. Max Everest-Phillips, 'Colin Davidson's British Indian Intelligence Operations in Japan 1915–23 and the Demise of the Anglo-Japanese Alliance' *Intelligence & National Security, Vol.*24 No. 5 (2009), pp. 674-699

11. Bose to Balfour, 2 February 1917, FO 800/210 TNA.

12. Quoted in Popplewell, *Intelligence and Imperial Defence*, p. 284

13. Ibid.

14. Best, Antony, *British Intelligence and the Japanese Challenge in Asia, 1914-1941* (Basingstoke: Palgrave/Macmillan, 2002), p. 26

15. 'German peace overtures to Japan- Conversation with Japanese Ambassador', 4 May 1916, CAB 37/147/10; Germany informed by Japan that there could be no separate peace negotiations, 18 May 1916 CAB 37/148/9 TNA

16. Bangkok to Berlin (German) 2 January 1916, and Shanghai to Berlin (German) 26 February 1916, ADM 223/667 TNA; Hall (DNI) minute 27 May 1916, ADM 137/371 TNA

17. Quoted in Everest-Phillips, 'Colin Davidson's British Indian Intelligence ... ', p. 683; Davidson (Yokohama) to Greene, 22 August 1914 FO371/2694/205638/23 TNA

18. Ibid.

19. Quoted in ibid., p. 688

20. Quoted in ibid., p. 688

21. Ibid., p. 691

22. Ibid.

23. Ibid., pp. 681-2; General Officer Commanding Singapore to War Office, 27 September 1916, FO 371/2789

24. Greene to Grey, 7 August 1916, FO 371/2789 TNA

25. Greene to Balfour, 15 January 1917, FO 371/3065 TNA

26. Greene to Grey, 15 January 1917, ibid.

27. Davidson to Greene, 17 January 1917, Ibid.

28. Cumins to Davidson, 29 July 1917 FO 115/2235 TNA

29. Ibid.

30. Quoted in Popplewell, *Intelligence and Imperial Defence*, p. 286
31. 'Report by agent Se.' authored by Davidson, 26 September 1917 FO 371/3069 TNA
32. Ibid.
33. Max Everest-Phillips, 'Colin Davidson's British Indian Intelligence Operations in ... ', p. 683
34. Davidson to Greene, 22 August 1916, FO 371/2694 TNA
35. Davidson to Greene, 29 September 1916, FO 371/2694 TNA
36. Davidson to Greene, 22 August 1916, FO 371/2694 TNA
37. Ibid.
38. Greene to Grey, 6 September 1916 FO 371/2694 TNA
39. Hackett, *Yamagata Aritomo in the Rise of Modern Japan*, p. 337
40. Balfour to Greene 13 February 1917, FO 371/2693 263898/83924/23 TNA
41. Everest-Phillips, 'Colin Davidson's British Indian Intelligence Operations in ... ', p. 683
42. Ibid., p. 695
43. Everest-Phillips, Max, 'The Pre-War Fear of Japanese Espionage: Its Impact and Legacy', *Journal of Contemporary History*, Vol. 42, No. 2 (Apr. 2007), pp. 246
44. Ibid.
45. Military Intelligence (MI2c) memorandum, 14 July 1917, WO 106/869 TNA.
46. Campbell to French (MI1a) 8 January 1918 FO369/1171 104197/86366/223 TNA.
47. Quoted in Popplewell, *Intelligence and Imperial Defence*, p. 285
48. Ibid.
49. Ibid., p. 282
50. Everest-Phillips, 'Colin Davidson's British Indian Intelligence Operations in ... ', p. 691.
51. Ibid.
52. Everest-Phillips, 'The Pre-War Fear of Japanese Espionage p. 252.
53. Everest-Phillips, 'Colin Davidson's British Indian Intelligence Operations in ... ', p. 695.
54. Judd, Alan, *The Quest for 'C': Mansfield Cumming and the Founding of the Secret Service* (London: Harper Collins, 2000), p. 443.
55. Kennard (Rome) to Oliphant (FO) 18 September 1919, FO371/3816 TNA

56. 'Report of the Anglo-Japanese Alliance Committee' 14 January 1921, FO371/6672 F1169/63/23 TNA
57. Quoted in Ong, *Operation Matador*, pp. 4-5
58. Ibid.
59. Quoted in Wiji Seki, 'Winston Churchill (1874–1965) and Japan', quoted in Cortazzi, Hugh, ed. *Britain and Japan: Biographical Portraits*, Vol. VI (London: Global Oriental, 2007), p. 3, 11
60. Best, *British Intelligence and the Japanese Challenge in Asia*, p. 91

5 Helping the Imperial Navy

1. Ferris, John, 'A British 'unofficial' aviation mission and Japanese Naval developments, 1919–1929' *Journal of Strategic Studies*, Vol.5, Issue 3 pp. 416-439
2. Evans, David C. & Peattie, Mark R. *Kaigun: Strategy, Tactics, and Technology in the Imperial Japanese Navy, 1887–1941* (Annapolis, MD: Naval Institute Press, 2012), pp. 17-19, 181, 248, 301; Peattie, Mark R. *Sunburst: The Rise of Japanese Naval Air Power, 1909-1941* (Annapolis, Maryland: Naval Institute, 2006), pp. 62, 537
3. Best, Anthony, *British Intelligence and the Japanese Challenge in Asia, 1914–1941*, p. 88.
4. Hoare, J.E. 'Ernest Cyril Comfort: The Other British Aviation Mission and Mitsubishi 1921–24' in Hugh Cortazzi ed. *Britain and Japan: Biographical Portraits*, Vol. VI (New York: Brill, 2007), p. 184-85
5. Evans & Peattie, *Kaigun*, pp. 301-302
6. Hoare, J.E. 'Ernest Cyril Comfort', pp. 186-87
7. Ibid., p. 188
8. Evans & Peattie, *Kaigun*, pp. 303-304
9. Branfill-Cook, *Torpedo*, pp. 113-116; In 1946 Oyagi was interviewed by US naval intelligence on torpedo technology, see http://www.fischer-tropsch.org/primary_documents/gvt_reports/USNAVY/USNTMJ%20Reports/USNTMJ-200D-0471-0529%20Report%200-01-2.pdf

6 No War with Japan

1. Statement by First Sea Lord, Standing Committee, 30 November 1922, ADM 116/3165 TNA

2. 'Statements at the Imperial Defence Committee 5 January 1925' Political outlook in the Far East, February 1925, c.p. 120(25) CAB 24/172/20 TNA

3. Ibid.

4. Quoted in Maurer John H. 'Winston has gone mad': Churchill, the British Admiralty, and the Rise of Japanese Naval Power, *Journal of Strategic Studies*, Vol.35, No.6. (2012), p. 776

5. Quoted in ibid.

6. On 1 September 1923 an earthquake (the *Great Kantō*) caused the death to approximately 140,000 people. Captain Malcolm Kennedy was in Japan with his family. He was attending foreign language training. His house collapsed and he managed to rescue his wife and son.

7. Quoted in Maurer John H. 'Winston has gone mad', pp. 776-77

8. Minutes of the 26th Meeting of the Standing Defence Sub-Committee, the Committee of Imperial Defence, 30 Nov. 1922, ADM 116/3165 TNA

9. Quoted in ibid.

10. Quoted in Maurer, 'Winston has gone mad', p. 781

11. Quoted in ibid.

12. Churchill to Baldwin, 15 Dec. 1924, ibid., p. 783

13. Churchill to Sir Roger Keyes, 22 March 1925, quoted in ibid, p. 783

14. Quoted in Maurer, 'Winston has gone mad', p. 783

15. All quoted in ibid. 786

16. All quoted in ibid. 787

17. All quoted in ibid. 787-88

18. Jeffery, Keith, *MI6: The History of the Secret Intelligence Service* (London: Bloomsbury, 2010), p. 257

19. Best, *British Intelligence and the Japanese Challenge in Asia, 1914-1941*, p. 91

20. Jeffery, *MI6*, p. 257

21. Best, *British Intelligence and the Japanese Challenge in Asia*, p. 87

22. Quoted in ibid., p. 88

23. Ibid.

24. Ibid., p. 90.

25. Ibid., p. 91.

26. Ibid., p. 96.

27. Ibid.

28. Quoted in Maurer, 'Winston has gone mad', p. 792
29. Ibid., p. 97.
30. Memorandum on Secret Service Funds, 9 October 1935 CAB 127/371 TNA

7 *The Aviator and the Submariner*

1. MI5 to Menzies (SIS) 11 August 1924, KV2/328 TNA
2. Cases in connection with the Air Ministry, 23 June 1926, KV2/328 TNA
3. Ball (MI5) to Menzies (SIS), 11 August 1924, KV 2/328 TNA
4. Boyle to Harker, 3 April 1928, KV 2/328 TNA
5. Notes on the case of Squadron Leader Rutland, RAF KV 2/328 TNA
6. Case History of F.Rutland, undated, KV 2/332, p. 16
7. Harker to Boyle, Note Squadron Leader Rutland, 27 January 1926, KV 2/328 TNA
8. SIS station (Paris) to SIS, 31 July 1924, KV 2/328 TNA
9. SIS report, 31 July 1924, KV 2/328 TNA
10. Letter to Ball, 25 July 1924, KV 2/328 TNA
11. MI1c to Ball (MI5), 18 July 1924 KV 2/328 TNA
12. Frederick Joseph Rutland, 31 December 1941, KV 2/333 TNA
13. Quoted in Haire, Emily, *Anglo-French intelligence liaison, 1909-1940* (PhD Thesis, Queen's University Belfast, 2014), pp. 123-25
14. Extract from a letter of British sent to the Admiralty from the British naval attaché, Tokyo, dated 20 January 1925, KV2/328 TNA
15. Case History, undated, KV 2/332, p. 16
16. Letter to Military Intelligence (MIc)18 September 1924, KV 2/328 TNA
17. Frederick Joseph Rutland, 31 December 1941, KV 2/333 TNA
18. KV 2/337, p. 23.
19. Everest-Phillips, Max, 'Reassessing pre-war Japanese espionage: The Rutland naval spy case and the Japanese intelligence threat before Pearl Harbor', *Intelligence and National Security*, Vol.21, No.2 (2006), p. 268
20. Naval attaché (London) to Minister of Marine (Tokyo) 19 June 1933, KV 2/ 338 TNA
21. Note ref.no21, SIS to MI5, 26 June 1933, KV 2/338 TNA

22. Frederick Joseph Rutland, 31 December 1941, KV 2/333 TNA
23. Ibid.
24. Director of Naval Intelligence (Tokyo) to Naval Attaché (London), 24 June 1933, KV 2/338 TNA.
25. Director of Naval Intelligence (Tokyo) to Naval Attaché (London), 27 July 1933, KV 2/338 TNA.
26. Naval attaché (London) to Director of naval intelligence (Tokyo), 8 March 1934, KV 2/338 TNA. This could refer to another spy under recruitment and not Rutland; otherwise, the name Shinkawa would have appeared at the beginning of the line not declassified. The document was stamped that the original is retained in the department under section 3(4) of the Public Record Act 1958.
27. Note 8 August 1934, KV 2/329 TNA
28. Note 9 February 1935, KV 2/329 TNA
29. Sinclair (SIS) to Kell (MI5), 23 January 1935, KV 2/330 TNA
30. Letter to Liddell (MI5), 4 February 1935, KV 2/330 TNA
31. Cowgill (SIS) to Liddell (MI5), 19 February 1942, KV 2/333 TNA
32. Frederick Joseph Rutland, 31 December 1941, KV 2/333 TNA
33. 'Communications' KV 2/330 TNA
34. Note, 4 July 1934, KV 2/329 TNA
35. Naval attaché (London) to director of Naval intelligence (Tokyo), 22 May 1935, KV 2/339 TNA
36. Frederick Joseph Rutland, 31 December 1941, KV 2/333 TNA
37. Intercepts enclosed in KV 2/339 TNA; Everest-Phillips, 'Reassessing pre-war Japanese espionage', p. 271
38. Ibid.
39. FBI report on Rutland, 2 July 1943, KV 2/336 TNA
40. Ibid.
41. Ibid.
42. Loureiro, Pedro, 'The imperial Japanese Navy and espionage: The Itaru Tachibana case". *International Journal of Intelligence and Counterintelligence.* Vol. 3 No.1, (1989), pp. 105-121
43. 'Squadron leader Rutland', note by the Naval Intelligence Department, 18 August 1943, KV 2/336 TNA
44. Frederick Joseph Rutland, 31 December 1941, KV 2/333 TNA
45. File on Rutland, KV 2/337, p. 1. unsigned letter to Rutland, 17 November 1941. KV 2/332 TNA
46. Philby to Young, 20 May 1946, KV 2/337 TNA

47. 'W' Reports, 23 March 1927, KV2/691 TNA
48. Note ref. no.31a, 26 January 1927, KV 2/688 TNA
49. Note ref. no.70a, KV 2/688 TNA
50. Copies of references, KV 2/688 TNA
51. Ibid.
52. Ibid.
53. Note ref. no. 70a, KV 2/688 TNA
54. Note ref. no. C/2115, 25 January 1927, KV 2/688 TNA
55. Note ref. no. C/2205, 24 February 1927, KV 2/ 688 TNA
56. Ibid.
57. Statement of Witness, George Calcutt, HMS Dolphin, 28 March 1927, KV 2/691 TNA
58. Statement of Witness, George Arthur William Johns, 26 March 1927, KV 2/691 TNA
59. Note by B2 ref. no. 57a, 26 March 1927, KV 2/691 TNA
60. Note ref. no. C2964, 19 December 1927, KV 2/872 TNA; Note ref. no. C 2988, 22 December 1924, KV 2/872 TNA
61. B2 note relation to Mayers, Colin, 18 April 1929 KV 2/689 TNA
62. Report ref. no. 938342, 24 April 1930, KV 2/689 TNA
63. SIS to Young (MI5), 16 December 1943, KV 2/689 TNA

8 The Memorandum of War

1. Piggott, Broken Thread, p. 223
2. Stephan John J. The Tanaka Memorial (1927): authentic or spurious?' Modern Asian Studies Vol. 7 No.4 (1973), pp. 737-739
3. MacKillop (Foreign Office, Far Eastern Department) 27 July 1931 FO 371/15446 TNA
4. D.M. to M.W. on CX 1124 of 27.7.1931, 29 July 1931, ibid.
5. M.W. to MacKillop, CX 1124, 14 August 1931, ibid
6. Stephan, 'The Tanaka Memorial', p. 740
7. Japan's Positive Policy in Manchuria, FO 371/15446 TNA
8. Stephan, 'The Tanaka Memorial', p. 741
9. Ibid., p. 742

9 The Ambassador

1. The Air Battle over Shanghai -1932 available at: *http://www. republicanchina.org/Air-Battle-over-Shanghai-Suzhou-Hangzhou-1932.pdf*; Robert E. van Patten, Before the Flying

Tigers *AIR FORCE Magazine* June 1999; Christopher Thorne, 'The Shanghai Crisis of 1932: The Basis of British Policy *The American Historical Review* Vol. 75, No. 6 (Oct. 1970), pp. 1616-1639.

2. Ibid.
3. Piggott, *Broken Thread*, p. 244.
4. Perdoe, *Captain Malcolm Kennedy and Japan*, p. 116
5. Ibid.
6. Ibid.
7. Jeffery, *MI6*, p. 257, pp. 262-63.
8. Japanese naval attaché (London) to Deputy Chief (Tokyo), 6 March 1933, KV 3/338 TNA
9. Hirota, Foreign minister (Tokyo) to Japanese ambassador (London) 25 October 1933, HW 12/173 TNA
10. No.1952 Circular of the Ministry of Foreign Affairs dated 25 October 1933, HW 12/173 TNA
11. December 1933 memorandum quoted in Pardoe, *Captain Malcolm Kennedy and Japan 1917-1945*, p. 128
12. Jeffery, *MI6*, pp. 257, 262-63
13. Eiji Seki, 'Winston Churchill (1874–1965) and Japan', quoted in Cortazzi, Hugh, ed. *Britain and Japan: Biographical Portraits*, Vol. VI (London: Global Oriental, 2007), pp. 6-7.
14. Ibid.
15. Best, *British Intelligence and the Japanese Challenge*, pp. 126-27.
16. Ibid., p. 127.
17. Ibid., p. 128.
18. Ibid.
19. Jeffery, *MI6*, p. 257, pp. 262-63.
20. Ibid.
21. Ibid., p. 246.
22. Quoted in Pardoe, *Captain Malcolm Kennedy and Japan 1917-1945, p. 185 note 419*
23. Diary entries quoted in ibid.
24. Ibid.
25. Eiji Seki, 'Winston Churchill (1874–1965) and Japan', quoted in Cortazzi, Hugh, ed. *Britain and Japan: Biographical Portraits*, Vol. VI (London: Global Oriental, 2007), p. 2.
26. Jeffery, *MI6*, pp. 265-66

10 *A Spy Close to the General*

1. NID Japanese section. Japan; War Plans against Hong Kong and Singapore, 25 May 1937 ADM 223/495 TNA
2. Report no 0487/37 by Director of Naval Intelligence, 2 June 1937, ADM 223/495 TNA
3. Memo by the Director of Plans 10 June 1937, ibid.
4. 'Japanese secret service', SIS to Robertson (MI5) 22 November 1937, KV 3/295 TNA
5. Ibid.
6. Ibid.
7. 'Japanese secret service' SIS to MI5 (Robertson) 13 April 1938 KV 3/295 TNA
8. Ibid.
9. SIS to MI5 (Robertson) 24 November 1937 KV 3/295 TNA
10. 'Japanese wartime intelligence activities in Northern Europe' 30 September 1946, p. 14, RG 226 Entry 212 Box 8 WN 24486 United States National Archives and Records Administration (NARA)
11. 'Japanese wartime collaboration with the Polish intelligence services' 2 October 1946, p. 12, ibid.
12. 'Heroic leader of Polish military intelligence in the West commemorated in Morocco' 2 February 2013. Available at: <http://www.mfa.gov.pl/en/c/MOBILE/news/heroic_leader_of_polish_military_intelligence_in_the_west_commemorated_in_morocco? accessed 26 March 2015
13. 'Japanese wartime intelligence activities in Northern Europe' 30 September 1946, pp. 14, 25 September 1946, RG 226 Entry 212 Box 8 WN 24486 National Archives and Records administration (NARA) United States
14. 'Japanese wartime collaboration with the Polish intelligence services' 2 October 1946, p. 1, ibid.
15. Ibid., p. 2
16. Ibid.
17. Ibid., p. 3
18. Ibid., pp. 3-4
19. 'Japanese wartime intelligence activities in Northern Europe' 30 September 1946, p. 4, RG 226 Entry 212 Box 8 WN 24486 NARA ibid.

20. Japanese wartime collaboration with the Polish intelligence services' 2 October 1946, p. 6, ibid.
21. Ibid., p. 7
22. Ibid., p. 8
23. Ibid., p. 9
24. Ibid.
25. Schellenberg, Walter, *The Labyrinth: The Memoirs of Walter Schellenberg, Hitler's Chief of Counterintelligence* (New York: Da Capo, 1999), p. 125; Doerries, Reinhard, *Hitler's Last Chief of Foreign Intelligence: Allied Interrogations of Walter Schellenberg* (New York: Routledge 2003), pp. 215-216.
26. Schellenberg, *The Labyrinth*, pp. 125-127; Doerries, Reinhard, *Hitler's Last Chief of Foreign Intelligence,* p. 216.
27. Ibid., pp. 125-130
28. See 'Japanese wartime collaboration with the Polish intelligence services', 2 October 1946, p. 10, RG 226 Entry 212 Box 8 WN 24486 NARA
29. Schellenberg, *The Labyrinth* pp. 133-135.
30. 'Japanese wartime collaboration with the Polish intelligence services' 2 October 1946, p. 10, RG 226 Entry 212 Box 8 WN 24486 NARA
31. Ibid., p. 9.
32. Ibid., p. 10.
33. Ibid., p. 4.
34. Ibid.
35. Ibid., p. 5.
36. Ibid.
37. Ibid.
38. Ibid, p. 6.
39. Ibid.
40. Japanese wartime intelligence activities in Northern Europe' 30 September 1946, p. 11, RG 226 Entry 212 Box 8 WN 24486 NARA
41. Ibid.
42. Ibid., pp. 35-38, 41
43. Ibid., pp. 13, 42-43, 46, 47, 50
44. Reports referring to Kure (see Appendix 1) ADM 116/5757 TNA
45. Ibid.

46. Reports referring to Yokosuka (see Appendix 1) ADM 116/5757 TNA
47. Ibid.
48. Ibid.
49. Ibid.
50. Ibid.
51. Ibid.
52. Ibid.; one is reminded of the co-star of Sean Connery in *Your Only Live Twice*, the noted Japanese actress Akiko Wakabayashi, who played a spy in the port of Yokohama.
53. Reports referring to Yokosuka (see Appendix 1) ADM 116/5757 TNA.
54. Ibid.

11 *A Double Agent*

1. Japanese naval attaché (London) to director of naval intelligence, 29 January 1934, KV 2/636 TNA
2. Abstract of a letter of Oka to Greene dated 12 October 1934, KV 2/364 TNA
3. Report, 26 March 1934, KV 2/ 634 TNA
4. Note on meeting with Greene, 26 March 1934, KV 2/364 TNA
5. Ibid.
6. KV 2/ 634 TNA
7. Japanese naval attaché (London) to director of naval intelligence, 7 February 1934, KV 2/636 TNA
8. Japanese naval attaché (London) to director of naval intelligence, 20 December 1934, KV 2/636 TNA
9. Ibid.
10. Ibid.
11. Ibid.
12. Oka to Greene, 9 Friday 1933 [possibly a typing mistake; 1934 the correct year] KV 2/634 TNA
13. Oka to Greene, 6 November 1934, KV 2/634 TNA
14. Note dated 12 November 1934, KV 2/634 TNA
15. Japanese naval attaché (London) to director of naval intelligence, 17 January 1935, KV 2/636 TNA
16. Sinclair (SIS) to Kell (MI5), 30 January 1935, KV 2/636 TNA
17. Japanese naval attaché (London) to director of naval intelligence, 20 March 1935, KV 2/636 TNA

18. Ibid.
19. Japanese naval attaché (London) to director of naval intelligence, 1 February 1935, KV 2/636 TNA
20. Foreign Office to Kell (MI5) 14 October 1935 KV 2/ 634 TNA
21. 'Interview with Mr Greene' and note on the 14 December 1937 interview of Greene with the director of naval intelligence, all in KV 2/635 TNA
22. Ibid.
23. Ibid.
24. Ibid.
25. Edition enclosed in KV 2/365 TNA
26. Ibid.
27. Report to A2, 3 March 1938, KV 2/635 TNA
28. 'Secret Agent in Spain' by Herbert Greene, Supplement review in KV 2/365 TNA
29. Special Branch report, 1 September 1937, KV 2/635 TNA
30. Enclosed note on William Herbert Greene in a letter by Lt Col Norman, 12 December 1939, KV 2/635 TNA
31. Biographical note 'William Herbert Greene', KV 2/635 TNA

12 Manipulation

1. Ronald minute. 31 July 1939, FO 371/23571 F8107/3027/23
2. Quoted in Best, *Avoiding War*, p. 163
3. Clive to Vansittart 25 July 1935, FO 371/19334 F4680/4680/23
4. Major General F.S.G. Piggott minute 23 March 1938 on Sir A. Clark Kerr to Lord Halifax 16 March 1938 FO 262/2016 153/70/38
5. Best, *Avoiding War*, p. 92
6. Piggott, *Broken Thread*, p. 244
7. Ibid., p. 282; Extract from military attaché's report No.18 of 13 November 1936; Military attaches visit to Manchuria and North China, WO 106/5584
8. Ibid.
9. Ibid.
10. Ibid., p. 297
11. Ibid., p. 326
12. Ibid., p. 329
13. Ibid.
14. Ibid.
15. Ibid., p. 330

16. Notes on a conversation with the Ambassador on Wednesday evening, May 19th, the day before Sir Robert Clive left Japan, WO 106/5584 TNA
17. DMO & I 10 August 1937, WO 106/5584 TNA
18. Piggott to Craigie, 18 November 1937, WO 208/1214 TNA
19. Ibid.
20. R.H.H. to Piggott, 20 October 1937, WO 106/5584 TNA
21. Howe to Craigie 25 May 1939, FO 371/23483 TNA
22. Craigie to Howe 30 June 1939, FO 371/23485 TNA
23. Quoted in Best, *Avoiding War*, pp. 164-165
24. Quoted in ibid., p. 93

13 Armies of Spies

1. Elphick, *Far Eastern File*, pp. 133-141
2. Japanese Intelligence Service, Far East Combined Bureau, 1 October 1940 KV 3/295 TNA
3. Samuels, *Special Duty*, p. 46
4. Ibid., p. 58
5. Japanese Intelligence Service, Far East Combined Bureau, 1 October 1940 KV 3/295 TNA p. 8
6. Ibid.
7. Ibid.
8. Ibid.
9. Ibid., p. 6
10. Ibid., p. 11
11. Ibid., p. 12
12. Extract from SEATIC No 133, dated 30 April 1945, WO 208/1346 TNA
13. Extract from: Allied Translation and Interpreter Section report No 230, dated 20 March 1944, WO 208/1346 TNA
14. Elphick, *Far Eastern File*, p. 82

14 Murder

1. Quoted in Fahey, John, *Australia's First Spies: The Remarkable Story of Australian Intelligence Operations, 1901-1945* (Melbourne: Unwin & Allen, 2018), p. 168
2. 'Japan: Blast all of You' Time magazine, 16 September 1940
3. Memo 29 December 1945, FO 371/46538 TNA

4. 'Arrest of British Subjects in Japan' Hansard, Debate, July 30, 1940 Vol.117 cc.1-3

5. Sir R. Craigie to Lord Halifax 31 July 1940, Fo371/24738 F3685/653/23 TNA

6. Craigie to Halifax 3 July 1940 quoted in Best, Antony, *Avoiding War: The Diplomacy of Sir Robert Craigie and Shigemitsu Mamoru, 1937-1941* (PhD Thesis, London School of Economics and Political Science, 1992), p. 243

7. Piggott, Francis, *Broken Thread: An Autobiography* (Aldershot: Gale & Polden, 1950), p. 309

8. Best, *Avoiding War*, p. 142

9. Ibid., p. 248

10. Churchill to Halifax 17 July 1940, FO 371/24660 F3572/27/10 TNA

11. Ibid., p. 249

12. Craigie to Chief Officer Intelligence Staff, Singapore, 10 June 1941 KV 3/295 TNA

13. Piggott, *Broken Thread,* p. 311

14. Felton, Mark, *Japan's Gestapo: Murder, Mayhem and Torture in Wartime Asia* (Barnsley: Pen & Sword, 2009), p. 58; Ovey to Foreign Office, 18 December 1941, KV 2/2470 TNA

15 False Alarm

1. Craigie to Eden, 3 February 1941, FO 371/27760 TNA

2. Captain of Intelligence Staff (Singapore) to Director of Naval Intelligence (Admiralty) 23 January 1941. WO 208/892 TNA

3. Japanese Minister (Bangkok) to Tokyo 28 January 1941, Consul E. Meiklereid (Sourabaya) to Captain of Intelligence Staff (Singapore) 1 February 1941, FO 371/27962 TNA

4. British consul at Sourabaya to COISM (Singapore) 1 February 1941, FO 371/27962 TNA

5. FECB Intelligence Survey No. 1822, 'Warning of Attack by Japan', 9 Dec. 1940, WO208/888 TNA

6. Ibid.

7. FECB Intelligence Survey No. 1822, 'Warning of Attack by Japan', 9 Dec. 1940, WO208/888 TNA

8. COS (41) Chiefs of Staff 43rd meeting 5 February 1941, CAB 79/9 TNA

9. 'Japanese Intentions' Joint Intelligence Subcommittee report, 5 February 1941, PREM 3/156 TNA; COS (41) 73 Annex 1 'Measures to Avert War With Japan' Chiefs of Staff report 6 February 1941, CAB 80/25 TNA

10. Eden to Halifax, 5 February 1941 FO 371/27962 TNA

11. Eden to Halifax 6 February 1941 FO 371/27962 TNA

12. 'Japanese Intentions', WO 208/855 TNA

13. Eden to Halifax, at 9 p.m. 6 February 1941 FO 371/27962 TNA

14. Best, Antony, *Britain, Japan and Pearly Harbor: Avoiding War in East Asia, 1936-41* (London: Routledge, 2006), pp. 141-42

15. Diary entry for 6 February 1941 in D. Dilks (ed.), *The Diaries of Sir Alexander Cadogan, 1938-1945* (New York: Puttman 1971), p. 353.

16. Hopkins and Butler conversation 6 February 1941 in Butler Papers quoted in best, Avoiding War, p. 293

17. 'Japanese Intentions' WO 208/855 TNA

18. JIC (41) 61 'Possible Action Against Japan', 7 February 1941 in appendix COS (41) Chiefs of Staff 46th meeting 8 February 1941, CAB 79/9; Eden and Chiefs of Staff meeting, 7 February 1941, CAB 79/9; COS (41)73 Annex 1 'Measures to Avert War With Japan' Chiefs of Staff report, 6 February 1941, CAB 80/25 TNA

19. Shigemitsu and Eden conversation, 7 February 1941, FO 371/27886 TNA

20. 'Japanese Intentions' WO 208/855 TNA

21. Eden to Craigie, 9 February 1941 FO 371/27962 TNA

22. Minute by Cadogan, 3 February 1941. FO 371/27886 TNA

23. Best, *Avoiding War*, p. 369

24. Memo by Director of Naval Intelligence to Foreign Office, 12 February 1941, WO 208/855 TNA

25. Craigie to Eden, 12 February 1941, FO 371/27886 TNA

26. 'Japanese Intentions' WO 208/855 TNA

27. Craigie to Eden, 14 February 1941, FO 371/27785 TNA

28. Butler note for Eden 14 February 1941, quoted in Best, *Avoiding War*, p. 293

29. 'Japanese Intentions' report dated 15 February 1941, WO 208/855 TNA

30. Best, *Britain, Japan and Pearly Harbor*, p. 143

31. Eden to Halifax, 21 February 1941, WO 208/855 TNA

32. Churchill to Cadogan, 16 February 1941, PREM 3/252/6A TNA
33. Ibid.
34. 'Japanese Intentions', WO 208/855 TNA
35. News report for 17 February, WO 208/855 TNA
36. 'Japanese Intentions' WO 208/855 TNA
37. Both articles enclosed in WO 208/855 TNA
38. Craigie to Foreign Office, 20 February 1941, F0371/27887 TNA
39. 'Japanese Intentions' WO 208/855 TNA
40. Ibid.
41. Captain of Intelligence Staff (Singapore) to Director of Naval Intelligence (Admiralty) 1 March 1941, WO 208/892 TNA
42. Appreciations and notes on probable future intentions, 1939-1941, Report by Major H. I. Chapman, M.I. 2C, 16 May 1941, WO 208/855 TNA
43. West ed. *The Guy Liddell Diaries*, Vol.1, p. 200

16 His Lordship

1. Sempill to Toyoda, 12 December 1924, summarized in report in KV 2/871 TNA
2. Brief notes regarding certain leakages of confidential Air Force Information recently dealt with by MI5, KV 2/871 TNA
3. Sempill to Toyoda, 10 December 1924, KV 2/871 TNA
4. Note ref. no. C2964, 19 December 1927, KV 2/872 TNA; Note ref. no. C 2988, 22 December 1924, KV 2/872 TNA
5. Note ref. no. C2964, 19 December 1927, KV 2/872 TNA; Note ref. no. C 2988, 22 December 1924, KV 2/872 TNA
6. Ibid.
7. All letters in 'Correspondence passing between Colonel The Master of Sempill and Teijiro Toyoda, Japanese Naval Attaché,' KV 2/871 TNA
8. Ibid.
9. Ibid.
10. Ibid.
11. Aide-memoire for a Foreign Office meeting, KV 2/871 TNA
12. Air Ministry to MI5, KV 2/871, 28 para. 1; report (undated; 1934) KV 2/873 TNA
13. Sempill to Piggott, 25 January 1928, KV 2/871 TNA
14. B2 (MI5) note, 17 October 1927, KV 2/872 TNA
15. Piggott to Sempill (amended draft; undated) KV 2/872 TNA

16. Hardie, Alex, 'Sempill, Japan, and Pearl Harbor: Traitor or Spy-Myth?', *International Journal of Intelligence and Counterintelligence,* Vol. No. (2022), p. 8

17. Quoted in Hardie, 'Sempill, Japan, and Pearl Harbor', p. 8

18. Alexander to Churchill, 8 October 1941, PREM 3/252/5 TNA

19. Kell to Swinton, KV 2/872 TNA

20. Slattery to Carter, 2 October 1940, forwarding Sempill's letter of 30 September 1940, KV2/872 TNA

21. Swinton to Churchill, 24 September 1941, PREM 3/252/5 TNA

22. Shigemitsu to Tokyo, 13 March 1941 in 'The Case of Lord Sempill', document ref. no. 797a, KV 2/872 TNA

23. Item 9, record for 13 March 1941, War Cabinet, CAB 65/18/7 TNA

24. Gooch to Carpmael, KV 2/872 TNA

25. Gooch to Vivian, KV 2/872 TNA

26. Quoted in Hardie, 'Sempill, Japan, and Pearl Harbor', p. 13

27. Ibid.

28. Young to Churchill, 17 December 1941, KV 2/872 TNA

29. Cadogan diary entry for 22 February 1941 quoted in Hardie, 'Sempill, Japan, and Pearl Harbor', p. 13

30. Morton to Jarret, 16 October 1941, PREM 3/252/5 TNA

31. Kamimura to Tokyo 13 September 1941, HW 12/268 TNA

32. Quoted in Hardie, 'Sempill, Japan, and Pearl Harbor', p. 18

33. Quoted in ibid., p. 18

34. Ibid.

35. Churchill to Eden, 20 September 1941, KV 2/872 TNA

36. West, Nigel ed., *The Guy Liddell Diaries*, Vol.I, 1939-1942 (New York: Routledge, 2005), p. 178.

37. Diary entry for 11 February 1941, ibid., p. 131

38. Churchill to First Lord of Admiralty, 6 October 1941, KV 2/872 TNA

39. Churchill to First Lord of Admiralty, 16 October 1941, KV 2/872 TNA

40. Hardie, 'Sempill, Japan, and Pearl Harbor', p. 19

41. C (Menzies) to Churchill, 4 December 1941, HW 1/294 TNA

42. Freeman, David, 'Winston Churchill & Lessons for Business Leader', July 2015, available at: https://winstonchurchill.org/publications/finest-hour/finest-hour-166/winston-churchill-lessons-for-business-leaders/ accessed 8 August 2022

43. Quoted in Owen, Frank, *The Fall of Singapore* (New York: Penguin Books, 2001), p. 65
44. Note by Liddell, 13 December KV 2/872 TNA
45. Note by the DSO (New Foundland), 16 March 1944, KV 2/873
46. Millis to Liddell, 28 February 1944, KV 2/873 TNA
47. Rothchild to Brown, 26 January 1942, KV 2/873 TNA
48. 'Lady Cecilia Sempill' enclosed in Nesbitt to Williams, 9 March 1944, KV 2/873 TNA
49. Hollis to Petrie, 23 June 1944, KV 2/874 TNA
50. Memo by Deputy Director General (MI5), 8 July 1944 KV 2/874 TNA
51. BiD (MI5) note, 30 April, 1947 KV 2/874 TNA
52. BiD (MI5) 21 April 1947, KV 2/874 TNA

Conclusion

1. Naval attaché (London) to Director of Naval Intelligence (Tokyo), 12 March 1934, KV 2/636 TNA
2. Director of Naval intelligence (Tokyo) to Naval attaché (London), 22 June 1935, KV 2/339 TNA
3. Director of Naval intelligence (Tokyo) to Naval attaché (London), 5 July 1933, KV 2/338 TNA
4. Director of Naval intelligence (Tokyo) to Naval attaché (London), 29 June 1935, ibid.
5. Director of Naval intelligence (Tokyo) to Naval attaché (London), 23 June 1933, ibid.
6. Air intelligence note, 24 December 1937, KV 2/635 TNA
7. Director of Naval intelligence (Tokyo) to Naval attaché (London), 13 March 1934, KV2/338 TNA
8. Director of Naval intelligence (Tokyo) to Naval attaché (London), 20 March 1935, ibid.
9. Director of Naval intelligence (Tokyo) to Naval attaché (London), 3 February 1934, KV2/636 TNA
10. Director of Naval intelligence (Tokyo) to Naval attaché (London), 4 July 1935, KV 2/339 TNA
11. Naval attaché (London) to Director of Naval Intelligence (Tokyo), 19 March 1934, KV 2/338 TNA
12. Naval attaché (London) to Director of Naval Intelligence (Tokyo), 4 June 1935, KV 2/339 TNA

13. See Wasserstein, Bernard, *Secret War in Shanghai: Espionage, Intrigue and Treason* (New York: Houghton Mifflin, 1999)

14. Fleming, Peter, *One's Company: A Journey to China in 1933* (London: Jonathan Cape, 1934), p. 155

15. 'Japanese and Russian Intelligence Systems', WO 106/6150 TNA

BIBLIOGRAPHY

Archives

Unpublished

The National Archives, Kew, Surrey, United Kingdom:
CAB (Cabinet Office) series
FO (Foreign Office) series
HW (Government Code & Cypher School) series
KV (Security Service) series
PREM (Prime Minister's Office) series
WO (War Office) series

National Archives and Record Administration, United States:
Record Group 226 Entry 212

Published

Fält, Olavi K. and Kujala, Annti eds (translation by Inaba Chiharu), 'Colonel Akashi's Report on His Secret Cooperation with the Russian Revolutionary Parties during the Russo-Japanese War' *Studia Historica*, Vol. 31 (1988)

Gilbert, Martin ed., *The Churchill War Papers*, Vol. 3 (New York: W.W. Norton, 2001)

House of Commons, 'Arrest of British Subjects in Japan' *Hansard*, Debate, 30 July 1940, Vol. 117 cc. 1-3

James, Robert R. ed., *Winston S. Churchill: His Complete Speeches, 1897–1963* (London: Chelsea House, 1974)

Office of Naval Intelligence; interrogation report available at: <http://www.fischer-tropsch.org/primary_documents/gvt_reports/USNAVY/USNTMJ%20Reports/USNTMJ-200D-0471-0529%20Report%200-01-2.pdf>

West, Nigel & Tsarev, Oleg eds, *Triplex: Secrets from the Cambridge Spies* (New Haven: Yale University Press, 2009)

Memoirs & Diaries

Dilks D. ed., *The Diaries of Sir Alexander Cadogan, 1938-1945* (New York: Puttman, 1971)

Lindley, Francis, *A Diplomat Off Duty* (London: E. Benn, 1947)

Piggott, Francis, *Broken Thread: An Autobiography* (Aldershot: Gale & Polden, 1950)

Shellenberg, Walter, *The Labyrinth: The Memoirs of Walter Shellenberg, Hitler's Chief of Counterintelligence* (New York: Da Capo, 1999)

West, Nigel ed., *The Guy Liddell Diaries*, Vol. I, 1939-1942 (New York: Routledge, 2005)

Movies

School of Spies, Yasuzô Masumura (1966)
The Bridge on the River Kwai, David Lean (1957)
The Thirty-Nine Steps, Alfred Hitchcock (1978)
Tinker, Tailor, Soldier Spy, Tomas Alfredson (2011)
You Only Live Twice, Lewis Gilbert (1967)

Books, Articles & Theses

Andrew, Christopher, *The Defence of the Realm: The authorized History of MI5* (London: Penguin, 2010)

Anonymous, 'Quit now, critics urge Johnson as Tory leadership race begins' *The Times*, 8 July 2022

Anonymous, 'Japan: Blast all of You' *Time* magazine, 16 September 1940

Anonymous, 'The Air Battle over Shanghai 1932' available at: <http://www.republicanchina.org/Air-Battle-over-Shanghai-Suzhou-Hangzhou-1932.pdf>

Anonymous, 'Heroic leader of Polish military intelligence in the West commemorated in Morocco' 2 February 2013, available at: <http://

www.mfa.gov.pl/en/c/MOBILE/news/heroic_leader_of_polish_military_intelligence_in_the_west_commemorated_in_morocco?>

Affeldt, Stefanie & Hund, Wulf D. 'Conflicts in racism: Broome and White Australia' *Race & Class*, Vol. 61, No. 2, pp. 43–61

Allison, Graham, *Destined for War: Can America and China Escape Thucydides's Trap?* (New York: Houghton Mifflin Harcourt, 2017)

Behringer, Paul Welch, 'Forewarned Is Forearmed: Intelligence, Japan's Siberian Intervention, and the Washington Conference' *The International History Review*, Vol. 38, Issue 3 (2016), pp. 1-16

Benesch, Oleg, *Inventing the Way of the Samurai: Nationalism, Internationalism, and Bushido in Modern Japan* (Oxford: Oxford University Press, 2014)

Berton, Peter, 'A New Russo-Japanese Alliance? Diplomacy in the Far East during World War I' *Acta Slavica Iaponica*, Vol. 11 (1993), pp. 57-78

Berton, Peter, *Russo-Japanese Relations, 1905–1917: From enemies to allies* (New York: Routledge, 2012)

Best, Antony, *Britain, Japan and Pearly Harbor: Avoiding War in East Asia, 1936-41* (London: Routledge, 2006)

Best, Antony, *British Intelligence and the Japanese Challenge in Asia, 1914-1941* (Basingstoke: Palgrave/Macmillan, 2002)

Best, Antony ed., *Britain's Retreat from Empire in East Asia, 1905–80* (New York: Routledge, 2017)

Best, Antony, *Avoiding War: The Diplomacy of Sir Robert Craigie and Shigemitsu Mamoru, 1937-1941* (PhD Thesis, London School of Economics and Political Science, 1992)

Bix, Herbert, *Hirohito and the Making of Modern Japan* (New York: Harper Collins, 2000)

Blake, George, *No Other Choice: An Autobiography* (New York: Simon & Schuster, 1990)

Branfill-Cook, Roger, *Torpedo: The Complete History of the World's Most Revolutionary Naval Weapon* (Barnsley: Seaforth Publishing, 2014)

Cortazzi, Hugh ed., *Britain and Japan: Biographical Portraits*, Vol. VI (London: Global Oriental/Brill, 2007)

Cortazzi, Hugh ed., *Britain and Japan: Biographical Portraits*, Vol. VIII (London: Brill, 2013)

Cook, Andrew, *Ace of Spies: The True Story of Sidney Reilly* (Stroud: The History Press, 2004)

Dickinson, Frederick, R., *War and National Reinvention: Japan in the Great War, 1914-1919* (Cambridge MA: Harvard University Asia Centre, 1999)

Doerries, Reinhard, *Hitler's Last Chief of Foreign Intelligence: Allied Interrogations of Walter Schellenberg* (New York: Routledge, 2003)

Drabkin, Ronald, *Beverly Hills Spy: The Double-Agent War Hero Who Helped Japan Attack Pearl Harbor* (New York: William Morrow, 2023)

Drabkin R. & Hart B. W., 'Agent Shinkawa Revisited: The Japanese Navy's Establishment of the Rutland Intelligence Network in Southern California' *International Journal of Intelligence and CounterIntelligence* Vol. 35 No. 1 (2022), pp. 31–56

Elphick, Peter, *Far Eastern File: Intelligence War in the Far East, 1930-45* (London: Corgi, 1997)

Evans, David C. & Peattie, Mark R., *Kaigun: Strategy, Tactics, and Technology in the Imperial Japanese Navy, 1887–1941* (Annapolis, MD: Naval Institute Press, 2012)

Everest-Phillips, Max, 'Reassessing Prewar Japanese Espionage: The Rutland Naval Spy Case and the Japanese Intelligence Threat before Pearl Harbor' *Intelligence and National Security*, Vol. 21 No. 2 (2006), pp. 258–285

Everest-Phillips, Max, 'Colin Davidson's British Indian Intelligence Operations in Japan 1915–23 and the Demise of the Anglo-Japanese Alliance' *Intelligence & National Security*, Vol. 24 No. 5 (2009), pp.674-699

Everest-Phillips, Max, 'The Pre-War Fear of Japanese Espionage: Its Impact and Legacy' *Journal of Contemporary History*, Vol. 42, No. 2 (2007), pp. 243-265

Fahey, John, *Australia's First Spies: The Remarkable Story of Australian Intelligence Operations, 1901-1945* (Melbourne: Unwin & Allen, 2018)

Felton, Mark, *Japan's Gestapo: Murder, Mayhem and Torture in Wartime Asia* (Barnsley: Pen & Sword, 2009)

Ferris, John, 'A British "unofficial" aviation mission and Japanese Naval developments, 1919–1929' *Journal of Strategic Studies*, Vol. 5, Issue 3 (1982), pp. 416-439

Ferris, John, *Behind the Enigma: The authorized history of GCHQ, Britain's Secret Cyber-Intelligence Agency* (London: Bloomsbury, 2020)

Fleming, Ian, *Casino Royale* (London: Jonathan Cape, 1953)

Fleming, Ian, *Moonraker* (New York: Signet Books, 1955)

Fleming, Peter, *One's Company: A Journey to China in 1933* (London: Jonathan Cape, 1934)

Fleming, Peter, *The Fate of Admiral Kolchak* (London: Rupert Hart Davis 1963; Birlinn Edition, 2001)

Frank, Richard, *Downfall: The End of the Imperial Japanese Empire* (New York: Penguin, 1999)

Frattolillo, Oliviero & Best, Antony eds, *Japan and the Great War* (Basingstoke: Palgrave Macmillan, 2015)

Freedman, Lawrence, 'Book review: Destined for War: Can America and China Escape Thucydides' Trap?' *PRISM: National Defense University*, 14 September 2017

Freeman, David, 'Winston Churchill & Lessons for Business Leaders', July 2015, available at: <https://winstonchurchill.org/publications/finest-hour/finest-hour-166/winston-churchill-lessons-for-business-leaders/> accessed 8 August 2022

Gough, Barry, 'Prince of Wales and Repulse: Churchill's "Veiled Threat" Reconsidered' Churchill Conference 2007 Proceedings Paper, available at: <https://winstonchurchill.org/publications/finest-hour/finest-hour-139/prince-of-wales-and-repulse-churchills-veiled-threat-reconsidered>

Greene, Graham, *The Confidential Agent* (London: Bloomsbury 1939)

Greene, Herbert, *Secret Agent in Spain* (London: R. Hale, 1938)

Hackett, Roger F., *Yamagata Aritomo in the Rise of Modern Japan, 1838–1922* (Cambridge, MA: Harvard University Press, 1971)

Haire, Emily, *Anglo-French intelligence liaison, 1909-1940* (PhD Thesis, Queen's University Belfast, 2014)

Hankey, Maurice, *Politics, Trials and Errors* (Oxford: Pen in Hand Publishing, 1950)

Hall, Simon, *Blinded by the Rising Sun: Japanese Military Intelligence from the First Sino-Japanese War to the end of World War II* (PhD Thesis, University of Adelaide, 2016)

Hardie, Alex, 'Sempill, Japan, and Pearl Harbor: Traitor or Spy-Myth?' *International Journal of Intelligence and Counterintelligence*, (2022) pp.1-36 available at <https://www.tandfonline.com/doi/full/10.1080/08850607.2022.2081048?tab=permissions&scroll=top>

Heere, Cornelis, *Japan and the British World, 1904-14* (PhD Thesis, London Schools of Economics and Political Science, 2016)

Jeffery, Keith, *MI6: The History of the Secret Intelligence Service* (London: Bloomsbury, 2010)

Jordan, John ed., *Warship* (London: Conway, 2008)

Judd, Alan, *The Quest for 'C': Mansfield Cumming and the Founding of the Secret Service* (London: Harper Collins, 2000)

Kemper, Steve, *Our Man in Tokyo: An American Ambassador and the Countdown to Pearl Harbor* (New York: Mariner, 2022)

Langer, William, *The Diplomacy of Imperialism, 1890-1902* (New York: Knopf, 1956)

Lea, Homer, *The Valor of Ignorance* (New York: Harper, 1909)

Linkhoeva, Tatiana, 'The Russian Revolution and the Emergence of Japanese Anticommunism', *Revolutionary Russia*, Vol. 31, No. 2 (2018), pp. 261-278

Loureiro, Pedro, 'The Imperial Japanese Navy and espionage: The Itahu Tachibara case' *International Journal of Intelligence and Counterintelligence*, Vol. 3 No. 1 (1989), pp. 105-121

Masuda, Hajimu, 'Rumors of War: Immigration Disputes and the Social Construction of American-Japanese Relations, 1905-1913' *Diplomatic History*, Vol. 33, No. 1 (January 2009), pp. 1-37

Matsusaka, Yoshihisa, *The Making of Japanese Manchuria, 1904–1932* (Cambridge, MA: Harvard Asia Center/Harvard University Press, 2001)

Maurer, John H., '"Winston has gone mad": Churchill, the British Admiralty, and the Rise of Japanese Naval Power' *Journal of Strategic Studies*, Vol. 35 No. 6 (2012), pp.775-797

Nagai, Yansuji, 'Diplomat's 1895 letter confesses to assassination of Korean queen' *Asahi Shimbun*, 12 November 2021, available at: <https://www.asahi.com/ajw/articles/14482741>

Nedved, Gregory J., 'The Sino-Japanese War of 1894-1895: Partially decrypted' *Cryptologia* Vol. 42, No. 2 (2017)

Nedved, Gregory J., 'Decryption in Progress: The Sino-Japanese War of 1894-1895' *Cryptologic Quarterly*, Vol. 36, No. 3 (2017)

Nish, Ian & Chapman, John, *On the Periphery of the Russo-Japanese War*, Part 1 Discussion Paper No. IS/04/475 April 2004 (The Suntory Centre, London School of Economics and Political Science, 2004)

O'Brien, Philips Payson ed., *The Anglo-Japanese Alliance, 1902-1922* (London: Routledge Curzon, 2004)

O'Neil, William D., *Military Transformation as a Competitive Systemic Process: The Case of Japan and the United States Between the World War* (Washington DC: CNA, June 2003) available at: <https://www.cna.org/archive/CNA_Files/pdf/d0008616.a1.pdf>

Ong Chit Chung, *Operation Matador, World War II: Britain's attempt to foil the Japanese invasion of Malaya and Singapore* (Singapore: Marshal Cavendish, 2011)

Orbach, Danny, 'The Military-Adventurous Complex: Officers, adventurers, and Japanese expansion in East Asia, 1884–1937' *Modern Asian Studies*, Vol. 53, No. 2 (2019)

Orbach, Danny, *Course on This Country: The Rebellious Army of Imperial Japan* (Ithaca: Cornell University Press, 2017)

Owen, Frank, *The Fall of Singapore* (New York: Penguin, 2001)

Paine, S. C. M., *The Sino-Japanese War of 1894-1895: Perceptions, Power, Primacy* (Cambridge: Cambridge University Press, 2002)

Paine, S. C. M., *The Japanese Empire: Grand strategy from the Meiji Restoration to the Pacific War* (Cambridge: Cambridge University Press, 2017)

Pardoe, J. M. R., *Captain Malcolm Kennedy and Japan 1917-1945* (PhD Thesis, University of Sheffield, 1989)

Parkinson, John, 'Wakamiya Maru off Tsingtao: September 1914' available at: <http://www.gwpda.org/naval/wtsing.htm>

Peattie, Mark R., *Sunburst: The Rise of Japanese Naval Air Power, 1909-1941* (Annapolis, Maryland: Naval Institute Press, 2006)

Popplewell, Richard, *Intelligence and Imperial Defence: British intelligence and the Defence of the Indian Empire, 1904-1924* (London: Routledge, 1995)

Saxon, Timothy D., 'Anglo-Japanese Naval Cooperation, 1914-1918' *Naval War College Review*, Vol. 53, No. 1 (Winter 2000), pp. 62-92

Rivera, Carlos R., *Big Stick and Short Sword: The American and Japanese Navies as Hypothetical Enemies* (PhD Thesis, Ohio State University, 1995)

Roberts, Andrew, *Churchill: Walking with Destiny* (London: Penguin, 2018)

Samuels, Richard J., *Special Duty: A History of the Japanese Intelligence Community* (Ithaca: Cornell University Press, 2019)

Samuels, Richard J., *Machiavelli's Children: Leaders and Their Legacies in Italy and Japan* (Ithaca: Cornell University Press, 2003)

Schencking, Charles J., 'The Imperial Japanese Navy and the Constructed Consciousness of a South Seas Destiny, 1872–1921' *Modern Asian Studies*, Vol. 33, No. 4 (October 1999), pp. 769–96

Schmid, Andre, *Korea between Empires, 1895–1919* (New York: Columbia University Press, 2002)

Sergeev, Evgeny, *Russian Military Intelligence in the War with Japan, 1904-05: Secret Operations on Land and at Sea* (London: Routledge, 2007)

Shillony, Ben Ami, *Revolt in Japan: The Young Officers and the February 26, 1936 Incident* (Princeton, NJ: Princeton University Press, 1973)

Siniawer, Eiko Maruko, *Ruffians, Yakuza, Nationalists: The Violent Politics of Modern Japan, 1860–1960* (Ithaca: Cornell University Press, 2008)

Snyder, Robert Lance, '"Shadow of Abandonment": Graham Greene's *The Confidential Agent*' *Texas Studies in Literature and Language*, Vol. 52, No. 2 (Summer 2010), pp. 203-226

Stephan, John J., 'The Tanaka Memorial (1927): authentic or spurious?' *Modern Asian Studies*, Vol. 7 No. 4 (1973), pp. 737-739

Takeshi Sugawara, *A Matter of Imperial Defence: Arthur Balfour and the Anglo-Japanese Alliance, 1894-1923* (PhD Thesis, University of East Anglia, 2014)

Thorne, Christopher, 'The Shanghai Crisis of 1932: The Basis of British Policy' *The American Historical Review*, Vol. 75 No. 6 (October 1970), pp. 1616-1639

Thorne, Christopher, *Allies of a Kind: The United States, Britain and the war against Japan, 1941-1945* (Oxford: Oxford University Press, 1978)

Tsukamoto, Katsuya, *Japan's 'Carrier Revolution' in the Interwar Period* (PhD Thesis, The Fletcher School of Law and Diplomacy, February 2016)

van Patten, Robert E., 'Before the Flying Tigers' *AIR FORCE Magazine* (June 1999)

Vinson, J. Chal, 'The Drafting of the Four-Power Treaty of the Washington Conference' *Journal of Modern History*, Vol. 25, No. 1 (March 1953), pp. 40-4

Wasserstein, Bernard, *Secret War in Shanghai: Espionage, Intrigue and Treason* (New York: Houghton Mifflin, 1999)

Weland, James E., *The Japanese Army in Manchuria: Covert Operations and the Roots of the Kwantung's Army Insubordination* (PhD thesis, University of Arizona, 1977)

Yoshihiro, Hirose, 'Yamagata Aritomo's Seiban Iken' (Opinion on the Taiwan Expedition) available at: https://www.surugadai.ac.jp/sogo/media/bulletin/Bunjo10-02/Bunjo10-02hirose.pdf

Zuckerman, Fredric S., *The Tsarist Secret Police Abroad: Policing Europe in a Modernising World* (Basingstoke: Palgrave/Macmillan, 2003)

INDEX